Race and Ethnicity in Latin America

Anthropology, Culture and Society

Series Editors:
Professor Vered Amit, Concordia University
and
Dr Jon P. Mitchell, University of Sussex

Published titles include:

RACE AND ETHNICITY IN LATIN AMERICA

Second edition

Peter Wade

PlutoPress
www.plutobooks.com

First published 1997
This edition published 2010 by Pluto Press
345 Archway Road, London N6 5AA and
175 Fifth Avenue, New York, NY 10010

www.plutobooks.com

Distributed in the United States of America exclusively by
Palgrave Macmillan, a division of St. Martin's Press LLC,
175 Fifth Avenue, New York, NY 10010

British Library Cataloguing in Publication Data
A catalogue record for this book is available from the British Library

ISBN   978 0 7453 2948 2   Hardback
ISBN   978 0 7453 2947 5   Paperback

Library of Congress Cataloging in Publication Data applied for

This book is printed on paper suitable for recycling and made from fully managed
and sustained forest sources. Logging, pulping and manufacturing processes are
expected to conform to the environmental standards of the country of origin.

10   9   8   7   6   5   4   3   2   1

Designed and produced for Pluto Press by
Chase Publishing Services Ltd, 33 Livonia Road, Sidmouth, EX10 9JB, England
Typeset from disk by Stanford DTP Services, Northampton, England
Printed and bound in the European Union by
CPI Antony Rowe, Chippenham and Eastbourne

Contents

Series Preface

Anthropology is a discipline based upon in-depth ethnographic works that deal with wider theoretical issues in the context of particular, local conditions – to paraphrase an important volume from the series: *large issues* explored in *small places*. The series has a particular mission: to publish work that moves away from old-style descriptive ethnography – that is strongly area-studies oriented – and offer genuine theoretical arguments that are of interest to a much wider readership but which are nevertheless located and grounded in solid ethnographic research. If anthropology is to argue itself a place in the contemporary intellectual world then it must surely be through such research.

We start from the question: 'What can this ethnographic material tell us about the bigger theoretical issues that concern the social sciences?'; rather than 'What can these theoretical ideas tell us about the ethnographic context?' Put this way round, such work becomes *about* large issues, *set in* a (relatively) small place, rather than detailed description of a small place for its own sake. As Clifford Geertz once said: 'anthropologists don't study villages; they study *in* villages'.

By place we mean not only geographical locale, but also other types of 'place' – within political, economic, religious or other social systems. We therefore publish work based on ethnography within political and religious movements, occupational or class groups, youth, development agencies, nationalists; but also work that is more thematically based – on kinship, landscape, the state, violence, corruption, the self. The series publishes four kinds of volume – ethnographic monographs; comparative texts; edited collections; and shorter, polemic essays.

We publish work from all traditions of anthropology, and all parts of the world, which combines theoretical debate with empirical evidence to demonstrate anthropology's unique position in contemporary scholarship and the contemporary world.

Professor Vered Amit
Dr Jon P. Mitchell

Preface to the Second Edition

A lot has happened in the study of race and ethnicity in Latin America since the first edition of this book appeared in 1997. There has been great increase in the amount of literature produced, especially in relation to indigenous social movements and also in relation to black people, or Afro-Latins or Afro-descendants as the current terminology often has it. A great deal of literature has come out of Latin American academies – most of it in Spanish and Portuguese, of course – as well as North American and European ones. There are new journals, such as *Latin American and Caribbean Ethnic Studies*, and new associations, such as the section for Ethnicity, Race and Indigenous Peoples, which is part of the Latin American Studies Association. There have been new theoretical focuses or more emphasis on ones that were already around – on sex and gender, on neoliberalism, on citizenship, on transnationalism and diaspora, on political ecology and biodiversity, on materiality and embodiment.

There have also been new overviews of the contemporary scene, including ones that deal mostly with Afro-descendants – for example, Whitten and Torres (1998), Andrews (2004), Dzidzienyo and Oboler (2005), Davis (2007) – and ones that deal mostly with indigenous people, and usually with indigenous movements, such as Sieder (2002), Langer (2003), Warren and Jackson (2003), Postero and Zamosc (2004) and Yashar (2005). The split between indigenous and black people in studies of Latin America, which is a recurrent theme of this book, while it has been overcome in some new scholarship (see Chapters 2 and 6), seems still to retain a good deal of force. Overviews that bridge the divide are fewer – see, for example, Leiker et al. (2007), Branche (2008) and the more synthetic overview of Latin Americanist anthropology in Poole (2008) – and seem to be popular among historians (see Chapter 2).

There has been an increasing geographical spread, especially in relation to what is sometimes called Afro-America. Although there is still a relative paucity of anthropological, ethnographic monographs – in English – on Afro-descendants in Latin America and although many of those that exist are on Brazil, overall there is now much more material on other parts of the region and I refer to some of this in Chapters 4, 5 and 6.

In preparing this second edition, I have remained true to the underlying idea of the first edition. The book is not intended to be an overview of black and indigenous people in Latin America, nor of the scholarly literature that describes and analyses them. Instead, my intention was, and still is, to give an outline of the changing perspectives that have guided scholars interested in race and ethnicity in Latin America and to illustrate, with concrete examples, how these perspectives have guided their research. This is easiest to achieve for the earlier periods, up until about the 1970s. Thereafter it gets a little more difficult, as the field expands and diversifies, and it becomes more tempting to produce an overview of current scholarship in all its themes and focuses. Still, I have tried to pull out the broad shape of the guiding perspectives, even if these are not as easy to see for the 2000s – not having the benefit of hindsight – as they are for previous periods.

I have revised all the chapters, adding new material that reflects recent work and directing the reader to a wider bibliography. Predictably, the chapters that have grown most are Chapters 5 and 6, which deal with recent approaches and themes. Chapter 6, for example, has more than doubled in size. The bibliography has also doubled in length. I have purposely biased the bibliography towards material available in English, despite the fact that there is a vast amount of material being produced in Spanish and Portuguese (not to mention French). The audience for this book is mainly in English-speaking countries (although a Spanish translation of the first edition was published by Abya-Yala in Ecuador) and it is with this in mind that I have made choices about what to include in the bibliography. I am very aware, however, that such choices are an integral part of the whole problematic of postcolonial and decolonial relations that structure the production of knowledge – a problematic that I discuss in more detail in Chapter 7.

I would like to thank the series editors, the editors and the production team at Pluto for their interest in publishing a second edition of this book and for working with me in their usual efficient and friendly way.

Peter Wade
December 2009

Introduction

All over Latin America, and indeed the world, racial and ethnic identities are becoming increasingly significant for minorities and majorities, governments and non-governmental organisations (NGOs). Once widely predicted to be on the decline, destined to be dissolved by political and economic modernisation, issues connected with race and ethnicity are taking on greater dimensions. Indigenous peoples and the descendants of African slaves – who are the focus of this book – have formed organisations and social movements that call for a variety of reforms to land rights, political rights, cultural autonomy and, in some cases, simply the right to life itself. In some cases, governments have adopted political measures, including constitutional reforms, that recognise the multi-ethnic composition of their nations and accord certain groups special rights, thus moving away from the classic republican nationalism of homogeneous citizenship in which everyone was equal before the state. Such rights, whether given or claimed, are generally in recognition of the historical legacy that these groups are held to have: as original owners of the land, as subjects of enslavement, as the victims of racisms.

In this book, I examine the different ways these issues have been understood over the years. Rather than simply describing the current situation in its many different facets, my aim is to give a critical overview of the debates about the significance of racial and ethnic identities and how to analyse them. To do this, I have taken a historical approach to theoretical perspectives on race and ethnicity in Latin America. On a practical level, I think that current perspectives are much easier to grasp when you know where they are coming from and what they are supposed to supersede. More theoretically, I strongly believe that knowledge is a process that has its own past – an archaeology or genealogy – which it is necessary to know in order to understand its current dynamic. As the metaphor of archaeology or genealogy suggests, present approaches build on, or are generated by, past approaches. It is wrong to simply debunk these as old hat, for three distinct reasons. First, while the earlier work done on race and ethnicity sometimes took a line that must be discarded, there were also valuable elements: we cannot now condone the frankly racist view of blacks and native Americans held by some early twentieth-century observers, but the intensive ethnographic fieldwork approach of the 1930s and 1940s set the tone for taking seriously the 'native' point of view in a – not unproblematic – fashion that later approaches would be foolish to deny. Equally, Marxist analyses popular in the 1970s have been subjected to extended critique, but their firm grasp of power inequalities and the importance of a historical analysis cannot be gainsaid.

Second, the perspectives of each period tell us a great deal about that time, about the relations between those studied and those doing the studying, and about the form that knowledge was expected to take. Thus the functionalist studies dominant from the 1930s through the 1950s spoke of a world in which indigenous societies could acceptably be studied as objects located 'in the field' – that is, in some notionally rural area, outside the domain of the anthropologist's urban home society, and also in the field of his (or more rarely her) interest and distancing scientific gaze. Nowadays, the realisation that these indigenous societies are located in and influenced (often negatively) by a broader field of social relations that *includes* the analyst and his or her society makes such an objectifying, scientistic stance much less acceptable. But newer perspectives are built on a critique of the older ideas and the older social order they were lodged in, so an understanding of those ideas and that social order is necessary. A postcolonial perspective makes little sense unless you know what a colonial perspective looked like; the same goes for postmodernist and modernist approaches.

Third, an attempt to understand the present that is uninformed by previous attempts risks not simply reinventing the wheel, but also falling into traps that have been fallen into and resolved in the past. A critical view on one's own perspective is achieved partly by having a good grasp of a range of possible perspectives, including ones that began some time ago.

It is also necessary to locate the academic study of black and indigenous peoples in a wider framework of how these peoples have been seen and understood by their observers, masters, rulers, missionaries and self-proclaimed protectors – not to mention how they have understood themselves. This is a huge area of historical analysis which I cannot encompass here, but it is worth thinking about the continuities between theological ponderings on the nature of the native American in the sixteenth century and anthropological approaches to the same subject 500 years later. One of the arguments running through this book is that, from a very early date, native Americans have occupied the institutional position of Other, as essentially different from their observers, whereas the descendants of black Africans have been located much more ambiguously, as both inside and outside the society of their masters and observers. This thread runs through colonial society, appears again in republican Latin American nations and is visible in the anthropological concentration on native Americans to the relative neglect of black people. This reveals that social anthropology, and social science in general, is not a wholly new take on understanding people that emerged in the late nineteenth century; it is part of a longer enterprise of *some* people (typically intellectual Westerners) understanding *other* people (typically colonial and postcolonial subjects, and the peasant and working classes of Western countries). This is another reason for taking historical view of debates about race and ethnicity in Latin America and it is all the more important when the rights that indigenous and black peoples in Latin America claim and are sometimes given (or have forced upon them) are themselves based on ideas about their historical traditions and status.

The structure of the book is as follows.[1] I start by looking at the concepts of race and ethnicity, since a clear grasp of what they mean must precede any further discussion. I then give a broad overview of blacks and indigenous people in Latin America since the conquest, comparing and contrasting their positions in colonial and postcolonial social orders, and in academic study. (It should already be plain by now that my concern is with native Americans and the descendants of Africans, not with the many other possible 'ethnic groups' of Latin America – Jews, Poles, Syrians, Italians, Germans, etc. Any attempt to include these diverse peoples as well would have been to court disaster.) The next two chapters examine theoretical perspectives on race and ethnicity at different periods, from the early twentieth century, through mid-century studies to the more radical approaches of the 1970s. Chapters 5 and 6 analyse in depth more recent developments that locate racial and ethnic identifications within the nation-state and the global context, and that have been influenced by postmodernism, postcolonialism and subsequent trends. The concluding chapter draws the threads together, attempting to find a balance among the different perspectives that have been analysed and reflecting what shape anthropology will be taking in a world which is at once more united by enabling technologies and yet more divided by inequalities of power.

1
The Meaning of 'Race' and 'Ethnicity'

'Race' and 'ethnicity' are not terms that have fixed referents. It is tempting to believe in a progressivist vision of social science that leads from ignorance towards truth – especially with the term 'race' which, in earlier periods, was commonly used in evidently racist ways that are now known to be manifestly wrong. It seems obvious that post-war understandings of the term 'race' are now 'correct'. But I argue that we have to see each term in the context of a history of ideas, of Western institutionalised knowledge (whether social or natural science) and of practices. Race and ethnicity are not terms that refer in some neutral way to a transparent reality of which social science gives us an ever more accurate picture; instead they are terms embedded in academic, popular and political discourses that are themselves a constitutive part of academic, popular and political relationships and practices.

This does not mean that academic (including social scientific) concepts are completely determined by their social context. Such a rigorously relativist position would be tantamount to abandoning the enterprise of systematic enquiry into our social condition. It would also ignore the fact that such enquiry is, to some extent, driven by the dynamic of its own search after 'truth': when new facts, or new combinations of facts, become increasingly at odds with established ways of thinking about certain sets of facts, this creates a dynamic for change. There are legitimate standards – of logic, coherence, evidence – which mean that not all accounts of 'reality' are equally valid; some are clearly wrong. My point is simply that academic concepts are not independent of their social context, that the search for knowledge is not a steady progress towards a fixed end, but a somewhat contingent journey with no necessary end at all.

This is especially the case with sociological or anthropological knowledge which, however methodologically sophisticated, can never pretend to the rigours of experimental technique that have helped the natural sciences achieve the high levels of prediction and control that underwrite their claims to truth. Part of the reason for this is that knowledge of society is based on people studying people, rather than people studying objects or non-humans, and – whatever the arguments about the level of self-consciousness of non-human animals – this creates a reflexivity, or circular process of cause and effect, whereby the 'objects' of study can and do change their behaviour and ideas according to the conclusions that their observers draw about those behaviour and ideas. Thus social scientists are faced with an ever-moving target which they themselves are partly propelling in an open-ended journey.[1]

In this chapter, I want to examine the concepts of race and ethnicity in their historical contexts and argue that we have to see both of them as part of an enterprise of knowledge. This knowledge has been and still is situated within power relations – which, as Michel Foucault has so famously argued, knowledge itself helps to constitute – and in which Western countries have had the upper hand.

RACE

Rather than starting with a definition of race which would seem to create a nice objective area of analysis against which previous approaches to the idea might then be judged more or less adequate, I will start with a look at how the term has changed in meaning over time, so that we can see what it has come to mean (without perhaps completely divesting itself of all its previous semantic cargo), rather than what it 'really' means.[2]

Race until 1800

Michael Banton (1987) gives a very useful outline of changing 'racial theories'. The word 'race' entered European languages in the early sixteenth century. Its central meaning was what Banton calls *lineage*, that is a stock of descendants linked to a common ancestor; such a group of people shared a certain ancestry which might give them more or less common qualities. This usage was predominant until roughly 1800. The overall context was a concern with classifying living things and there was discussion and disagreement about why things were different, how permanently they were different and so on. In the concept of race as lineage, the role of appearance was not necessarily fundamental as an identifier. Thus one 1570 English usage referred to 'race and stock of Abraham', meaning all the descendants of Abraham. This included Moses, who had two successive wives; one of these was a Midianite (descendant of Midian, a son of Abraham), the other was a black Ethiopian woman. All the sons of Moses by these two women would be of 'his race', whatever their appearance (Banton, 1987: 30).

In general terms, the Bible supplied the framework for thinking about difference: the theory of monogenism was accepted – all humans had a common genesis, being the progeny of Adam and Eve. The main explanations for human difference were environmental and this was seen as affecting both the social and political institutions of human society and bodily difference – often the two were not really seen as separate.

For example, the Swedish botanist Linnaeus (1707–78), whose *System of Nature* was published in 1735, divided up all living things into species and genera, setting the basis for later classifications of difference. He presented various accounts of the internal subdivisions of the genus *Homo*. In one such (Hodgen, 1964: 425), 'Americans' were characterised thus: 'Copper-coloured, choleric, erect. Paints self. Regulated by custom.'

What we would call cultural and physical features are presented together, showing that they were not necessarily seen as very different, but also showing that what we would now call cultural traits were seen as 'natural': such differences were *naturalised* without being *biologised* (see next section, below; see also Wade, 2002a).

Banton argues that the use of the term 'race' was quite rare between the sixteenth and eighteenth centuries – the period of the scientific revolution and the Enlightenment – and that ideas about the inferiority of non-European peoples, such as Africans, were not very widespread, especially among the major thinkers of the time. Thus he sees the oft-quoted Edward Long, son of a Jamaican planter, whose *History of Jamaica* (1774) is frequently claimed as showing typically racist attitudes, as an exception rather than the rule. Equally, he argues that Thomas Jefferson, who famously advocated abolition in his *Notes on the State of Virginia* (1787), may have thought of the gulf between blacks and whites in terms of species difference, but was criticised by others for his views.

Banton's concern here is to contest 'presentism', the judging of the ideas of previous historical eras by the standards of our own. This, he argues, tends to lump all these different people together indiscriminately as 'racists', thus losing sight of the complex ways people thought about difference.

This is all very well, but Banton presents us with a history of ideas which is rather divorced from its social context. Audrey Smedley (1993) gives a rather different picture in which the guiding thread of ideas about the supposed *superiority* of Europeans, or whites, runs through the varying and complex ways of conceiving of human difference. The Bible may have implied monogenesis, but it also provided a means for asserting that Africans were inferior. Different peoples were said to be the descendants of the various sons of Noah and Africans were sometimes argued to be the sons of Ham, cursed by Noah for having seen him when he was drunk and naked.[3] In medieval theology, blackness was often linked to the devil and sin, and Africans were often held to be inferior even during the early stages of this period (Jordan, 1977; Pieterse, 1992). Throughout the period Banton refers to, Europeans were generally thought of as more civilised and superior.

Smedley's account – like many others – lays emphasis on the social, economic and political conditions in which the ponderings about human difference took place: explorations of Africa, the conquest of the New World, colonialism, slavery. Following a lead set by Horsman's study of Anglo-Saxons' ideas about fulfilling their 'manifest destiny' of superior political leadership based on freedom and democracy (Horsman, 1981), she focuses on the English and suggests various factors that made them particularly prone to exclusivist ideas of themselves as superior. These factors included the relative isolation of north-eastern European peoples from Greek and Roman knowledge, at least until the Renaissance; the rise from the sixteenth century of capitalism, secularism and possessive individualism (based on ideas of personal autonomy, the importance of property-owning and the accumulation of wealth); the importance given to hierarchy, often defined in economic terms; and the English experience with the sixteenth- and seventeenth-century colonisation of the Irish who had already been relegated to the status of savages (that is, as supposedly bestial, sexually licentious, undisciplined, etc.). This sort of background set the scene for the brutal encounter of the English with the Africans and the native inhabitants of the New World, the usurpation of land as private property and the conversion of Africans into chattels.

Hall (1992b) makes a more general argument about Europe as a whole. He emphasises how the idea of Europe as an entity emerged during this period, from broader and more inclusive concepts of Christendom – which included, for example, black Christian Ethiopians seen as allies in holy wars against Islam (Pieterse, 1992: ch. 1). During the fifteenth century, non-European Christians were gradually excluded from the domain of Christendom itself and by the sixteenth century Europe had replaced Jerusalem as the centre of the known world. Despite internal wars and quarrels, Europe was being drawn together by mercantile capitalism and technological development (see also Jones, 1981). It was also being increasingly defined in opposition to Others – Africans, native Americans. The image of the wild man, the savage who reputedly existed on the peripheries of Europe (Taussig, 1987: 212), and of the infidel who had been fighting Christendom for the Holy Land were being increasingly supplemented and displaced by the image of the paganism and savagery located in Africa and the New World – although in all cases, ambivalence (for example, of hate and desire) attached to such images. In short, then, ideas about human difference, while they may have involved a concept of race that was diverse, contested and even not very central, were certainly powerfully structured by ideas of European superiority. Kant (1724–1804), the philosopher whose influence has been so important in Western thought, may not have written much directly about race, but he did comment thus: 'the fellow was quite black from head to foot, a clear proof that what he said was stupid', and David Hume (1711–76) could also state that 'the Negro' was 'naturally inferior to the whites' (Goldberg, 1993: 31–2).

Goldberg (1993) also paints a broad picture. He sees the concept of race as emerging with modernity itself – 'race is one of the central conceptual inventions of modernity' (1993: 3) – and as intertwined with basic ideas about morality. Whereas in previous eras, morality was defined in terms of virtue and correct behaviour, or of the prevention of sin, in the modern period, and with the discoveries, people began talking in terms of stocks or breeds of humans people with engrained, *natural* qualities. Human identity and personhood became increasingly defined by a discourse of race, certain races became defined as non-rational or aesthetically inferior (lacking in the 'natural' balance of beauty and harmony) and race could define certain people as fit for slavery.

Race in the Nineteenth Century

Banton (1987) then moves on to consider the concept of race as *type*. This concept, which built on existing ones and developed in diverse and contested ways during the nineteenth century, was based on the idea that races were permanent, separable types of human beings with innate qualities that were passed on from one generation to the next. Now everyone (or thing) that was alike in nature and appearance was thought to have descended from a common ancestor. Moses' sons, in this view, would not belong to the stock and race of Abraham: some would be considered to belong to the black race, while others might be mixed race, Semites or perhaps Caucasians. Within this overall view, typologies of humankind proliferated and there was heated debate about whether types were separate species or not. Polygenism – the theory that different human types had separate origins – gained ground, despite its divergence from biblical teachings (Anderson, 2006). Ideas about evolutionary change (in a pre-Darwinian sense), which had been present in the seventeenth century in concepts of the gradual progression from primitive forms of human life (of which the 'lower' peoples were often thought to be exemplars) towards supposedly superior forms, were adapted to ideas about racial types as stages on an evolutionary scale. Racial types were hierarchically ordered, as racial 'lineages' had been before, but now the basis of the hierarchy was thought of in terms of innate differences of 'biology', the term proposed by Lamarck, among others, in 1802 to describe the scientific study of living organisms (Mayr, 1982: 108). 'Natural' differences were increasingly seen as specifically 'biological' differences.

Stocking (1982: ch. 2) compares two French scientists of the early nineteenth century, Degérando and Cuvier. In his writings, Degérando hardly mentioned race and saw difference as environmental, although he did see 'primitive' peoples as being examples of previous stages in progression of humans towards European perfection. Cuvier, in a sign of things to come, expounded a 'static non-evolutionary tradition of comparative anatomy', and spent his time collecting (or rather stealing) bones and skulls for comparative measurement to assess racial difference. This was an early example of a whole industry of anatomical measurement, designed to specify racial typologies, with great attention being paid to the skull since brain size was held to correlate with superior intelligence. Although many of the practitioners of this science were medics and naturalists, anthropology was often the label they used for their investigations.

This was the age of scientific racism when 'even for self-pro-claimed egalitarians, the inferiority of certain races was no more to be contested than the law of gravity to be regarded as immoral' (Barkan, 1992: 2–3). The conceptual centrality which Goldberg asserts for race can also be seen in this statement by Robert Knox, Scottish medic and author of *The Races of Men* (1850): 'That race is everything, is simply a fact, the most remarkable, the most comprehensive, which philosophy has ever announced. Race is everything: literature, science, art – in a word, civilisation depends on it' (cited in Pieterse, 1992: 49).

The context for the rise of this science – and science it was held to be, even if it was bad science and immoral by today's standards – was the abolition of slavery and the slave trade. There is no easy correlation here, because the apogee of scientific racism was the end of the nineteenth and the beginning of the twentieth centuries, whereas first the slave trade then slavery itself were mostly abolished by 1863.[4] Also, some racial theorists were opposed to slavery on humanitarian grounds, while, conversely, some southern US slave-holders opposed racial typologies on religious grounds (Banton, 1987: 9, 45). But it is no coincidence that just as abolitionist opinion gained dominance in Europe, making the institutionalised inferiority of blacks morally insecure, theories began to emerge that could justify the continued dominance over blacks (not to mention native Americans, Asians and Orientals) in terms of supposedly innate and permanent inferiority, and now with the full power of scientific backing. In any case, slavery was partly opposed in terms of its unsuitability for a modern industrial society based on free wage labour (Eltis, 1987), rather than because it oppressed black people, so opposing slavery was no guarantee of a positive stance on racial equality.

The other main social context was the rise of imperialism which, following on from the first main phase of colonialism between about 1450 and 1800 based mainly on settler colonies and mercantile capitalism, began in the nineteenth century to expand rapidly into Asia, Africa and the Pacific, with less direct settlement and more emphasis on the extraction and cultivation of raw materials and on the sale of industrial goods. Goldberg continues his analysis of the intertwining of ideas of moral philosophy and racial theory in Western thought by arguing that, in the nineteenth century, utilitarianism became central and that, although the concept of race might not be directly invoked, the principles of utility and the collective good allowed authoritarian rule in which the most rational – the white colonisers – decided on rational grounds what was best for the less rational – the black colonised. Thus John Stuart Mill, the great exponent of utilitarianism, who followed his father into the colonial service in India where 6000 civil servants controlled vast areas of the subcontinent, preached the need to govern the lower, less civilised orders (Goldberg, 1993: 35).

Race in the Twentieth Century

The twentieth century saw a period of changes and contradictions during which the meanings attached to the term 'race' varied very widely. On the one hand, eugenics emerged as a convergence of science and social policy, the term coined at the turn of the century by Francis Galton, scientist and cousin of Charles Darwin. It was based on scientific racism and the idea that the reproductive capacities of biologically 'unfit' individuals (for example, the insane) and, more generally, the 'inferior races' should be restricted, just as the breeding of domestic livestock might try to eliminate unwanted traits. The movement had quite a strong influence in Europe and the US and also affected Latin America (Stepan, 1991); by the time it became part of Nazi policy in the 1930s, it had lost much ground elsewhere. On the other hand, however, this period also saw the dismantling of scientific racism.

The latter trend had several sources. Darwin's evolutionary theories indicated that it was no longer possible to think in terms of permanent racial types: breeding populations adapted over time. However, these ideas, published as early as 1871 (*The Descent of Man*) took a long time to impact and did not scotch scientific racism; rather the latter adapted to the former with the development of social evolutionism according to which superior, 'fitter' races were more 'successful' in terms of their capacity to dominate others (Stocking, 1982: ch. 6).

Franz Boas, the anthropologist, also played an important role in challenging scientific racial typologies (Stocking, 1982: ch. 8). A Jew with a background in physics, he left behind the anti-Semitism of late nineteenth-century Germany and migrated to the US where he did anthropometric research – measuring heads, as many others were doing at the time. He discovered that variation in head dimensions over a lifetime or between contiguous generations exceeded that found between 'races'. The very techniques of scientific racism could be used to undermine its theories. Boas went on to challenge theories of innate racial difference and hierarchy, but it would be wrong to see Boas as the hero single-handedly overthrowing scientific racism. Students of his – such as Ashley Montagu – were also very influential. More broadly, the rediscovery of Mendelian inheritance in 1900 paved the way for the establishment of the science of genetics. Mendel, hitherto a little-known Austrian monk, had discovered 40 years earlier that specific traits (in sweet peas) were controlled by specific elements (that is, genes) which were passed from one generation to another as independent components; this meant that the idea of 'type', based on a collection of traits passed down the generations as an unchanging bundle, was untenable.

The social context for these changes was varied: imperialism continued apace, legal racial segregation was solidly in place in the US and was gaining ground in South Africa, and the rise of the women's movement and working-class militancy aroused conservative fears of social degeneration which fed into the social reform drive of the eugenics movement. On the face of it, then, there was little reason why scientific racism should be undone. But science had its own dynamic here and the facts that were mounting up about inheritance and anthropometry simply no longer fitted into the racial typology paradigm. The racist ideology and atrocities of the Nazi regime in Europe and the upheavals of the Second World War, followed by the black civil rights movement in the US protesting against legal racial segregation, supplied the political drive to finally dismantle scientific racism. This was epitomised in the post-war UNESCO declarations on race which boldly stated that humans were fundamentally the same and that differences of appearance were just that and did not indicate essential differences in, say, intellect.

What happened, then, to the term 'race' in this context? Many biologists, geneticists and physical anthropologists – but not all – have reached the conclusion that, biologically speaking, races do not exist.[5] Genetic variation exists, but it is very difficult to take a given gene or set of genes and draw a line around its distribution in space to define a 'race'; nor can a term such as 'black' or 'white' be pinned down genetically in anything approaching a clear way. Furthermore, most psychologists agree that humans are, on average, the same in terms of their mental capacities; individual variation exists, of course, but there are no significant variations that correlate with categories such as 'black', 'Amerindian', 'white', 'African', 'European' and so on (Lieberman and Reynolds, 1996). Therefore, many natural scientists and the vast majority of social scientists agree that races are *social constructions*. The idea of race is just that – an idea. The notion that races exist with definable physical characteristics and, even more so, that some races are superior to others is the result of particular historical processes which, many would argue, have their roots in the colonisation by European peoples of other areas of the world.

The social constructedness of racial categories can be illustrated by a well-known contrast between North America and Latin

America. In the former region, the category 'black' supposedly includes anyone with a known 'drop of black blood'; thus someone known to have had a black grandmother will be assigned a black identity. In Latin America, to over-simplify a complex situation, there is a continuum of racial categories and often only people who look quite African in appearance will be identified as black; people of evidently more mixed ancestry will often be classed by a variety of terms denoting a position between black and white. Thus, for example, a Puerto Rican, used to not being classed as black in Puerto Rico, when she moves to the mainland US, may find herself suddenly identified as a black person. The reasons for this contrast are complex, but they are fundamentally historical in nature and connected with the type of colonial enterprise and sets of social relations established in each region (Marx, 1998). The point is that the term 'black' has no simple referent, even in the Americas: its meaning varies according to context.[6]

Now the notion that races are social constructs does not mean that they are unimportant – 'merely ideas', as it were. Clearly, people may behave *as if* races did exist and, as a result, races do exist as social categories of great tenacity and power. If people discriminate on the basis of their ideas of race, this is a social reality of paramount importance. Equally, people may lay claim to a racial identity that represents for them central aspects of their person – indeed in the US, racial identity is so politicised that no one is really complete without one.[7]

But if races are social constructions, what kind of social constructions are they? Social life is full of social constructions – gender is the one most commonly cited, but ethnicity, as we shall see, is also one, and class could also qualify. Is there something that lets us know when we are dealing with a *racial* construction? Many social scientists argue that races are social constructions built on phenotypical variation – that is, disparities in physical appearance (see Wade, 1993b, 2002a). The brute fact of physical difference exists and people have used these cues to create ranked social categories which are used to include and exclude and which are said to show more or less innate, natural differences which are passed on over generations: racial identification involves a discourse of naturalisation (Gilroy, 1982; Goldberg, 1993).

This common approach, while it is in my view mostly sound, does however assume that there is such a thing as the brute fact of phenotypical variation. It recognises that races do not exist as objective biological entities, but then tries to reconstruct an objective basis for recognising 'racial' distinctions by grounding them in phenotype. This glosses over the problem that the apparently 'natural fact' of phenotypical variation is itself socially constructed: the physical differences that have become cues for *racial* distinctions are quite particular ones: not just ones that show some recognisable continuity over generations (perhaps height, weight, hair colour, etc.), but ones that corresponded to the geographical encounters of Europeans in their colonial histories. It is specific combinations of skin colour, hair type and facial features that have been worked into racial signifiers.

Thus, to pick up the argument I started with, the concept of race is even more surely linked into a European history of thinking about difference, rather than a concept describing an objective reality that is independent of a social context. To see races as social constructions built on some neutral biological fact of phenotypical variation is to assert that we can recognise a racial categorisation independently of history and build a study of race on an objective basis. In fact, only certain phenotypical variations make racial categories and the ones that count have emerged through history. This means that races, racial categories and racial ideologies are not simply those that elaborate social constructions on the basis of phenotypical variation – or ideas about innate difference – but those that do so using the particular aspects of phenotypical variation that were worked into vital signifiers of difference during European colonial encounters with others (Wade, 1993b, 2002a).[8] It means that the study of race is *part of* that history, not outside it, and thus that what is to *count* as the study of race is not to be circumscribed by some objective definition about phenotypical variation but can change over time and is, ultimately, up for grabs. This is the only way we can include in the study of race the fact that a group of white US girls triggered an 'imitation race war at their virtually all white high school [in 1994] by dressing "black"'. This had nothing to do with phenotypical variation, but plenty to do with 'race' (Bernstein, 2003).

ETHNICITY

The term 'ethnicity' is at once easier and more difficult: its history is shorter and less morally loaded, but it is also used more vaguely – sometimes as a less emotive term for 'race'. The word 'ethnicity' arose in academic parlance and dates from the Second World War (Banks, 1996: 4; Eriksen, 1993: 3; Glazer and Moynihan,

1975: 1), but the word 'ethnic' is older. Based on the Greek word *ethnos*, meaning people or 'nation' (although the latter word has specific connotations since the rise of nationalism in the modern era), it was used in English to refer to heathens or pagans until the nineteenth century, when, with the apogee of scientific racial typologies, it was used as a synonym of 'racial' (R. Williams, 1988: 119). With the dismantling of scientific racism, it began to be used in the phrase 'ethnic group' – for example, by Julian Huxley in *We Europeans* (1936) – to talk about groups that were still seen as biological groupings, without being biological races (Lyons, 1996: 12). Thereafter, the word has generally been employed to refer to groups of people seen as minorities within larger nation-states – Jews or Poles in Brazil, Algerians in France. The proliferating usage of 'ethnicity' and 'ethnic group', both in academia and in popular parlance, is partly due to rapid processes of social change which have created new postcolonial nations and massive migrations: the terms 'tribe' and 'race', with which people often used to label the differences that seemed important in these contexts, were deemed inaccurate, demeaning or old-fashioned (Eriksen, 1993: 8–10). 'Ethnicity' has often been used in place of 'race' either because the very use of the word 'race' has been thought to propagate racism by implying that biological races actually exist or because, tainted by its history, it simply 'smelt bad'.

But what does 'ethnicity' mean? Banks collects a useful set of comments from anthropologists and concludes that ethnicity is 'a collection of rather simplistic and obvious statements about boundaries, otherness, goals and achievements, being and identity, descent and classification, that has been constructed as much by the anthropologist as by the subject' (1996: 5). Ethnicity is a social construction that is centrally about identifications of difference and sameness, but the same could be said of race, gender and class – so where does the specificity of ethnicity lie, if anywhere? Some commentators remain vague on this point, but the general consensus is that ethnicity refers to 'cultural' differences, whereas, as we saw above, race is said to refer to phenotypical differences – although some draw no real distinction between race and ethnicity (for example, Eriksen, 1993: 5). To give some substance to this rather bland definition, I will give some brief examples of how ethnicity has been understood.

Some early influential approaches emerged from the Manchester school of anthropology. Clyde Mitchell, for example, focused on the so-called Copper Belt mining towns of Northern Rhodesia (now part of Zambia). People from many different 'tribes' – as anthropologists then tended to call them – congregated on these towns and Mitchell observed that 'tribal' identities became more, rather than less, distinctive in an urban environment through opposition to each other. People categorised each other in terms of dress, speech, customs, appearance and so on. Ethnicity – as it was later to be called – was a way of categorising complex cultural differences and thus defining for individuals who was who and how to behave towards them. In the Kalela dance, urban migrants expressed these differences in a jovial form: as they danced on rest days in these mining towns, men from each 'tribe' caricatured the cultural traits of other groups and thus restated ethnic identities (Mitchell, 1956; see also Banks, 1996; Hannerz, 1980)

Abner Cohen criticised these social classification approaches and took a line that has since been characterised as an 'instrumentalist' or 'resource mobilisation' model (Banks, 1996: 39; B. Williams, 1989). The basic argument was that people used aspects of culture to signal boundaries and create in-groups that tried to control some useful resource or political power. Thus Hausa migrants in the Yoruba town of Ibadan in Nigeria manipulated aspects of their culture – customs, values, myths, symbols – to create an ethnically identified in-group that controlled long-distance trade in cattle and kola nuts. For Cohen, ethnic groups were informal interest groups (Cohen, 1969, 1974). This approach opposed the so-called 'primordialist' perspective, which implied that ethnic identity was just a basic feature of people's psychological make-up, a product of the way they classified people, for example. A similar instrumentalist line was taken in the US by Glazer and Moynihan (1975).

This gives some idea of what ethnicity as discourse of cultural difference might mean, but it remains rather unspecific: in Britain, different classes are often thought to have particular cultural features, even if class is principally based on economic differences; men and women also differentiate each other by reference to speech, cultural behaviour and so on. In this sense, ethnicity becomes an unsatisfactory residual analytic category: it includes all those forms of cultural categorisation where there is no other primary discourse of differentiation, such as wealth, sex, age, phenotype, etc.

My own angle on this problem is that ethnicity is, of course, about cultural differentiation, but that it tends to use a language of *place* (rather than wealth, sex, or inherited phenotype). Cultural difference is spread over geographical space by virtue of the fact that social relations become concrete in spatialised form. This creates a cultural geography, or in Taussig's phrase, a moral topography (1987: 253; see also Wade, 1993a: 51). People thus use location, or rather people's putative origin in certain places, to talk about difference and sameness. 'Where are you from?' is thus the 'ethnic question' *par excellence*. Of course, not all objective differences in location are important in terms of people's perceptions of cultural geography: as Barth (1969) pointed out many years ago, it is the people involved, not the analyst, who define what features constitute difference and sameness.

This approach gives us a handle on a commonly noted aspect of ethnicity, the fact that ethnic identities are 'nested' in a kind of Russian doll form. Rather than having a single and univocal ethnic identity, most people have multiple identities according to who they are interacting with and in what context. Thus northerners and southerners in one country or region may differentiate themselves (in England, Italy, the US), but identify as the same *vis-à-vis* people from a different country (English versus Italians), yet identify with those people in the face of broader differences (Europeans or 'Westerners' versus Africans).[9]

The place perspective also helps to understand why 'ethnicity' seems to have become a more common phenomenon in the modern world. Although people have doubtless always thought about difference in terms of place, and although people have migrated since the origins of the human species, it is reasonable to argue that with the onset of modernity and a global world – which, for argument's sake, I will say dates from the late fourteenth century and the Discoveries – people from different locations in their own cultural geographies have interacted with increasing intensity. The rise of nationalism from the late eighteenth century (in the US, then Latin America and Europe), the later phases of imperialism (for example, the carve-up of Africa) and postcolonial migrations (for example, from former colonies to former colonial nations) all instigated periods of intense redefinition of boundaries and of social collectivities in which the question of origin in a cultural geography as a defining feature of difference and sameness has become very salient. In this sense, then, as with race, ethnicity and ethnic categorisations are part of a particular history. To see ethnicity as a language of cultural geography is not a final, objective definition, but reflects the importance of changing cultural geographies for people in the modern world.

RACE AND ETHNICITY: IS THERE A DIFFERENCE?

From the argument so far it may seem that race and ethnicity are distinct concepts. There are, however, two sets of reasons why some people might argue that they are the same. First, some people who do not effectively distinguish between race and ethnicity argue that 'race' should be jettisoned as a term with too much invidious history; they prefer to talk about ethnic relations and ethnic minorities (or, less often, majorities – it is often forgotten that, for example, Anglo-Saxon North Americans are just as 'ethnic' as Italian-Americans). A variant on this view argues that 'ideas of "race" may or may not form part of ethnic ideologies and their presence or absence does not seem to be a decisive factor' (Eriksen, 1993: 5). Anthias and Yuval-Davis do distinguish between race and ethnicity as modes of social categorisation (1992: 2–3), but also see racism as the 'discourse and practice of inferiorizing ethnic groups' (1992: 12). The second set of reasons is more complex and I will argue through it before returning to the first problem.

The dismantling of the biological concept of race and its general acceptance, at least in social sciences, as a social construction has brought about a recognition of the mutability of race – the comparison between North and Latin America discussed earlier is an example. Racial identities are now seen in somewhat the same way as ethnic identities: they are contextual, situational, multivocal. This view is an inevitable result of seeing races as social constructions, which by their nature must depend on shifting social relations, but more recently it also owes a lot to post-structuralist and postmodernist social theories (see Chapter 5). Very briefly, these have led to a critique of a concept of identity as an essential entity, based on the Enlightenment version of the subject as a sovereign, autonomous, rational actor. Freudian theories of the subconscious, Marxist theories of the determination of human consciousness by economic structures and French structuralist theories of the existence of innate structures of human consciousness which underlie diverse cultural expressions – all these have undermined the Enlightenment view of the subject and led to current views of the subject as fragmented, multiple, unstable and decentred (Hall, 1992a). A corollary of this is an anti-essentialist view of identity: a person, and even less a group or category, does not have an underlying essence or centre that defines overall character (Landry and MacLean, 1993: ch. 7). 'Women' or 'whites' are internally heterogeneous groups: like subjects, these categories are fragmented and decentred (that is, they have no defining centre). In this view, then, races are like ethnic groups.

It may be objected that racial identifications cannot be as flexible as this sort of view implies: social categories that use physical, bodily cues to assign identities do not seem that open to 'decentring'. There are two issues here. The first is that bodily cues can be used to mean various things: thus a certain skin tone and hair texture in the US might mean 'black', whereas in Latin America it might mean '*mulato*': bodies themselves are socially constructed. In addition, bodies are not immutable: plastic surgery is the most obvious example (Edmonds, 2007), but hair-straightening, skin-lightening and sun-tanning are all ways of altering the body that can have an impact on racial identification – and Michael Jackson is only a recent example. The second issue is that anti-essentialism does not necessarily contest the apparent fixity of racial identifications: rather, the point is that the fact that someone is 'black' or 'white' or 'indigenous' does not therefore say everything about that person. S/he may also be old/young, female/male, homosexual/heterosexual, rich/poor and so on: there are cross-cutting identifications. Thus the point remains that racial identifications seem similar to ethnic identifications: both are partial, unstable, contextual, fragmentary.

My view is that a distinction, based on the approaches to race and ethnicity that I have argued for above, is worth maintaining, although I admit that it cannot be a radical one. The distinction should not be that racial identifications are imposed by a majority on a discriminated minority, while ethnic ones are chosen by in-group members for themselves (Banton, 1983: 106). Instead, my point is that to deny a specific role to racial identifications, as Eriksen (1993) does, or to discriminations based on them, as Anthias and Yuval-Davis (1992) do, is to blur the *particular history* by which these identifications come to have the force they do. To identify oneself or others as 'Serb' in Eastern Europe is to invoke a particular, relatively local history; to identify oneself or others as 'black', 'indian'[10] or 'indigenous' in much of the Western world is to invoke, distantly or immediately, a long history of colonial encounters, slavery, discrimination, resistance and so on. This does not mean that ethnic histories cannot be long and conflictive, but I think it is necessary to highlight the history of race by calling it by its name.

Neither does this approach mean that racial identifications or racisms are everywhere the same, or that if racism departs from the biologistic version of late nineteenth-century scientific racism it does not really qualify as racism (an implication of some accounts – for example, Smedley [1993] and Banton [1987] – that treat scientific racism as a kind of ideal type). There are different racisms, but, in my view, they are linked in historically varied ways to that history of colonial encounters. The meanings attributed even nowadays to 'black' or 'white' in South America, the Caribbean, South Africa, Europe, the US, and also Australia are not independent of each other nor of that history. Racism today in much of Europe, for example, is different from earlier versions in that it depends less on attributions of biological inferiority (although these have not disappeared either). Instead, the so-called new or cultural racism depends on ideas about deeply engrained cultural difference (Barker, 1981; Solomos, 1989; Wetherell and Potter, 1992). Yet many of the current images of blacks, whites, Asians, etc. resonate with previous images: race has been, as Goldberg (2008) puts it, 'buried alive'.

Racial and ethnic identifications do, however, overlap, both analytically and in practice. At an abstract level, both race and ethnicity involve a discourse about origins and about the transmission of essences across generations. Racial identifications use aspects of phenotype as a cue for categorisation, but these are seen as transmitted intergenerationally – through the 'blood' – so that ancestral origin is important; likewise ethnicity is about origin in a cultural geography in which the culture of a place is absorbed by a person (almost 'into the blood') from previous generations (Porqueres i Gené, 2007). On a more practical level, if ethnicity invokes location in a cultural geography, it may be the case that the phenotypical traits used in racial discourse are distributed across that geography: in Colombia, for example, 'blacks' are located in certain parts of the country (Wade, 1993a). Also, ethnic identifications may be made within a single racial category and vice versa, so that any individual can have both racial and ethnic identities.

RACE, ETHNICITY AND CLASS

A final theoretical area that needs to be broached is that of the relation between race, ethnicity and class. Here I shall refer mainly to the debates about the relation between race and class, since theoretically this has been the main terrain of dispute and because the issues under debate are basically the same for the case of ethnicity. I will refer to some non-Latin Americanist literature, because much of the debate has occurred outside the context of Latin America and because, in subsequent chapters, I will be looking in detail at race, ethnicity and class in Latin America.

The parameters of this debate were defined by discussions for, against and within Marxism (for more detail, see Anthias and Yuval-Davis, 1992: ch. 3; Gilroy, 1982; Omi and Winant, 1986). The central question was whether race could be 'explained' in terms of class, or more broadly economics. A classic Marxist approach to race argued that the underlying determinant of capitalist societies is the opposition between the owners of capital (the bourgeoisie) and the non-owners (the proletariat); this division, while not fully developed historically, determines much of what happens at all levels in a society. Racial categories must be related to this division and, if they exist, it is because the bourgeoisie has created them in order to (a) better dominate a particular fraction of the workforce, who are categorised as naturally inferior and good only for manual work, and (b) divide the workers into antagonistic racial categories and thus rule them more effectively. In these arguments, the origins of racism were located in the class relations of colonialism and the basic functions of racism remain essentially the same over time. This is a simplified version of a classic Marxist argument, but it set up one extreme in the debate.

Critics of this position might admit that domination of labour and divide-and-rule tactics were important parts of a racially stratified system and they might admit the colonial origins of racism, but they attacked the crude class reductionism of this approach. For a start, it is clear that racial categories can affect economic factors: as we shall see in the next chapter, the fact that Africans became slaves while native Americans were formally exempted from this category was due, among other things, to ideas about Africans and native Americans. Thus the determinations run both ways. Second, the way that racial identifications have changed over time, even in one capitalist country, cannot be easily explained in terms of changing class structures. Thus, changes in racial relations in the US during this century – for example, legal desegregation – while they may be related to the changing needs of capitalists for a better skilled and more flexible workforce, are also the product of black resistance – as *blacks*, more than as black *workers* – and the dismantling of scientific racism. Third, racism becomes an element of false consciousness, a misapprehension of 'reality': either the bourgeoisie invents it and imposes it on the gullible working class, or the working class somehow invent it for themselves. Neither option really captures the power and 'reality' of racial identifications in daily life. Fourth, class diversity within the oppressed racial category is hard to account for – for example, the position of middle-class blacks.

Over the years, Marxist-oriented writers shifted positions in a variety of ways to take account of these problems (Solomos, 1986). In broad terms, the tendency has been to attribute more 'autonomy' to racial factors, seeing them as having an impact on economic and class structures and as not reducible to class determinations. Racism could be seen as an ideology which paradoxically, as Anthias and Yuval-Davis (1992: 69–70) pointed out, actually *determines* the location of racialised groups in the class structure: the Marxist starting point is more or less reversed in that ideology is determinant. John Rex, taking a Weberian approach that is close to some revisionist Marxist positions, argued a similar line (Hall, 1980: 314; Rex, 1986).

Other approaches, not necessarily divorced from Marxist influences, have tried to avoid the idea that race is 'merely' ideology that intervenes, however autonomously, in class relations. For them race is a level of experience and cultural reality in its own right. Thus, for Gilroy, the struggle of blacks in Britain for civil rights or against police harassment is part of the way the working class is constituted as a political force (1982: 302). In an echo of Hall's resonant phrase that 'race is the modality in which class is "lived"' (Hall, 1980: 340), Gilroy asserts that the postcolonial economic and social crisis of British society is '*lived* through a sense of "race"' (1993b: 22). Omi and Winant oppose all forms of class reductionism and instead analyse 'racial formations' and 'racial projects' as *sui generis* social phenomena that may be related to class factors, but in which people have their own interests and goals that are defined in terms of racial identifications and meanings (Omi and Winant, 1986; Winant, 1994).

More recent approaches, then, have tended to move away from treating race and class 'as two distinct sets of relations, which interconnect in some essential way' and which are involved in some kind of mutual determination (Anthias and Yuval-Davis, 1992: 75). Rather, and as part of a postmodernist move away from the 'big theories' of social thought – such as Marxism – which try to encompass all phenomena within one totalising and inevitably reductionist explanation, the emphasis is on the multiple ways in which people may identify differences and sameness, struggle, mobilise, and make alliances and enmities. Feminist theory has been an important force in moving in this direction, both in terms of social theory and political action, showing, for example, that black women have different interests from black men, or Asian women from white women (Anthias and Yuval-Davis, 1992: ch. 4; hooks, 1991; Knowles and Mercer, 1992). This has led, particularly in the US and Europe, but increasingly in Latin America, to debates about the cultural politics of identity and difference which, some claim, distract attention from basic issues of economic inequality (for example, Fry et al., 2007a; Marable, 1995: ch. 16).

Issues of economic exploitation and inequality have taken on greater force in the wake of neoliberal policies in Latin America (and worldwide), which have opened markets to global trade, reduced state protection and welfare, pushed down wages for the poorer sectors of the labour force and increased poverty (see, for example, Perlman, 2005). In this context, Goldberg (2008) insists on recognising race and racism as vital forces in today's world and sees them as global forces that – as arguably they have always done – operate across national boundaries. He challenges what he identifies as the tendencies of neoliberalism to mask talk of race and racism, focusing instead on the individual or 'culture', and diverting attention from structural forces of oppression, which involve race, but also class. Thus he equally insists on grasping the political-economic domination and inequality – and resistance – that race and racism involve, rather than focusing on cultural identities. In this sense, then, the debate has been reshaped, but has not gone away.

CONCLUSION

The arguments arrayed above will be important in examining race and ethnicity in Latin America. The differences and similarities between the categories 'black' and 'indian', for example, cannot be understood without a clear idea of what racial and ethnic identifications involve. It has often been argued that 'black' is a racial identification, while 'indian' is an ethnic one. I will be arguing that the difference is not quite so straightforward. Nor can the differences and similarities between Latin America and the US in terms of racial identities and racism be grasped without knowing what these terms mean. Again, it has commonly been said that the US is (or was) the home of 'real' racism, a deep racism based on genetics, while Latin America is characterised by a more superficial racism of appearance or phenotype. I will argue that such an opposition is misleading.

2
Blacks and Indigenous People in Latin America

The study of black and indigenous people in Latin America has, to a great extent, been divided into, on the one hand, studies of slavery, slavery-related issues and 'race relations' and, on the other, studies of 'indigenous people'. Colonial historiography has recently brought the two together to some extent in synthetic overviews (for example, Fisher and O'Hara, 2009; Restall, 2005; see also Lockhart and Schwartz, 1983), but the divide is a deep-seated one. In this chapter, I look at why this divide exists. I argue that the roots of the split go back to the fifteenth century and have spread right through the colonial period, the republican period of nation-building and into the scholarship and politics of the twentieth century. I will also be arguing in this book that such a division is not, ultimately, very helpful and only hides interesting contrasts and similarities between blacks and indigenous people in Latin America.

AFRICANS AND 'INDIANS' IN COLONIAL LATIN AMERICA

At the time when the Spanish and Portuguese arrived in the New World, Africans were a well-known category of person. Some of this knowledge derived from classical texts, religious sources and travellers' tales; but some of it derived from direct contact with Africa, by virtue of voyages of exploration down the West African coast from the 1430s which had resulted in African slaves entering Lisbon from the 1440s. By 1552, 10 per cent of the population of Lisbon comprised slaves (Saunders, 1982: 55). In addition, the primary experience of the Iberian people (and other Europeans) with Africans was of the Moors, both during the Crusades in the Holy Land and as a result of the Moorish occupation of the Iberian peninsula, from which they were only finally expelled in 1492, after almost 800 years of continuous presence. It is true that Christianity had existed in Ethiopia since the second century and African Christians had fought alongside Europeans in the Holy Wars: in medieval Europe, cults formed around particular Ethiopian figures

(Pieterse, 1992: 25). Part of the motive for Portuguese explorations in Africa was the search for the legendary Christian kingdom of Prester John, and Bakongo kings in what is now Angola converted to Christianity as early as 1491. However, because of the long-standing Muslim presence in many areas of Africa – mainly those between the Saharan and sub-Saharan zones – the region as a whole tended to be seen as infidel territory and during the fifteenth century this status was reaffirmed in several papal bulls (Saunders, 1982: 37–8).

In contrast, native Americans were a conundrum. There was a good deal of uncertainty about their status, whether they had the use of reason, whether they were real humans, whether they were brutal savages or, alternatively, represented some version of human existence before the Fall (Hulme, 1986; Mason, 1990; Pagden, 1993). Images in colonial discourse are rarely one-sided and with respect to Africans there was ambivalence – infidel or pagan versus Christian, slaves versus trading partners – but this was particularly evident with respect to native Americans. The dual image of the noble and the ignoble savage that was to flower in the eighteenth century (Meek, 1976) was already captured in the constant representation of indigenous people as cannibals (Mason, 1990) alongside the image of them as innocent beings (Pagden, 1982).

Some of this ambivalence, and the difference between Africans and native Americans, is evident in the issue of slavery. At the time of European contact with Africans and indigenous American people, slavery was considered a normal, if usually temporary, status. There was justification in the Bible and in Aristotelian philosophy for enslavement of the captives of a 'just war' (such as one against infidels), Christians and Moors had enslaved each other, and slaves from the Balkans and the Black Sea area were being used in sugar plantations in Cyprus and Sicily. The conquistadors were keen on enslaving indigenous people in the New World and they received some backing from the regal authorities. Indigenous people could be legitimately enslaved if they were classed as cannibals or Caribs (from which the word cannibal derives) – which in the Caribbean context simply meant those who resisted Spanish rule (Hulme, 1986). One reaction among Spanish thinkers and theologians was to label the indigenous people as 'natural slaves', a category deriving from Aristotelian thought and designating a person incapable of autonomy (Pagden, 1982: 29–30). But there was little agreement on all this and others in the clergy questioned whether a war could ever be 'just' when waged against those who had never known Christianity and who had been defined as vassals of the Crown in

Crown territory. The terrible brutality of the conquistadors and the manifest decline of the indigenous population added strength to these arguments, as did contact with the Aztecs and the Incas whose cities and rule of law were signs of 'rationality'. This was the substance of the famous 1550–51 debates between Bartolomé de las Casas and Juan Ginés de Sepúlveda, but already by 1542 slavery of indigenous people had been outlawed in Spanish colonies. Portugal followed suit in Brazil in 1570. Such legislation was often ineffective in rooting out slavery, which continued in many peripheral areas and especially in Brazil where indigenous slaves fed the north-eastern sugar plantations (Hemming, 1987; Lockhart and Schwartz, 1983: 71–2)

For Africans and their descendants, in contrast, there was little questioning of the propriety of enslavement. There was legal provision for manumission (individual freedom), reflecting the concept of slavery as a temporary condition, and a good number of slaves became free through this means – mostly by self-purchase after years of saving (Bowser, 1972; Klein and Vinson, 2007). Otherwise, slaves gained freedom by escaping and, as part of this process, perhaps forming resistant settlements of 'maroons' – from the Spanish term for them, *cimarrones* – known as *palenques* in much of Spanish America and *quilombos* in Brazil (Heuman, 1986; Price, 1979; Thompson, 2006). But it was not until slavery as an institution was challenged and dismantled during the early nineteenth century that black people as a category began to be freed in the Americas. During the early period of the slave trade, Africa was infidel territory and the Portuguese had papal authority to wage a 'just war' there; slavery was legitimated as a positive good for infidel Africans; and much of the enslaving was done by Africans themselves, thus masking the question of its legitimacy. Once the slave trade was well under way and the mines and plantations of the colonies so dependent on it, there was little incentive to question such a central institution.

Indigenous people and Africans thus had different locations in the colonial order, both socially and conceptually. Indigenous people were, officially, to be protected as well as exploited; Africans were slaves and, although they had rights enshrined in legislation, this was piecemeal and uneven – although the Spanish did produce a code in 1789 – and the main concern was with control, rather than protection. This difference continued through the colonial period. Ideally, the Spanish would have liked to maintain three separate categories: Spanish, indigenous people and Africans; rulers, tributaries and slaves. Indeed, the authorities talked of the *república de españoles* and the *república de indios*, the latter based on the indigenous community, created and constrained by legislation. Such an ideal was undermined from the start by the possibility of slave manumission, which created the beginnings of a class of free blacks. It was also weakened by the fact that Spaniards' American-born offspring were no longer simply Spaniards, but *criollos* (creoles). In addition, from early on, indigenous people moved into urban areas and Spaniards usurped indigenous land, while some indigenous people became direct dependents of the developing rural hacienda: both processes weakened the link of the indigenous people to the communities that, in great part, defined their identity as indigenous people (Harris, 1995b: 354–9).

Most of all, the ideal of separation was undermined by *mestizaje*, mixture. The main meaning of this term is sexual mixture, but implied is the spatial mixture of peoples and the interchange of cultural elements, resulting in mixed and new cultural forms. Spaniards, creoles, indigenous people, free blacks and slaves interbred – destitute Spaniards with free black women, indigenous princesses with aristocratic Spaniards, runaway slaves with indigenous women, Spanish masters with slave women, free blacks with indigenous people and creoles – and their offspring were recognised as mixed people of various kinds. Racial nomenclature was variable and dozens of labels existed, but *mulato* was the term often used for someone of supposedly black–white mixture, *zambo* for black–indigenous mixture and *mestizo* for indigenous–white mixture. Not all *mestizos* were 'mixed', however, since an indigenous person who disavowed his or her origins could attempt to 'pass' into this category. All these actually or nominally mixed people, in their turn, interbred with others. Some *mulatos* were slaves, but most mixed people were free and in many areas they soon outnumbered Spaniards, creoles, indigenous people and slaves (Cope, 1994; Klein and Vinson, 2007; Mörner, 1967; Rout, 1976).

This proliferating mixture was not, however, unstructured. On the contrary, it was powerfully shaped by race, class and gender. Whites were firmly at the top of the pile, slaves and indigenous people at the bottom. White men had the power to control white female sexuality and marriage, while they could also abuse and/or maintain informal sexual relations with darker-skinned, lower-class women with relative impunity (Powers, 2005; Wade, 2009b).

In terms of race, the Spanish attempted to maintain categorical distinctions for whites and between indigenous people and the rest.

Indio was a specific administrative category – in many ways, a fiscal category, since the typical indigenous person was one who lived in an indigenous community and paid tribute, in labour or goods (Harris, 1995b: 354). It was also a census category, since it was important to enumerate indigenous people as a working and tributary population. In Brazil, where there was less in the way of a dense, sedentary indigenous population that could be easily exploited through existing systems of political stratification, authorities were less concerned with maintaining strict barriers, but indigenous people still had a specific administrative status. In short, *indio* was an institutionalised identity.

There was nothing comparable for blacks. The status of slave, of course, was very specifically defined and slave was a central census category. But many blacks were free and they fitted into much vaguer categories which lumped together everyone who was not either white, indigenous or slave. Thus in New Granada (the basis of today's Colombia), the residual census category was simply *libre* (free person) which included *mestizos*, *zambos*, freed blacks and *mulatos*, and sometimes indigenous people who had evaded their formal indigenous identity by leaving their communities (Wade, 1986). In Brazil, the middle category was free people which, again, included a broad mixture of people (Alden, 1987: 291). In Cuba (Martinez-Alier, 1989), reference was usually made to *pardos* (roughly, 'light browns'), and sometimes also to *morenos* ('dark browns'). In Mexico, while some local censuses used detailed categories such as *mestizo*, *mulato* and free black, others simply classed all the racially mixed population as *casta* (Seed, 1982: 577).

This system of socioracial stratification is often termed the *sociedad de castas*, after the term *castas* (breeds, castes) which was applied variously to the middle strata or everyone below the top strata (Katzew, 2004). The term is not used for Brazil and there is evidence that the situation there was more fluid (Mörner, 1967), but the basic situation seems to have been similar (Russell-Wood, 1982: 67–83). In this society, whites, and specifically white men, were at the top, indigenous people and blacks, especially females, at the bottom and positions in the middle were defined by various criteria of status, among which colour and descent were very important, without being definitive. Thus occupation could influence one's 'racial' classification in a census, as could the position of one's spouse – although the term 'racial' might not be used, being signified, in Mexico for example, by the term *calidad* or quality (McCaa, 1984; Seed, 1982). People jockeyed for position and trans-

Atlantic litigation might take place if someone who claimed to be white felt he had been insulted by being called a *mestizo* (Jaramillo Uribe, 1968: 181–6).

There has been debate about how open this system was in the Spanish colonies and, in particular, how important 'race' was in defining position within it. Chance (1978) and Mörner (1967) see a relatively open society in which race had a declining role to play as *mestizaje* made racial identifications more indeterminate. Jaramillo Uribe (1968), Carroll (1991) and McCaa (1984) give a greater role to people's ideas about racial ancestry and identity. For Brazil, Russell-Wood (1982: 78) talks of the emergence of a 'meritocracy' during the eighteenth century, but admits that 'the free coloured had to fight to overcome … discrimination and prejudice', while Lockhart and Schwartz (1983: 403) say that in this period the merchant-planter elite saw the mixed middle strata as a threat in a social order in which 'definitions of social conflict were often perceived in terms of colour rather than economic class'. The role of racial distinctions is often given salience by more recent studies (for example, Martínez, 2008; Silverblatt, 2004) and various historians argue that a greater concern with race became evident among elites in the later eighteenth century, as they felt the need to protect their position against encroaching *mestizos* and worried more about the racial status of marriage partners, feeling a greater need to protect white women's honour (Gutiérrez, 1991; Twinam, 1999). It seems probable that there is no single answer and that a lot depended on local factors, but it seems clear that ambiguity and room for manoeuvre was greatest in the middle ranges: for those at the bottom of the pile, labelled indigenous and black (or worse, slave), there was less flexibility (Wade, 1993a: 9).

The point is that within this system, indigenous people had a relatively institutionalised position, whereas blacks did not: some were in the category of slave, others in that vague middle category of *castas*, *pardos* or *libres*. It also seems that, although both sets of people suffered great hardship in practical terms, indigenous people were seen in some sense as superior to blacks. This is evident from marriage regulations which allowed whites to marry indigenous people, while restricting unions with blacks and mulattoes. The authorities set out regulations in 1778 which forced whites under 25 years to seek parental approval of their marriage, thus impeding unions thought to be unsuitable, especially for young women (Martinez-Alier, 1989: 11). But intermarriage with indigenous people was not formally restricted, since 'their origin is not vile like that of other *castas*' (Mörner, 1967: 39). The Mexican Audiencia, reviewing these regulations, commented on marriage between indigenous people and blacks or mulattoes, recommending that parish priests be ordered to warn the indigenous and his parents of the serious harm that 'such unions will cause to themselves and their families and villages, besides making the descendants incapable of obtaining municipal positions of honour in which only pure Indians are allowed to serve' (cited in Mörner, 1967: 39).

In sum, then, indigenous people and blacks had different relationships to the official structures of bureaucracy. Since the relationship between law and social order is notoriously difficult to establish, it would be dangerous to argue that this difference translated directly into an identical difference in popular colonial perceptions of blacks and indigenous people, or in conditions of material welfare. Indeed, indigenous people were often treated extremely badly. But the laws themselves, especially those of the late colonial period, were in part a reflection of white elite concerns and it is clear that the category *indio* was not simply a legal fiction, but an everyday reality, reconstituted through daily practice.

BLACK AND INDIGENOUS PEOPLE IN THE NEW REPUBLICS

With independence, the former Spanish colonies began to dismantle the administrative trappings of empire, although Brazil gained independence as an empire in its own right until it became a republic in 1891, while Puerto Rico and Cuba remained colonies of Spain until 1898. Under the pervasive influence of European liberalism, the status of indigenous and, more particularly, indigenous land came under attack. There were widespread moves to disestablish indigenous communities and undermine the existence of a separate category of people who had a legal position distinct from that of simple citizen. These were frequently ineffective and in the Andes 'there were strong local vested interests in maintaining a distinctive category of Indians' (Harris, 1995b: 363). Legal discriminations against mixed bloods were gradually removed and by 1854 slavery was abolished in the new republics; it was retained in Brazil until 1888, in Puerto Rico until 1873 and in Cuba until 1886 (Bauer, 1984; Grieshaber, 1979; Halperín Donghi, 1987). However, ideas about race and about categories of people called *indios*, *negros*, *mestizos*, etc. were by no means removed from the national panorama. Again, there was a distinct difference between the images of blacks and indigenous people in debates about the identity of the new nations – or empire in the case of Brazil.

Ideas about race were crucial elements in discussions about national identity in a world where European and North American nationalisms already dominated the stage. Latin American elites wanted to emulate the modernity and progress of these nations and accepted in broad terms the tenets of liberalism which saw in science, technology, reason, education and freedom of the individual the underlying forces of progress. But these modern and progressive nations either had no significant black or indigenous populations, or, in the case of the US, kept them strictly segregated. In contrast, most Latin American countries had substantial numbers of *mestizos*, blacks and indigenous people. Worse still, by the late nineteenth century, the theories of human biology accepted in Western scientific racism relegated blacks and indigenous people to a permanently inferior status and condemned mixed-bloods as degenerate.

Latin American elites tried to deal with this contradiction by adapting Western theories of human difference and heredity. The racial determinism of European theories was often avoided and emphasis placed instead on the possibility of improving the population through programmes of 'social hygiene', improving health and living conditions. Lamarckian theories about the hereditability of characteristics acquired during a single lifetime were popular, since these held out the hope of lasting improvement of 'the race' (Stepan, 1991). Many states imposed campaigns to control or eradicate prostitution, for example, which indicated the gendered nature of these ideas: women were often seen as a potential source of 'contamination' of the nation (Findlay, 1998; Guy, 1991). The idea of the degeneracy of the *mestizo* was contested, and indeed in nations such as Colombia or Mexico mixedness became a symbol of a distinctive Latin American identity, free from the slavish emulation of European or North American masters (Minna Stern, 2003).

On the other hand, the type of mixedness invoked was often itself biased towards whiteness: European immigration was often encouraged or even sponsored by the state, and, more generally, the process of mixing could be seen as a progressive *whitening* of the population. Mixture would supposedly bring about the elimination of blacks and indigenous people and the creation of a mixed society that was at the distinctly whiter end of the spectrum. Such a vision was almost magical, since every instance of race mixture must logically be a darkening as well as a whitening, but the vision was sustained, on the one hand, by eugenic notions that white 'blood' was stronger than other types and would naturally dominate in the mixture and, on the other, by immigration policies which tried to restrict the entry of blacks and encourage European immigration in a 'war on blackness' (Andrews 2004: 118). These ideas and processes were common, in varying ways, to Brazil, Venezuela, Cuba, Argentina, Bolivia and Colombia, among others (Andrews, 2004: ch. 4; Appelbaum et al., 2003; Graham, 1990; Helg, 1995; Naro, 2002; Sanjinés, 2004; Skidmore, 1974; Smith, 1997; Stepan, 1991; Wade, 1993a; Wright, 1990).

In the attempt to delineate a distinctive national identity, reference could be made (or could not be avoided) to the historical roots of the nation. From the 1920s, the 'indian' became a prime symbol of national identity in countries such as Mexico and Peru: both countries created government departments for indigenous affairs, while Peru recognised the 'indigenous community' as a legal entity and Mexico created academic institutes dedicated to the study of indigenous peoples. In Brazil, an agency was set up in 1910 for the 'protection of the indian'. This, in broad terms, was the ideology of *indigenismo*. This term covers a variety of perspectives, but the central notion was that indigenous people needed special recognition and that special values attached to them. Very often, it was a question of exotic and romantic symbolism, based more on the glorification of the pre-Columbian indigenous ancestry of the nation than on respect for contemporary indigenous populations. Thus the reality was often one of continued discrimination and exploitation. In addition, the future was generally envisaged as being integrated and *mestizo* in colour.

Manuel Gamio, for example, who became director of the Instituto Indígena Interamericano in Mexico, undertook archaeological investigations of Teotihuacán and also began studies of contemporary indigenous communities. At the same time, his overall perspective was integrationist and conformed to the typical ideas of nation-building based on education and incorporation (Brading, 1988; Hewitt de Alcántara, 1984: 10). For Mexico, 'postrevolutionary *indigenismo* … represented yet another non-Indian formulation of the "Indian problem"; it was another white/mestizo construct … part of a long tradition stretching back to the Conquest' (Knight, 1990: 77). For many – but not all – *indigenistas*, indigenous people were 'proto-citizens, incapable of rising to the level of citizen without state tutelage' (Dawson, 2004: xx). In Brazil, as well, 'every indigenist project aimed to solve the problem of transforming the Indian from … "savagery" to the superior stage of "civilization"'

(Lima, 1991: 246), while the representation of *índios* required they remain 'passive figures to be molded by Euro-Brazilian ideologies' (Ramos, 1998: 83). On the other hand, some *indigenistas* adopted much less integrationist positions. Peruvians José Carlos Mariátegui (1895–1930) and Víctor Raúl Haya de la Torre, for example, took a more radical line, wedding socialism and *indigenismo* and modelling the future nation on the supposedly socialist aspects of ancient Andean indigenous culture (Chevalier, 1970; Hale, 1984). Elites in Cuzco in the Peruvian Andes also developed a 'pro-Indian' version of *indigenismo* in the 1920s, which they used to contest ideologies of *mestizaje* coming out of Lima (de la Cadena, 2000: 85). Such a view responded in part to the fact that a dense indigenous population still lived in the Andes. Whatever the variety, however, the point remains that indigenous people were often seen as a special category, needy of the specific attention of intellectuals, the state and the Church.

Blacks were much less likely to be symbolised in this way and were rarely held up as the symbols of a glorious heritage. Only in Cuba and Brazil, with their very large black populations, was there a positive revaluation of blackness in some quarters, although, again, this tended to be integrationist in tone, with the emphasis on the emergence of a mixed society in which a black input was valued as long as it was under control. Even then, the trend was mainly literary, with little discernible impact on government policy.

In 1920s and 1930s Cuba, there was a trend of *afro-cubanismo* in literary circles with authors such as Alejo Carpentier and Nicolás Guillén leading the way (Bueno, 1993; McGarrity and Cárdenas, 1995: 92; Prescott, 1985). Franco (1967: 103–32) argues that this was inspired by the European avant-garde view of primitivism as an alternative to scientific rationality. Afro-Cuban music was also making a big impact within the country and internationally (Manuel, 1995; Moore 1997; Roberts, 1979). Even though there were strong elements in these trends of the appropriation by whites of exotic aspects of black culture – blacks were an infrequent sight in the dance orchestras that played Afro-Cuban music (Díaz Ayala, 1981: 158; Moore 1997) – it was nevertheless a departure from the image of blacks as simply backward and inferior.

In Brazil, musicologist Mário de Andrade also accepted African musical elements as a valuable part of a mixed Brazilian national music (Reily, 1994), at a time when samba was becoming a central musical icon of the nation (Vianna, 1999). But it was Gilberto Freyre who was central to producing a vision of Brazil that went beyond the dilemmas created by scientific racism which had branded the country as racially hybrid and therefore inferior (Needell, 1995; Skidmore, 1974: 184–92). Policies of whitening through immigration still existed, but by Freyre's time scientific racism was on the wane – in any case some Brazilian thinkers had tried to avoid the most determinist versions of it. As Andrews contends (2004: 153), from about 1930, the frank attempts by Latin American states to whiten their national populations, at least as a policy measure, gradually gave way to a process of de facto 'browning'.

Freyre's aim was to redefine the Brazilian nation as mixed – and proud of it. Even so, his view was highly assimilationist. In his book, *Brazil: An Interpretation*, for example, he stated:

> Brazil stands today as a community from whose experiment in miscegenation other communities may profit. Probably in no other complex modern community are problems of race relations being solved in a more democratic or Christian way than in Portuguese America. And Brazil's experiment does not indicate that miscegenation leads to degeneration. (1951: 98–9)

This declared Brazil to have actually benefited from race mixture, since this had solved problems of race relations. He also said that Brazilians generally feel that 'nothing is sincerely or honestly Brazilian that denies or hides the influence of the Amerindian and the Negro': *authentic* Brazilian identity was therefore mixed (1951: 122). On the other hand, he declared: 'Negroes are now rapidly disappearing in Brazil, merging into the white stock' (1951: 96) and although 'Brazil still has to face the problem of assimilating certain Amerindian tribes as well as those groups of Negroes whose culture remains largely African', this was not a major problem since:

> the general tendency among broad-minded Brazilians [he admits that not all of them are] is to maintain, towards Africans as well as Indians, a policy of slow and intelligent assimilation, in which the assimilating group may incorporate into its culture certain values of general interest or artistic importance. (1951: 119)

Some of this – not all – was very optimistic, indeed naive, stuff when applied to the realities of Brazilian social structure and culture, but it was an attempt to redefine Brazilian identity as something other than a slavish copy of Euro-American nations and yet still 'complex [and] modern'; it is, in effect, a redefinition of modernity away from whiteness towards hybridity – a move that prefigures more postmodern discussions that also welcome Latin America's hybrid nature (García Canclini, 1989; Schwarz, 1992: 1–18; see also Wade, 2004).

The central point, however, is that the sort of redefinition of national identity attempted by some Cuban and Brazilian intellectuals and scholars was, in the Latin American context, limited in comparison to that attempted for indigenous people. Most important, perhaps, these attempts were at the level of image, representation and literary and musical productions; they rarely involved state policy. *Indigenista* approaches generally did involve policy, thus continuing the tradition of reifying indigenous people as an object of official attention.

BLACK AND INDIGENOUS PEOPLE IN POLITICS AND SOCIAL SCIENCE

The different location of blacks and indigenous people in the political and imagined space of the nation did not receive much attention from scholars until recently, but it seems to me of great importance: it has had significant political consequences and has also affected the way each category has become an object of study in academia. Colombia is a good example of this difference and its consequences.

Indigenous people in Colombia have suffered terrible discrimination and abuse and still suffer today. Yet legally and conceptually they have a special position. Legislation in 1890 reaffirmed the existence of indigenous *resguardos* (reserves) and indigenous councils to govern them. In 1941, the state created an institute of ethnology whose main purpose was to study indigenous society and history. Since the beginnings of its academic institutionalisation in the country in the 1940s, the majority of anthropology has focused on indigenous people. The premier Gold Museum in Bogotá focuses exclusively on pre-Columbian indigenous people, even though there were important gold-working traditions in the regions of Africa whence came a good part of the population of the country. Indigenous mobilisation to fight for land and rights has been a significant force since the 1960s and important concessions – on paper at least – have been won. Legally, indigenous people, who formed about 3 per cent of the nation's population by 2005, owned about 30 per cent of its territory in the form of reserves – although practical enforcement of that ownership is a different matter (DANE, 2006). In the 1991 constitutional reform, indigenous groups won important rights, including the right to two seats in the Senate (Arocha, 1992; Jackson, 1995; Wade, 1993a: 352–5, 1995a).

Blacks, in contrast, according to Friedemann (1984) have been made 'invisible' in the nation – systematically ignored, marginalised and belittled. I would argue that things are not quite so straightforward, in the sense that, for over a hundred years, commentators on Colombian national identity have always recognised the existence of blacks, and Colombia also underwent its own musical and artistic form of *negrismo* in the mid-twentieth century (Wade, 2000), but it is true that this recognition has often been disparaging, exoticising or caricatured. It is certainly true that, until the 1990s, they were rarely studied academically – not constituting the cultural Otherness that anthropology has sought among indigenous people – and that politically they have generally been seen as ordinary citizens, even while in practice they suffer racial discrimination (Wade, 1993a). Black political mobilisation has been much weaker than that of indigenous people and in the 1991 constitutional reform, black groups fared much worse in terms of extracting concessions on land rights and cultural recognition – although in both respects they did make ground-breaking steps in the direction of being constituted as a specific cultural, political and conceptual category within the nation (Arocha, 1992; Friedemann and Arocha, 1995; Restrepo, 2002; Wade, 1995a, 2002b).

This contrast, in my view, has its roots in the history I have outlined above. The result of this history in academic terms has been the general separation of studies of blacks from those of indigenous people – with some notable exceptions, such as Whitten (1981a) and Taussig (1980, 1987). A second result has been the historical neglect of blacks in relative terms – with the main exception of Brazil where, even so, indigenous people have been the domain of anthropology, while blacks have generally been studied by sociologists. In the face of this, one tendency has been to focus on blacks, bemoaning their neglect in academic circles compared to studies of indigenous people and seeking to redress it: this highlights the differences between 'black' and 'indigenous' as categories by focusing on them separately. The recent increase in studies of Latin American black people, Afro-Latinos and Afro-descendants, with some exceptions, tends to fit into this trend (for brief overviews, see Andrews, 2009; Wade, 2006a). Another tendency is to see blacks and indigenous people as rather similar: both are seen as minorities in nation-states intent on a future of homogeneity; both are at the bottom of a ladder which represented parallel hierarchies of wealth, education, civilisation and race; both are inputs into the progressive, modernising process of whitening the nation (Stutzman, 1981; Whitten, 1985; Wade, 1993a).

Neither perspective is wholly right nor wrong. The point is to bring blacks and indigenous people into the same overall theoretical perspective, especially in the context of the Latin American nation, while also recognising the historical, political and conceptual differences that do exist between these categories. Blacks and indigenous people have both been characterised as Others, located in the liminal spaces of the nation, but they have fitted in different ways into what I call the structures of alterity. The apparent 'invisibility' of black people in Colombia, for example, has not been due to a simple process of discrimination – indigenous people have, if anything, suffered even greater discrimination – but due to the precise mode of their insertion into the structures of alterity. They have not been institutionalised as Others in the same way that indigenous people have. Interestingly, however, since the 1990s there has been the appearance of blacks on the public political stage in Colombia, Brazil, Nicaragua and other countries where constitutional measures recognise the special status of blacks in general or particular groups of blacks (see Chapter 6). In some sense, this corresponds to a relocation of 'blackness' in structures of alterity in ways that make it look increasingly like 'indigenousness'. This phenomenon has helped spur a number of recent studies that place blackness and indigenousness in the same theoretical frame, while recognising their differences (for example, Anderson, 2007, 2009; Arruti, 1997; French, 2009; Hale et al., 2003; Hooker, 2005; Ng'weno, 2007b; see also Andrews, 2009: 201–3, Safa, 2005). These studies indicate that, in some contexts, black and indigenous groups make important alliances, despite the different sorts of relationships they may have to the state. In other contexts, both 'black' and 'indigenous' identities may emerge from a common historical and cultural background (French, 2009).

BLACKS AND INDIGENOUS PEOPLE, RACE AND ETHNICITY

Another way that the split between blacks and indigenous people was introduced into social science was with the virtually unquestioned assumption that the study of blacks was about racism and race relations, while the study of indigenous people was about ethnicity and ethnic groups. The principal idea underlying this was that the category 'indigenous' or *indio* does not depend on phenotypical signifiers. As I mentioned above, during the colonial period, the identity of *indio* depended partly on being located in an indigenous community; leaving that community, which might also involve leaving aside typically 'indigenous' clothing and language, was a step on the path to becoming a *'mestizo'*. Studies in the twentieth century reinforced this: 'indigenous' was – and to a large extent still is – seen as a category defined by cultural signifiers (clothing, language, place of residence, etc.) and the boundary between indigenous and *mestizo* is potentially crossable by manipulating those signifiers (Bourricaud, 1975; de la Cadena, 2000; Guss, 2006: 296–7; Harris, 1995b; van den Berghe, 1974a: 15). In contrast, 'black' is often seen as a category defined by more fixed phenotypical criteria that cannot be manipulated in the same way.

There are two sets of problems here. The first is that it is wrong, in my view, to see indigenous people simply as an ethnic group or set of ethnic groups. The category *indio* was an integral part of the colonial encounters within which the discourse of race emerged and, for example, the debates about the fate of the nation that took place in Colombia in the late nineteenth and early twentieth centuries talked in similar terms about the supposed failings of 'indian blood' and 'black blood'. From a macrohistorical perspective, then, 'indian' was a racial category and retains strong elements of this history. Hendrickson (1991: 290) notes that in Guatemala the categories *'indio'* and *'ladino'* (*mestizo*) are referred to explicitly as labels of *raza* (race) as well as ethnic group. Many authors note that indigenous people face 'racism', even while they refer to them as ethnic groups (for example, Harris, 1995b: 371; Watanabe, 1995; Whitten, 1976). Recent approaches are less coy than previously about seeing indigenous people through the analytical lens of race. Nelson (1999), for example, has no qualms about seeing Guatemala in this way; neither does Hale (2006). Poole (1997) refers openly to race for the Andes, de la Cadena's book (2000) has many more index entries related to race than to ethnicity, while Weismantel (2001) develops a flexible approach to race in the Andes that sees it as something that can be accumulated in and on the body, rather than something that is fixed at birth (see also Orlove, 1998). García (2008: 219) uses the concept of race and resists 'dichotomous views that separate phenotype and culture, biology and history', and Hooker (2009: 17), confronting a situation where 'indigenous peoples suffer from racial discrimination and racialized groups make claims relating to language, culture and territory', seeks to overcome the 'artificial division between race and culture in theories of multiculturalism'.

This brings us to the second set of problems, which relates to the microscale. There is no doubt that, on an individual level, '*indios*' can become '*mestizos*'; it is also true, however, that 'blacks' (*negros*) can become '*mulatos*' or '*pardos*' or '*morenos*'. As I argued in the previous chapter, it is mistaken to assume that, just because racial signifiers are bodily, they are completely fixed. Part of this assumption comes from the classic US case where racial identification has been very rigid and an attempt has been made to create very tightly bounded categories of black and white. Even there, 'passing' occurs, so that an individual who is classed as black in some circumstances 'passes' for white in others; and blacks may also lighten their skin and straighten their hair. Spike Lee, in his film *Jungle Fever* (1991), cleverly plays with US racial identifications by introducing a dark-skinned character who seems at first to be African-American, but turns out, from his speech, to be Italian-American – and rabidly anti-black. The main point is that it is wrong to extrapolate from the US case to racial identifications in general. The Latin American material shows that, for example, the same individual dressed shabbily and smartly will be identified with different colour terms that locate the person on a scale between black and white. These terms are not dependent on phenotype alone, because the context of somatic features alters people's classification – and even perhaps perception – of these features (Sansone, 2003: ch. 1; Solaún and Kronus, 1973). It is also widely reported that 'the blacks' is often a term used more or less synonymously with 'the poor' (for example, Harris, 1952) or more widely that poverty and blackness are seen as strongly suggesting each other (Streicker, 1995; Twine, 1998: 119), indicating again that economic status influences racial classifications. Thus identifications of 'black' are malleable, as well as those of 'indigenous'. Race is not just about fixity (Wade, 2002a).

It is also worth bearing in mind, however, that such malleability is not complete. The indigenous migrant from the highlands of Peru who becomes a domestic maid in Lima is on her way to becoming a *mestizo* woman, but her background is not forgotten; the term *cholo* is frequently used to identify people who are seen as 'between' indigenous people and *mestizos* (Radcliffe, 1990). Equally, people who, by local standards, have *typically* indigenous or black somatic features have a hard job losing that identity, even if they are not publicly labelled as indigenous or black (Watanabe, 1995: 31). Of course, physical signs are in the eye of the beholder. Nelson (1999: 231) tells the story of a woman who always told her son never to sit next to an indigenous women on the bus, lest he be mistaken for her son (and thus an *indio*). To Nelson the young man looked very non-indigenous; to the mother, something in his appearance might suggest to an observer that he was indigenous. In Latin America, people are generally quite sensitive to the possibilities of ancestry that can be inferred from appearance, so such signifiers, even when they are so subjectively perceived, cannot be erased completely by changing other cues.

This is not to argue that the categories of black and indigenous are therefore exactly the same in terms of the processes of identification they involve. Each category has a different history with different possibilities and modes of construction and transformation, modes that also depend on local contexts. The use of 'race' to talk about black identity and 'ethnicity' to talk about indigenous identity separates phenotype from culture, as if the former was not itself culturally constructed. Both 'indigenous' and 'black' are, in my view, categories that have aspects of racial and ethnic categorisation.

In sum, then, I think it is necessary to bring blacks and indigenous people into the same theoretical frame of reference, while recognising the historical differences between them and the consequences of these at a political level. However, as the succeeding chapters will show, blacks and indigenous people have generally been dealt with separately.

3
Early Approaches to Blacks and Indigenous People, 1920s to 1960s

There were essentially two overlapping contexts for thinking about and studying indigenous people in Latin America before the Second World War. On the one hand, there was the 'problem' of indigenous people in the national frame with which *indigenista* thought in all its varieties was concerned. This was a theme debated by intellectuals and politicians, and policy was always a central issue since the 'problem' was that of how (or sometimes whether) to integrate indigenous people into the modernising nation (Poole, 2008).

The other context was that of international social science, shaped by the North American and European academies. This was never disconnected from the first context and indeed increasingly integrated with it, in the sense that some of the Latin Americans concerned with policy issues of (non-)integration in their countries were themselves trained in Euro-American social science – after all, a School of American Archaeology and Ethnography was founded in Mexico by German-American Franz Boas as early as 1909. However, although policy was not irrelevant in this context, it tended to take a back seat to 'scientific' study. Here functionalism was an important theoretical perspective from about the 1930s up to at least the 1960s. In anthropology, this approach tended to focus on particular (non-Western) communities with the aim of discovering their internal mechanisms of social integration. The method was intensely ethnographic, based on living in the community for a long period and preferably learning the local language, and issues of social change and national context tended to be sidelined in favour of studying structural and cultural patterns within the community. In Latin America, there was also a concern with left-wing political orientations and social justice, although this flowered towards the end of the period under discussion in this chapter. Other influences in the academic context included North American cultural ecology which, beginning in the 1940s, attempted to see cultural patterns and social structure as ecological adaptations; and, finally, French structuralism, which was important for many anthropologists and was pioneered in the Latin American context by Claude Lévi-Strauss who first did fieldwork in Brazil in the 1930s; the full impact of this theoretical approach was not felt, however, until the 1960s.

Geographically, there were three main areas of study: the Andes, Mesoamerica (particularly Mexico) and Amazonia. In the latter area, although *indigenismo* was an internal policy issue in Brazil from at least 1910 (Lima, 1991; Ramos, 1998), questions of racial and ethnic identities and relations were not broached in an academic context until late in the period under review and, when they were, the concern was mainly with indigenous people as victims of genocide. Initially, then, I will be concerned with the first two areas, with a principal focus on Mexico.

Mallon notes a difference between Mexico – where the forces and ideology of *mestizaje* took precedence, defining *mestizos* as central and indigenous people as peripheral – and the Andes, where the indigenous population was much larger and there were more 'bi-polar' constructions based around images of the indigenous highlands and plateaus and the white/*mestizo* coast and valleys (Mallon, 1992: 35–8, 1995). Nevertheless, common to both areas was a basic conceptual division between indigenous people and *mestizos*. Thus in Mexico, the rural *mestizos* were seen as peasants and class was the central analytic category for historians and anthropologists; in contrast, indigenous people lived in peripheral regions and could be studied in their own terms. Similarly in Peru, indigenous people were seen as 'traditional', gradually being incorporated into the modern market economy which was the domain of *mestizos* and thus becoming *mestizos* themselves, perhaps via the intermediate category of '*cholo*' (Mallon, 1992, 1995). In general, then, class was associated with *mestizos* and, although the word was not necessarily used, ethnicity with indigenous people. At the same time as an overall modernisationist perspective implied that class would eventually erase ethnicity, and although *indigenistas* were concerned with problems of integration into national society, or the lack of it, there was a sense that indigenous people could be studied as isolated groups and communities.

Another common feature uniting Mesoamerica and the Andes was the difference between the so-called closed corporate indigenous communities and the more open integrated communities. The distinction was initially made for Mesoamerica where the closed communities were those that had attempted to maintain a certain defensive isolation – for example in central and southern Mexico (including Chiapas) and in highland Guatemala, (Nash, 1970; Wolf, 1955). The contrast was with more open communities, often in more lowland areas, that had historically been more integrated and had a correspondingly weaker 'indigenous' identity. The same distinction was later made for Peru, contrasting the highlands to the coastal regions (Grieshaber, 1979: 120).

Functionalist approaches in Mexico

In Mexico, studies of indigenous people in the 1930s and 1940s were mainly in the classic functionalist mode (for Peru, see Degregori and Sandoval, 2008). On the one hand, *indigenistas* such as Manuel Gamio were interested in researching pre-Columbian indigenous history and in studying contemporary indigenous people in order the better to 'improve' their lifestyle and integrate them (Sittón, 2008). As part of this trend, Mexicans and some early North American anthropologists were carrying out ethnographic studies of the ways of life of the indigenous people who seemed the most 'traditional' and untouched. Mexican scientists, including anthropologists, also undertook biological studies of traditional indigenous communities with the aim of diagnosing 'problems' and helping assimilation (Minna Stern, 2003).

On the other hand, US anthropologists such as Robert Redfield began in the 1920s the functionalist study of so-called 'folk' communities – ones that were indigenous, but were also far from untouched, having had a long experience of interaction with non-indigenous people (as, in reality, had even the most apparently isolated communities). His footsteps were accompanied and followed by important scholars, including Ralph Beals, Oscar Lewis and George Foster. In the 1950s, the Harvard Chiapas Project sent scores of anthropologists, graduate students and professionals – including Evon Vogt and Francesca and Frank Cancian – to the Chiapas region of south-eastern Mexico to do community studies which were often still highly functionalist in approach, despite the mounting critiques directed at this approach for its assumptions of integration and harmony, and its neglect of history, conflict and the wider context (see Hewitt de Alcántara, 1984: chs 1 and 2, for a discussion of this period).

These anthropologists differed widely amongst themselves – for example, Lewis (1951) restudied Tepoztlán, the subject of an early book by Redfield (1930), and found envy and dissent instead of harmony and cooperation – but with regard to ethnic or race relations, many of them had rather little to say. Redfield dealt tangentially with the issue by means of his folk–urban continuum, which posited an ideal-typical traditional pole of the almost untouched community at one end, going through the folk community and the local town, to the regional city at the other end. Along the continuum, people's values and social relations gradually became more 'modern' (by which he meant more individualistic, more secular, less homogeneous and more governed by class structures and the market). Change, or 'acculturation', occurred through contact of more traditional with more modern ways. Apart from the obvious flaws of such a one-way dynamic, based more on the decontextualised exchange of attitudes than on economic and political relations, there is little here that tells us about ethnic and racial identifications. On the contrary, the implication was that the difference between 'indigenous' and '*mestizo*' could be measured on a linear scale of the presence or absence of objective traits and attitudes: this hardly captures the complex processes of contextual identification of self and other that lie at the heart of identity.

More direct treatments of ethnic relations, however, did exist in the functionalist mould. Sol Tax (1942), Melvin Tumin (1952) and John Gillin (1951) wrote on the topic in relation to Guatemala, as did Redfield himself at a later date (Redfield, 1956). Gillin and Tumin argued that indigenous people and *mestizos* (or *ladinos* as they were called there) had relations of 'caste' – that is, two very separate groups were divided by a strong social barrier similar to the black–white boundary of the US at the time – and there was a good deal of argument about the appropriateness of this term to cover a variety of local contexts (see Aguirre Beltrán, 1979: ch. 8). Mexico, for example, was often seen as being more fluid.

Despite this usage, the functionalist approach to interethnic relations tended to emphasise harmony and interdependence rather than conflict and exploitation. As Hewitt de Alcántara notes (1984: 64–6), scholars such as Sol Tax and Manning Nash made use of concepts of pluralism, originally derived from the work of J.S. Furnivall on Burma. Pluralism tried to account for the continued existence of different cultural groups in a single society in terms of their common participation in certain institutions, especially economic and political ones; this was what created underlying social integration. Although later versions of pluralism emphasised the existence of coercion in this situation, 'members of the Tax-Nash school supposed that Indian people and non-Indian people interacted principally because they needed each other and received a necessary service during the exchange' (Hewitt de Alcántara, 1984: 66). That is, a benign and harmonious interdependence and complementarity underlay ethnic relations. Indigenous people were poor because they were isolated and had yet to acquire the knowledge, skills and technology for a more prosperous life. Economic development should be planned so as to allow this, without imposing total cultural assimilation.

One common corollary of these functionalist and pluralist approaches was the idea that indigenous culture was traditional and thus a brake on the process of modernisation that was widely assumed to be occurring or at least desirable. The classic formulation of this view was actually developed in relation to peasants rather than indigenous people and is found in George Foster's notion of 'limited good' based on his work in the *mestizo* village of Tzintzuntzan from 1948 onwards (Foster, 1967). According to Foster, peasants thought that the sum total of value available to them all was limited; thus anyone who became richer was doing so at the expense of others; this generated intense envy, conflict and distrust, and these psychological dispositions inhibited expansion and growth. This world view was the result of centuries of colonial domination, but had crystallised into a self-perpetuating attitude. Critics of Foster pointed out that his argument tended to blame the poor for being poor, that their poverty depended much more on external circumstances than their psychological attitudes and that, if opportunities for growth were presented in the appropriate form, 'traditional' peasants would take advantage of them (Long, 1977: ch. 3).

Reading between the lines of this body of work, one finds the underlying premise – typical of a community-level functionalist approach – that cultural groups are relatively unproblematic entities: 'there is a group, named X, which has given boundaries and a certain culture and social structure within those limits'. The question of how those boundaries were constituted and re-constituted or the idea that the culture of the group might change while the boundary remained did not really enter into the picture.

Interethnic Relations in Chiapas

An illustration of these tendencies can be found in an article by Ben Colby and Pierre van den Berghe (1961) on ethnic relations in Chiapas, southern Mexico. This is an interesting article, because it is constructed partly in opposition to the preceding functionalist, pluralist trend, while it also explicitly retains some of its ideas and its more hidden assumptions. The authors gave a detailed picture of the social structure of San Cristóbal de las Casas, a colonial town and regional centre of Chiapas, and they included some of the surrounding rural area with its indigenous communities. The inhabitants of San Cristóbal mostly called themselves *ladinos* and were ranked by class; higher-class people were whiter, lower-class people were darker-skinned and more 'indigenous-looking'. The indigenous people as such, however, did not live in the town – where they become 'rapidly ladinoized' – but in the rural areas. Socially, *ladinos* ranked higher than indigenous people in all respects.

Ladinos and indigenous people also had different cultures and Colby and van den Berghe listed these in a table that summarised differences in religious orientations, social relationships, family relationships, attitudes to work and so on. In a typically pluralist vein, these differences were underlain by basic forces of integration, institutions in which everyone participated: the Catholic Church, local and federal government (although the data the authors supplied tend to undermine the idea of the latter as an integrative influence, since local government was entirely in the hands of the *ladinos*, while the local programmes of the Instituto Nacional Indigenista (INI) were run by a national administration), and the regional economy in which *ladinos* bought indigenous people's goods (at exploitative prices) and indigenous people and *ladinos* 'exchanged services' (that is, the former worked for the latter at low rates of pay). These economic exchanges were 'one of the major foci integrating ladino and Indian cultures' (1961: 780).

Ladino–indigenous relations were described as paternalistic – presaging the comparative treatment of race relations that van den Berghe would later publish (1967) that distinguished between competitive and paternalistic forms of race and ethnic relations. This meant that indigenous people acted submissively and were treated with benign condescension if they knew their place. This resulted in a degree of social segregation, since *ladinos* and indigenous people never interacted on equal terms. However, relations of godparenthood, for example, crossed such boundaries as indigenous people sought *ladinos* to be godparents to their children. Indigenous people could 'pass' into the *ladino* group by speaking good Spanish and dressing and behaving like a *ladino*; they might then 'still be called an Indian', but would be treated as *ladinos* (1961: 783). This ambiguity was not clarified by the authors, although it is difficult to see how being treated as a *ladino* could include being called 'an indian' when the status implications of such a label were so strong. Overall, because the ethnic line was flexible, they foresaw a gradual move from this paternalistic system, inherited from the colonial past, to an 'integrated, *mestizo*–hispanic society' (1961: 789). In contrast, in some areas of Guatemala, the ethnic line was more rigid and this created a more competitive situation as some indigenous people became wealthier, but were not allowed to cross the ethnic line.

This all gives quite a useful picture of ethnic relations and, as they noted, it paralleled to a great extent the accounts given by Tax, Gillin, Tumin and Redfield of Guatemala. However, there are a number of problems. First, each group was reified as a fairly homogeneous entity with its own culture, the traits of which could be enumerated in a table. It was implied that moving from one group to the other meant a switch in cultural traits. The possibility that indigenous people who passed into the lower class of the *ladino* group retained some of their cultural traits was not envisaged, nor was the idea that culture might change while ethnic boundaries persisted. Second, the ladino group was admitted to be highly class-stratified in a way that itself mirrored a *ladino*–indigenous divide – that is, the poor *ladinos* were all 'indigenous-looking' – but this apparently had no effect on how upper-class *ladinos* treated lower-class ones, nor how lower-class *ladinos* treated indigenous people (some of whom, for example, must have been their kinsfolk). We are asked to believe that all *ladinos* treated all indigenous people in the same way.

Third, the *ladino*–indigenous boundary was shown to be permeable, but the way the boundary itself persisted remained unclear. The boundary was assumed to exist of its own accord, but it must be the case that it was maintained by the actions of individuals who made identifications. The behaviour of lower-class *ladinos* towards indigenous people thus becomes crucial, but, as already noted, it was not dealt with. The reasons for the persistence of the boundary in the form it took were also unclear. Putting aside the statement that the differences in ethnic relations observable between Chiapas and northern Guatemala derived 'from a difference in the flexibility in the ethnic line' (Colby and van den Berghe, 1961: 787) – which appears to be a tautology, since the differences in ethnic relations *are about* the flexibility in that line – the only solid explanation given was that, in Mexico, a policy of cultural assimilation had existed since the 1910–1917 revolution, thus making passing a relatively acceptable tactic. The idea that the boundary might still exist, whatever its flexibility, because it was economically advantageous for *ladinos* to exploit indigenous people was not entertained.

Fourth, the authors noted that the modernisation programmes of the INI had been strongest in the indigenous villages nearest San Cristóbal, but that it was precisely these villages that had shown 'reactive resistance' and had maintained cultural distinctiveness (1961: 778). This observation was left in the air, but it showed that modernisation did not necessarily lead to ladinoisation, as their analysis would have supposed; it also indicated that elements of culture could change while leaving the ethnic line intact or even strengthened, and it undermined their optimistic prediction of a move towards an 'integrated *mestizo*–hispanic society' as indigenous people rose in education and wealth. Finally, although the activities of the INI were discussed, there was little sense of the place of indigenous people as a category in the nation-state or of how local hierarchies reproduced national ones.

In sum, then, this analysis still carried within it a large quantity of functionalist baggage. Van den Berghe was soon to change and, after a period working in South Africa, and influenced no doubt by the less benign visions of pluralism produced by M.G. Smith for the Caribbean (1965) and Leo Kuper for South Africa (Kuper and Smith, 1969), his own approach moved away from functionalism, although he retained the concept of pluralism (see Chapter 4). Others also began to see ethnic identity as more flexible and not destined to disappear with development. Hinshaw's 1964 restudy of a community in Guatemala, first studied by Tax in 1937, showed that 'Panajacheleños [had] acculturated in these respects [of dress, language and employment] while remaining Indian in identity' (Tax and Hinshaw, 1970: 192). Nash (1958) had already found similar patterns, but his argument that industrial technology did not mean cultural disintegration in an indigenous community was directed more at proving that indigenous people were amenable to modernisation – along the lines of Tax's (1953) argument that Guatemalan indigenous people were 'penny capitalists' – than at showing the contextual nature of ethnic identity.

The Analysis of Colonialism

There were also important currents within Mexico at this time – which in the late 1960s and 1970s found echo in Peru (where several Mexican anthropologists did research) – that went against the functionalist flow (Hewitt de Alcántara, 1984: ch. 2; Sittón, 2008; for Peru, see Degregori and Sandoval, 2008). The driving force here was an analysis of colonialism, which was being undertaken especially in Britain and France in the context of post-war decolonisation, but had also been part of the Marxist-influenced radical thought of the Peruvians José Carlos Mariátegui and Víctor Raúl Haya de la Torre in the 1920s and 1930s that influenced scholars all over Latin America. Mexicans Gonzalo Aguirre Beltrán and Julio de la Fuente were among those who, according to van den Berghe (1974b: 2), arrived at a 'happy marriage of Marxist class theory and Chicago anthropology' and this allowed them to emphasise inequality and exploitation while also dealing with ethnic and racial identities, a concern that was developed by others, such as Pablo González Casanova (see Chapter 4).

Julio de la Fuente – who started out as a Marxist, was attracted by functionalism and indeed worked with that founding father of functionalism, Malinowski, on a study of Mexican markets in the early 1940s (Malinowski and de la Fuente, 1982) – worked on interethnic relations in the Chiapas region and came to the conclusion that the label 'indigenous' was a tool used by *mestizos* to ascribe inferior status to those perceived as different and thus legitimate their exploitation (de la Fuente, 1965; Hewitt de Alcántara, 1984: 46–8). In the 1950s and 1960s, Aguirre Beltrán developed the concept of 'regions of refuge'. As with de la Fuente, there was a strong Marxist influence in his work and he focused on unequal exploitative relations between urban and rural dwellers in rather isolated regions. In these 'regions of refuge', urban dwellers used ascriptions of indigenous identity to legitimate social stratification: 'the class struggle between the elite and the illiterate masses takes on the tones of an interethnic battle' (Aguirre Beltrán, 1979: 93).

In both these approaches, there was an implicit challenge to the assumption that the boundary between indigenous and *mestizo*, and the categories it separates, were just 'there', as pre-constituted objective facts to be investigated. The implication, albeit not really explored by either scholar, was that both are constructed in processes of exploitation and unequal exchange. This prefigured the 'instrumentalist' approach to ethnicity that I outlined in Chapter 1. Nevertheless, some of the same problems emerge as with the functionalists: not enough attention was paid to the way the boundary is constructed and maintained; the implication that all *mestizos* exploit all indigenous people did not sit well with the realities of boundary-crossing. There was thus a tendency – as in other analyses of 'the colonial situation' – to create two static homogeneous groups of colonisers and colonised: as Aguirre Beltrán said for the Chiapas region, 'social mobility scarcely exists' (1979: 93), a comment which fails to capture any sense of process. Also, partly due to the Marxist influence, there is the problem of 'reducing' these ethnic and racial identifications to economic determinants, thus denying them their own dynamics.

BLACKS: INTEGRATION IN A CLASS SOCIETY

As with indigenous people, one way of approaching blacks was as a 'problem' in processes of nation-building and, as with indigenous people, this overlapped strongly, especially among Latin American academics, with the scientific study of blacks as bearers of particular ways of life. The latter occurred first in countries that had large and culturally quite distinctive black populations, principally Cuba and Brazil, which had both continued to purchase African slaves as late as the 1870s (Curtin, 1969: 234), with slavery persisting into the last decades of the nineteenth century. In other countries, such as Colombia and Venezuela, blacks were considered within the general perspective of the future of the nation and its racial constitution, but were not a focus of study until later (Wade, 1993a; Wright, 1990).

Among the first specialists on blacks were Raimundo Nina Rodrigues in Brazil and Fernando Ortiz in Cuba – the latter for example published an important study in 1906. Both scholars were, at this stage, deeply enmeshed in the scientific racism of the day. Ortiz was engaged on a long-term study of Afro-Cuban criminality and the underworld culture, the aim of which was to investigate these with a view to eliminating them as backward elements in the nation's progress. Ortiz clearly saw Afro-Cubans as inferior at this early stage of his career. Phrenology – the study that drew a link between head form and aspects of character – was popular at the time as part of the more fringe domains of racial science and the Italian phrenologist Cesare Lombroso contributed a preface to Ortiz's first book on Afro-Cuban criminality (Ortiz, 1973 [1906]; see also Ortiz, 1984).

In Brazil, the early studies of medic Nina Rodrigues – himself of mixed race – made him 'the most prestigious doctrinaire Brazilian racist of his era' until he died in 1906 (Skidmore, 1974: 58). His legacy was soon overshadowed first by scholars such as the physician Arthur Ramos and the sociologist Edison Carneiro, who both published on Afro-Brazilian culture from the 1930s, and then by the writings of Gilberto Freyre. As mentioned in the previous chapter, from the 1930s Freyre became a central figure in Brazilian views on blacks and national identity (Needell, 1995). Redefining what it meant to be Brazilian was not, however, a purely inward-looking endeavour: Brazil was being represented on the international stage as well. Here Freyre was making a comparison between Brazil and the US that was a vital part of Brazil's self-image and, for decades to come, of academic writing about comparative race relations in the Americas (Marx, 1998; Seigel, 2009).

Freyre was claiming that Brazil was, compared to the US, a 'racial democracy'. This argument, as made by Freyre or as developed later, held that slavery had been more benign in Brazil, the Portuguese colonists more tolerant of race mixture, abolition had been less disruptive and contested, there was no strict segregation, no lynching, and so on. This led to a more tolerant, mixed society that, while it might be strongly divided by class, was 'with respect to race relations ... probably the nearest approach to paradise to be found anywhere in the world' (1959: 9). Frank Tannenbaum added scholarly weight to this argument in his book *Slave and Citizen* (1948), which argued that Iberian slave law (which allowed manumission) and the influence of the Catholic Church had both helped integrate blacks into Latin America slave societies in ways that contrasted with Anglo-Saxon America. There has been great debate about whether slavery was, in fact, more benign in Latin America than in the US or, say, Jamaica and the upshot has been that it was impossible to generalise in these broad terms; too much depended on local factors (Davis, 1969; Graham, 1970; Lombardi, 1974). Still, it was undeniable that, in Latin America generally: (1) blacks were freed more frequently than in the southern US; (2) race mixture was more common; and (3) the products of that mixture were recognised more readily as socially distinct from their parents. In the US: (1) freedom for blacks was limited and highly controlled; (2) race mixture occurred, but was repressed; and (3) the offspring of mixed unions were not really accorded a social space of their own – the early recognition of a mixed, 'mulatto' category was partial and evaporated during the nineteenth century so that mixed-race people were basically classified as blacks.

Harris (1974) thought that Tannenbaum was wrong about the law and the Church, and that the reasons for these differences were economic and political. In Brazil, the lack of a solid indigenous population meant Africans were the main workforce, but there was a labour market gap, so to speak, between white masters and slaves. This was best filled by freed slaves who, as it happened, were generally mixed, since the 'mulatto' children of white men with slave women were obvious candidates for being freed. Recognition of mixed people as a specific category was then a natural consequence. In the US, a plentiful supply of poor whites filled that gap and the competitive relations established between white and black ensured that the category 'black' would be heavily policed with racism and legal restrictions that tried to make all blacks slaves and deny intermediate racial categories.

Harris's argument was undermined by the existence of a recognised middle racial category in the northern European Caribbean colonies, where it did not seem to be economically necessary, but emerged perhaps more as a political buffer between a tiny white elite and a huge slave population (Jordan, 1969). Hoetink (1969) also pointed out the importance of the existence of a solid white family structure in inhibiting race mixture and, above all, the recognition of mixed people as socially different: both race mixture and recognition were more likely to occur where colonists tended to be single men. Marx (1998), on the other hand, emphasised the post-slavery nation-building context: the US was trying to unify a nation divided by civil war and did so by including all whites in a privileged category *vis-à-vis* all blacks; in contrast, Brazil increasingly based notions of national unity on a more generalised inclusiveness, apparently ignoring colour and thus contrasting itself to the US.

Whatever the precise reasons for the emergence of the difference (see Daniel, 2006; Foner and Genovese, 1969; Marx, 1998; Wade, 1986), the point remains that it is hard to argue that some generalised tolerance was at the roots of the Latin American pattern. This pattern is, it is true, characterised by complex processes of mixture that have, in most areas, stopped the emergence of relatively clear US-type black–white boundaries, but, as we shall see in ensuing chapters, this does not mean that Latin America is the polar opposite of the US, as racial paradise is the opposite of racial hell. Both societies were slave societies, built on racially ranked stratification; they developed in different ways, but they also share a good deal in terms of the hierarchisation of racial identities. In that sense, the 'contrast' between Brazil and the US is, in part, a rhetorical and political device (Seigel, 2009). Nonetheless, the idea of Brazil as a racial democracy, which Freyre popularised, has been very influential and set the agenda for much of the study of blacks in Latin America generally.

Race and Class in Brazil: The UNESCO Studies

One of the results of the differences explored in Chapter 2 between the status of blacks and indigenous people in the intellectual – and especially anthropological – panorama was that there never really emerged a tradition, functionalist or otherwise, of doing intensive ethnographies that had as their object the explication of the internal characteristics of particular black communities. Although some community-based studies were done, the aim was to illuminate something about Brazilian race relations. Blacks were not seen, in the same way as indigenous people often were, as Others to be studied in their own right, as a separate category; they were seen, as indigenous people only sometimes were, in terms of their relations to others in the nation.

Donald Pierson's *Negroes in Brazil: A Study of Race Contact at Bahia* (1942) fits into such a trend and also into the comparative race relations approach implied in Freyre's work. Bahia as the blackest, most African-looking area of Brazil has tended to attract academic attention and Pierson found there a 'multiracial class society' (1942: 336). In his view:

> In Bahia there is probably little or no race prejudice in the sense in which that term is used in the United States. There are no castes based on race; there are only classes. This does not mean that there is nothing that might properly be called prejudice but that such prejudice as does exist is *class* rather than *caste* prejudice. (1942: 331)

He was using the word 'caste' here as it had been used in the US to characterise the deep-seated black–white segregation of the southern US, hedged about with complex rules of etiquette that defined the appropriate behaviour between whites and blacks, irrespective of their economic status, as that between master and servant. In contrast, Pierson found that 'relations between the races in Brazil have *always been*, to a considerable extent, intimate and cordial' (1942: 335, emphasis added). The putative historical depth given to this cordiality – Sérgio Buarque de Holanda had already written about the 'cordial man' as a central figure of the Brazilian national character (Linger, 1992: 8) – implies the idea of a benign Brazilian slavery and, as to the future, Pierson envisaged: 'the gradual but persistent reduction of all distinguishing racial and cultural marks and the fusing, biologically and culturally, of the African and the European into one race and one common culture' (1942: 337).

The problems with such an approach are manifold and more evident now that racial and ethnic identifications did clearly not disappear, and have recently become more salient. Suffice to say at this stage that Pierson had thrown the baby out with the bath water: for him, Bahia was not like the US; therefore race was more or less irrelevant. The fact that, according to his own figures, 98 per cent of blacks were in the lower class, while 86 per cent of whites were in what he called 'the intelligentsia' (that is, the upper class), had to be explained, in his approach, in terms of past discriminations (for example, of slavery) which had placed blacks at the bottom, but which now (almost magically) were purely 'class' discriminations. Racism played no further role in maintaining inequality and this was evident to Pierson because relations were 'cordial'. The possibility that racism could operate in different ways than in the US was not explored.

It was this 'traditional' vision of Brazil purveyed by Freyre and Pierson (Toplin, 1971) that was vital when, after the horrors of Nazi racism and as part of the final dismantling of scientific racism and eugenics, UNESCO – headed at the time by Arthur Ramos – decided to undertake a study of race relations in Brazil that, within the overall UNESCO initiative on attacking racism (Barkan, 1996), would show the world how to get things right in this respect (Maio, 1999).[1]

The UNESCO studies covered very different areas of Brazil and this is important when assessing the results of their research. One UNESCO team, headed by Charles Wagley and including Thales de Azevedo, Luiz Costa Pinto, Harry Hutchinson, Marvin Harris, Ben Zimmerman, focused on north-east and central Brazil, including Rio. Another team, headed by Roger Bastide and Florestan Fernandes, and including Oracy Nogueira, focused on southern Brazil, especially São Paulo. In this latter region, the black presence was more recent and there was a large white population, much of which was of relatively recent European origin; race relations there were arguably more conflictive than in the north-east where Pierson had also worked. Also, Fernandes was more radical in his views than many of the northern team; he later became part of the so-called São Paulo school, with Fernando Henrique Cardoso and Octavio Ianni, which was purged from São Paulo University by the military government in 1969.

The results of the UNESCO studies varied a good deal, but overall there was little evidence to sustain the idea of a racial democracy. Most researchers reported evidence of racial prejudice and discrimination (for example, Azevedo, 1953; Bastide and Fernandes, 1955; Nogueira, 1955; Wagley, 1952). Rather than attempting to summarise all these studies – which have been reviewed elsewhere, I will look in some detail at a couple of significant examples.[2]

Marvin Harris carried out an anthropological study of the town of Minas Velhas in Minas Gerais (Harris, 1952). In this study he detailed at length the negative and racist stereotypes that surrounded the image of *negro* in the town, but then explained that whites never actually behaved on the basis of these stereotypes because there was 'no status-role for the Negro as Negro, nor for the white as white' (1952: 63) – that is, the image of *negro* was an ideal type that did not correspond to a real individual; there was no actual category of people agreed to be *negros*; the term was virtually an insult and the word *preto* was more commonly used for dark-skinned people. In reality, people's status was determined by a number of criteria – mainly wealth and occupation – of which racial identification was only one. Here the implicit comparison with the US is clear: an opposition was set up between a system in which the racial criterion did define everything (the US 'caste' system in which, as Malcolm X so pithily put it, a black person with a PhD was still called a 'nigger') and one in which it was merely one factor among others (the Brazil 'class' system).

Harris then looked in more detail at the social structure of the town and defined three ranked groups on the basis of wealth and occupation. These, he said, represented the town's actual status groups – they defined who associated with whom on equal social terms. He then analysed whether race could place a person in a different group from that for which their wealth and occupation qualified them. He found that race was a secondary diagnostic in that this almost never happened: there was only one black man who qualified economically for Group A status but was denied full social participation in it because he was black (1952: 68). However, he admitted that, since race and class criteria overlapped so much, this did not actually tell us much. That is, each group was more or less homogeneous with respect to both economic and racial criteria: only 4 per cent of the top group were non-white, while only 20 per cent of the bottom group were white (1952: 70). Thus to say *rico* (rich) was the same as saying *branco* (white), while *pobre* (poor) and *preto* were also virtually synonymous. Harris went on to say that, in the middle group, there was evidence that racial criteria were creating a split. People in that group divided over their basic identification with the rich whites as against the poor blacks. This was evident, for example, in the creation of competing carnival celebrations for *brancos-ricos* and *pretos-pobres* which tended to split the middle group. Thus there was 'no justification for dismissing race as a chimerical side-effect of the class structure' (1952: 77).

Harris's study was flawed in a number of ways. He admitted that the overlap between race and class severely undermined the whole procedure of assessing race as a diagnostic of rank. A better way of proceeding might have been to define status groups independently, simply on the basis of who associated with whom on equal terms, and then see how homogeneous these groups were with respect to race and class criteria. Even this would have come up against the same problem, but we might then have known more about what happened with the significant minority of whites in the bottom class: how did they treat the blacks and mixed-race people in their class? Did they have greater chances of upward economic mobility because they were white and might get favourable treatment from richer whites? Harris's analysis was too static (and indeed the economy of the town itself was too stagnant) to answer such crucial questions.

Nevertheless, Harris went on to make more sweeping statements about race in Brazil, for example in *Patterns of Race in the Americas*, first published in 1964. Here he said that, 'the issue of racial discrimination is scarcely a vital one' and that 'as far as behaviour is concerned, "races" do not exist for the Brazilians' (1974: 63, 64). Yet Thales de Azevedo, working in Bahia, had concluded that 'coloured people are still considered to be part of a biological and social category characterised by traits thought to be inferior to those of whites' (1953: 103, my translation). For Harris, class was the main factor in ranking: 'It is class which determines who will be admitted to hotels, restaurants and social clubs' (1974: 61). Yet in 1951, the black US dancer Katherine Dunham had complained of being refused admittance to a São Paulo hotel and the ensuing fuss had led to the passage of the Afonso Arinos Law prohibiting such discrimination (Skidmore, 1974: 212). Azevedo had also found that 'often blacks do not encounter barriers because, knowing the prejudices of the whites, they avoid certain places' (1953: ch. 7, my translation).

Harris (1970) also argued that Brazilian modes of racial classification led to the 'maximization of ambiguity': there were dozens of terms commonly used to classify people by their appearance and the same individual might be classified in different ways by different people. This was in contrast to the US, where racial terminology was simpler and more agreed upon. Since 'the *sine qua non* of any thorough-going minority system is a foolproof method of separating a population into superordinate and subordinate groups' (Harris,

1974: 54), Brazil could not have such a system. The problems here are, first, that although many terms are used to classify people in Brazil, and elsewhere in Latin America, other research has indicated that, in practice, people operate with basic conceptual prototypical categories for ordering that variety that correspond roughly to black, white and indigenous and the first-level mixtures between these three (Sanjek, 1971; Whitten, 1985: 42). Surveys carried out in 1976 and 1995 elicited many colour terms, but over 95 per cent of respondents only used six or seven terms (Telles, 2004: 82). Second, it may be true that there is not a 'thorough-going minority system' in Brazil or elsewhere in Latin America, but this hardly clarifies the role that race evidently does play. Telles (2004) shows that, although Brazilians' racial classifications are ambiguous, key categories such as *moreno*, *negro* and *branco* still operate and underpin racial exclusions based on those categories. As with Pierson, the baby is being thrown out with the bath water if the only example of a 'minority system' is implicitly taken to be the US under Jim Crow segregationist legislation. It is necessary to grasp that in Brazil – and in other contexts, such as Colombia – a collective consensus on the boundaries of categories such as 'white', 'black', 'brown' and 'indian' may not exist, but this does not stop people making, *in particular contexts*, specific racialised identifications of self and other, which may change according to context but which still have important structural consequences in terms of labour markets, housing markets, police harassment, marriage choices and so on.

Fernandes (1969) was more emphatic about the existence of racism in São Paulo society and his book, which drew on the research done in the 1950s, documented in detail how blacks and whites felt about each other and about racism. However, the detail of the work – which in any case is rather abstract, since there is little concrete ethnography and many decontextualised anecdotes and interviews – is set within Fernandes' overall understanding of race and capitalism. He saw an overall process in which slavery places 'blacks' and 'mulattoes' – Fernandes did not distinguish greatly between these categories – at the bottom of the social hierarchy. Abolition occurred under the pressures of capitalist expansion and the demand for free labour. Freed blacks were not integrated, however, due to their lack of education and skills necessary for the capitalist labour market, or as Fernandes called it 'the competitive social order'. The heavy white immigration that occurred in southern Brazil between 1880 and 1930 merely exacerbated this situation, displacing blacks from the labour market and causing a stage of marginality in which alcoholism, crime, broken families and so on undermined even further their ability to compete. Nevertheless, immigration expanded the competitive social order, bringing modernisation and, over time, the gradual integration of blacks.

Fernandes saw, then, a gradual shift from a traditional society based on paternalism, with blacks 'knowing their place', towards a democratic capitalism within which racial discrimination would have no function; racial identities would decline in the face of class. The racism that Fernandes documented so carefully was, in his view, an anachronism, a hold-over from previous times, but it would remain unless there was proactive effort on the part of whites to remove it; white indifference was also to blame for lack of black integration. The result that he found in the 1950s was what he called a system of 'accommodation' (1969: 391): individualistic mobility was permitted for a small number of blacks and mixed-race people, while the rest remained in the lower strata, kept in place by negative stereotypes and racial discrimination, by white indifference and by the lack of a concerted political challenge by blacks and mixed-race people. Racial prejudice was usually dissimulated and many blacks (especially those who accepted their place in the system) themselves denied its existence. Those blacks who did achieve some upward mobility tended to distance themselves from other blacks, associating with and perhaps marrying white people; this too made black political mobilisation difficult.

There are clearly problems with Fernandes' idea that there was an overall shift in progress from a traditional to a modern society in which racial identity would be, by definition, irrelevant. Bastide (1957) was less sanguine and saw a continuing role for racism in a competitive society, a position also taken by van den Berghe (1967: ch. 3). Nevertheless, the details of Fernandes' analysis of the practice of accommodation capture, in my view, many salient aspects of racial identifications in Brazil and elsewhere. To take just one example, accommodation serves, in his view, to mask the realities of racial prejudice. In 1995, the São Paulo newspaper *Folha* carried out a national survey on attitudes to race. Of those identified as white, 89 per cent said they thought whites were racially prejudiced (although they denied being prejudiced themselves). Of those identifying as black, 91 per cent said whites were prejudiced. But one question asked people who identified themselves as blacks and *pardos* ('browns') if they had ever been subject to discrimination; 77 per cent said no (although this was 64 per cent for blacks alone).[3]

So although there is a generalised recognition of the existence of racism (Bailey, 2004), it is very often something that 'other people' practice and suffer from. Ethnographic studies also comment on the 'silence' of Brazilian black people about experiences of racism (Sheriff, 2001: ch. 3; Twine, 1998: ch. 7) and this helps maintain a 'cordial racism'. In my experience in Colombia, some blacks denied being discriminated against: I believe this is because to admit being a victim was, in their view, to admit to being the type of person who might be discriminated against – not only black, but, by association, untrustworthy, stupid and so on – as if it might be their fault that they were discriminated against (Wade, 1993a: ch. 13).

There is, however, a strong tendency in Fernandes' work to take 'black' and 'mulatto' as unproblematic categories. Harris goes too far in using the ambiguity of classification to argue for the irrelevance of race identities, but the blurring of racial categories, their contextual nature and the whole ideology of 'whitening', which valorises whiteness and opens the limited possibility of black and mixed-race people renegotiating their own and their children's racial identity, are vital aspects of the situation in Brazil and elsewhere that are suggested, but that do not receive they attention they need in Fernandes' work.

In sum, then, the UNESCO studies undermined the idea of a racial democracy in Brazil and, in some cases, detailed many aspects of how racism worked in a non-US, non-'caste' system. However, there was still a tendency to deny the significance of race or to see it as declining over time: Brazil was seen as basically a class society. It is important that these studies were almost always in implicit comparison with the US: the latter's 'caste' system was the home of 'real' race relations and racism against which other societies could be measured. The idea that one could think in terms of different forms of racism and race relations without necessarily opposing them was not easily entertained at that time. There was also a general tendency in these studies to reify racial categories (Fernandes) or to deny them completely for the Brazilian case (Harris); the idea that racial categories are in a constant process of reconstitution through people's practice and exist contextually and interactively was not current, and it was this that gave rise to some of the problems in seeing what racial identities meant in Brazil. Since they were not like those in the US – where their reification by analysts was understandable given their relative social solidity – they somehow eluded observers' analytical grasp.

CONCLUSION

There are two main trends underlying these early studies that I want to highlight. First, the idea that racial and ethnic identities were destined to disappear: this was evident in much intellectual thought, including that of some *indigenistas*, about the nation. This was a general tendency in social thought at the time, but in Latin America especially, the association of blacks and indigenous people with the past has been very strong: they have been associated with primitivism, slavery, antique modes of production, traditionalism and so on. Even the trends in *indigenismo* and *negrismo* that sprang up in the 1920s and 1930s (see Chapter 2) were mostly based on valuing these associations, rather than challenging them. The idea, argued by Gilroy (1993a), that blacks in the Atlantic diaspora have been in the vanguard of modernity – prefiguring its crises of identity and critiquing its contradictions – was barely conceivable.

The second trend is the taking for granted of racial and ethnic identities. These were generally conceived as being concrete things 'on the ground' which could be put under the microscope. People might pass from one to another or one might argue that they did not exist except as 'mere' ideas (as did Harris, 1952), but in general there was an impoverished analysis of the relation between ideas and practice – groups existed and people had ideas and feelings about them. The interactive, recursive relation between the groups as perpetually reconstituted collectivities in action and the groups as perpetually re-imagined communities in thought was not grasped.

4
Inequality and Situational Identity: The 1970s

By the middle of the 1960s, the growing influence of radical perspectives in social science was apparent. Marxism had been a constant presence in Latin American social science – as I showed in the previous chapter, it had influenced writers from José Carlos Mariátegui in 1920s Peru to Aguirre Beltrán in 1960s Mexico – but now it took on new force, often channelled through ideas about dependency which could be more or less distant from classical Marxism.

Dependency theory had emerged after the war and incorporated various different strands in Latin America. On the one hand, there was the analysis of unequal terms of trade associated with Raúl Prébisch and the Economic Commission for Latin America; this position, which was not really a Marxist one, argued that Latin America was disadvantaged by unfavourable terms of trade with Europe and the US and needed economic protection to allow more independent industrial development. On the other hand, there was the Marxist analysis of imperialism which, as developed by Lenin, Rudolf Hilferding and Rosa Luxemburg, related imperial expansion directly to the internal dynamics of the capitalist mode of production. This was the kind of approach developed by André Gunder Frank who, concentrating more on capitalist exchange than production, understood the poverty of the Third World as a result of the expropriation of resources from the periphery, through a chain of exploitative metropolis–satellite relations, to the centre. This is not the place to enter into an assessment of development theory (see Kay, 1989), but the point is that inequality and mechanisms of exploitation were an increasingly important focus of attention for those whose gaze had been fixed on smaller domains of interethnic relations. Thus, during the 1970s and into the next decade, many debates centred on the relative roles of class and ethnicity or race.

At the same time, the analysis of ethnicity was advanced by anthropologists such as Frederick Barth (1969), Abner Cohen (1969, 1974) and A.L. Epstein (1978). This established ethnic identity as a more flexible, contextual construct and worked against the tendency to reify social groups that had been common. In the introduction to his edited collection, Barth (1969) argued that ethnic groups were socially constructed and that the focus of analysis should be the boundaries of the group. He criticised the current conception of ethnic groups as self-perpetuating entities with given sets of cultural attributes. He emphasised that ethnic groups exist *in relation to* others; people establish boundaries on the basis of criteria that seem important to them, whether or not an outside observer can appreciate these differences. Boundaries continue to exist when people and cultural information cross them and they may have a different character depending on what differences are being emphasised by the actors concerned in a given situation. Although Barth himself did, at times, suggest that ethnic identity was, in the end, a rather inflexible, permanent aspect of a person (Banks, 1996: 13–14), he established the basis for seeing ethnic identity as *situational*: if it is established in relation to something else, then it will vary depending on what that something is.

In short, then, both these overall trends moved away from the emphasis on 'isolated' communities in functionalist anthropology and located ethnic groups more in the context of the nation and in history, and more in terms of economic inequality and processes of the social construction of identity. Ethnic identities were also understood as phenomena that were not necessarily destined to fade away with 'modernisation' and 'acculturation'; being flexible and being connected to inequality, there was no inherent drive for their disappearance.

INDIGENOUS PEOPLE: ETHNICITY, DEPENDENCY AND RESISTANCE

Some of the changes that occurred in this period can be judged by looking again at Pierre van den Berghe. In 1969, he and Colby published *Ixil Country: A Plural Society in Highland Guatemala*, which retained the pluralist approach they had used before but was now tempered with a greater emphasis on economic and political domination. Ethnic boundaries were related not only to the way that people cooperated and exchanged services, but also to the way that one group dominated another. Van den Berghe then moved his area of research to Peru where he studied the community of San

Jerónimo, near Cuzco. Dependency theory was influencing Peruvian social scientists such as Enrique Mayer, Fernando Fuenzalida and Aníbal Quijano (Degregori and Sandoval, 2008) and the approach showed clearly in van den Berghe's work too.

In one article on the subject, he began with the uncompromising statement that 'throughout the world, the practical import of ethnicity is intimately linked with the unequal distribution of power and wealth' (van den Berghe, 1975: 71). He avoided, however, any tendency to assume that class is automatically more significant than ethnicity. Van den Berghe then outlined the 'sociology of dependence approach', as elaborated by Peruvian researchers such as Fernando Fuenzalida and José Matos Mar, according to which 'Peruvian social structure is conceived as a multitude of binary relations of dependence and domination', forming 'chains of dependence' that 'converge at the apex into the national, and beyond it, the international ruling oligarchy' (1975: 73; see also Long, 1977: ch. 4; van den Berghe, 1974a: 16). Indigenousness, in this scheme, was defined as 'the low end of a dependency chain on nearly all dimensions of unequal relations' (1975: 74). The strength of this approach, for van den Berghe, was that ethnicity is anchored in power relations; thus culture does not by itself define ethnic boundaries, since it is impossible in Peru to neatly separate indigenous from *mestizo* culture; rather, power differences define that boundary. He admitted that this approach 'tends to submerge ethnicity too much under class', resulting in the attempt, for example, to understand indigenous people as peasants rather than indigenous people (p. 75). He emphasised that there were specifically cultural aspects to the situation – for example, ethnic difference makes the system of domination 'all the more difficult to shake' (p. 77); or there were the local power-brokers of indigenous origin who used their knowledge of Quechua the better to manipulate their former peers (p. 77).

Ethnic boundaries in general should, in van den Berghe's view, be defined both objectively (in terms of objective cultural traits) and subjectively (in terms of what people say they are) – elsewhere van den Berghe rejected what he took to be Barth's extreme subjectivist position (actually less so than he suspects) which, he said, argued that 'an ethnic group is whatever anybody says it is' (1974b: 5). In Peru, however, ethnic boundaries were to a great extent 'defined subjectively, relatively and situationally' (1975: 73). Thus the upper class of San Jerónimo might be seen as *mestizo* by local standards, but as *cholo* by the upper class of Cuzco; the term '*cholo*' did not define a group of people, but was a relational term, used to deprecate individuals that the speaker saw as inferior.[1] Likewise, there was little consensus as to who was *mestizo* and who indigenous, with some people classing most others in the town as *mestizos* and others labelling them indigenous. This, however, was not very typical of the Andes and in many other areas the indigenous–*mestizo* line was much more sharply drawn (1975: 82). In any event, although boundaries were flexible in this way, important differences of power and wealth were evident in the town and these corresponded to ethnic differences: indigenous was low status, *mestizo* was higher.

Van den Berghe retained, however, an important element of his previous position: Peru was a relatively open system which allowed 'considerable mobility' from the indigenous group to the *mestizo* group, in which, therefore, 'the subordinate group steadily decreases in proportion' (1975: 83, 78). The fact that this seemed to contradict his idea that the indigenous–*mestizo* boundary was maintained by power relations rather than cultural difference was not addressed, unless the (unlikely) argument was that the hierarchy of these power relations was itself diminishing.

François Bourricaud was less positive about the future of Peruvian society. In an important article (1975), he was critical of dependency theory because the simple fact of dependence could not explain the peculiarities of Peru, 'which is a mixture of very heterogeneous elements strangely combining great rigidity with great fluidity'. This is why, he said, 'the cholo emerges as a key character': it was the *cholo* who represented 'the element of mobility in a system which neither encourages nor stresses mobility' (1975: 357). Ultimately, however, Peru could not crystallise as a nation around either the symbol of *cholo* (which is too pejorative a term), or indigenous or *mestizo*; in Peru there was neither a class nor a caste system, there was only heterogeneous change, the direction of which Bourricaud admitted he was uncertain about (1975: 386).

Rodolfo Stavenhagen was also more cautious in his views – this time with reference to the Chiapas highlands. He saw relations of colonialism and class coexisting over a long period of time as aspects of stratified interethnic relations. Class relations were tending to displace colonial ones, but this did not necessarily mean the erasure of indigenous ethnic identity. In common with other Mexican social scientists of the time who critiqued ideas of 'acculturation' (Sittón, 2008), Stavenhagen emphasised the persistence of 'Indian cultural identity independent of stratification' (1975: 206) which occurred when indigenous people moved up in the ranking system without loss of identity. In addition, the loss of ethnic identity by indigenous people could be interpreted as a negative move, heralding proletarianisation and even marginalisation rather than upward mobility (1975: 215).

Judith Friedlander, working in Mexico, addressed the logic of van den Berghe's argument about culture, but in a different way. In her view, indigenous culture in Hueyapan was constantly changing, taking on traits that were being discarded by the Mexican upper classes as they redefined their identity and acquired new symbols. But:

> despite the fact that the 'content' of Hueyapan culture is always changing, the 'structural' relationship of Indian to hispanic remains the same. The villagers are still Indians by virtue of the fact that they continue to lack what the elite continues to acquire.

Meanwhile the Hueyapeños themselves 'do not make the distinction between their "culture", which has been changing, and their "class", which has remained virtually the same' (1975: 71); they saw their culture as basically the same as during colonial times. Friedlander's and van den Berghe's views of indigenous culture as a changeable, flexible construct thus contrasted with the image of indigenous culture as static, conservative and traditional that was a corollary of George Foster's notion of 'limited good'. That some people, including indigenous people themselves, might *see* indigenous culture as static and traditional is true, but this puts the issue on a different footing, opening up a more complex approach to competing discourses about indigenous culture (see Chapter 7).

Ideas about the persistence of ethnic boundaries despite cultural change and the consequent possibility of ethnic identities that might persist in a changing form were also reflected in studies on urban migrants. The process of urbanisation had been widely assumed to lead to cultural homogenisation and the submergence of 'traditional' ethnic identities into urban class identity; urbanisation was, after all, seen to be a central dynamic in modernisation. Research by Roberts (1974), Doughty (1972) and Isbell (1978: ch. 8) indicated that this was not necessarily the case, showing that strong links between city and village often existed, and that rituals and festivals from village life were adapted to city settlements. This indicated cultural continuities but said little about ethnic identification. In fact, self-identification as indigenous or perhaps *cholo* among migrants was often avoided, since these terms were associated with the rural backwardness that many migrants wished to avoid. However, these labels did not disappear. Bourricaud (1975: 384) argued that in Lima terms such as 'indigenous' and '*cholo*' were used by some migrants to describe other migrants; and none of these migrants would 'be recognised by anyone outside their own circles as anything other than *cholos*' (see also Radcliffe, 1990). In La Paz, Bolivia, the proportion of indigenous people in the population declined from 81 per cent in 1860 to 30 per cent in 1909, mainly due to changes in how people classified themselves (and were classified by others). Yet in the 1950s, there were experiments in *indigenista* theatre that created – temporarily – a space for indigenous identities that were more than just quaint folklorism (Bigenho, 2006). In the 1970s, the so-called Fiesta del Gran Poder (the worship of a particular image of Christ) became a central expression of identity for indigenous urban migrants. It was, however, rather ambiguous. Identified clearly as a '*cosa de indios*' (an indian thing) by the city's upper and middle classes, the Fiesta increasingly centred on La Morenada ('dance of the blacks'), in which indigenous people dressed up as colonial blacks – what might be called ethnic identification through 'racial displacement' (Guss, 2006: 319–20). Categorisations based on perceived cultural (and physical) differences were thus still an important part of everyday urban life.

Internal Colonialism and Resistance

Directly connected to dependency approaches and the analysis of colonialism was the development of theories of internal colonialism. One of the first to use the idea was the Mexican Pablo González Casanova, building on Aguirre Beltrán's notion of region of refuge (see Chapter 3):

> Internal colonialism corresponds to a structure of social relations based on domination and exploitation among culturally heterogeneous, distinct groups. If it has a specific difference with respect to other relations based on subordination, it inheres in the cultural heterogeneity that is historically produced by the conquest of some peoples by others. (1965: 33)

The idea was simply that relations of exploitation between regions within a country paralleled those between colonising and colonised countries: the existence of a territorial distinction; the monopolisation of trade and (sometimes) control of production in the colonised territory by an external elite that was ethnically and/or racially distinct; the control of the colony's institutions by that elite; and the subordination of the colonised population in political, economic and cultural terms to the coloniser's priorities (González Casanova, 1971; Hechter, 1975; van den Berghe, 1974b: 6). The difference from the 'regions of refuge' idea – and Aguirre Beltrán disapproved of González's concept, partly because it conflicted with his own underlying conviction that integration and acculturation were the way forward (Sittón, 2008) – was that the internal colony was not an isolated backward region, dominated by a local elite, that could be modernised through integration into the nation. Instead the colony was already integrated into national and international circuits of capitalist production and exchange (Hewitt de Alcántara, 1984: 113). The idea that exploitation was the driving force behind ethnic and racial distinctions was, however, very much the same.

The theory of internal colonialism was used extensively to characterise the position of indigenous communities or regions in Latin America. Norman Whitten used it, for example, in his analysis of Ecuadorian jungle Quechua on the borders between Amazonia and the Andes (1975, 1976). These people were not homogeneous, but had a clear self-identification which was becoming clearer, not merging with *mestizo* culture: 'Lowland Quechua ethnicity [has to be understood] as a rational response to expanding opportunities in the money economy under the continuance of internal colonialism in Ecuador' (1975: 47).

Whitten (1976) focused on an indigenous *comuna* (roughly, a reserve) established in 1947, near the growing colonist town of Puyo. The *comuna* was established by the state partly to offset foreign encroachment; the land around it quickly passed into the private ownership of *mestizo* colonists: as such the *comuna* represented 'a special aspect of national expansion and, increasingly, a basis for indigenous survival' (1976: 240). Whitten used the concept of internal colonialism partly because of the special legal status of the *comuna*, which created a separate territory within the nation, and because of the strong racial ideology of mixedness as the basic characteristic of Ecuadorian national identity, which was 'a powerful mechanism for exclusion of the non-mixed' (1976: 251, 275); thus *mestizos* – who might identify as *blancos* (whites) in the local context to further differentiate themselves from indigenous people – were the colonisers of indigenous territory. The labelling of indigenous people by *mestizos* created an expanding generalised category of *indio* to which *mestizos* contrasted themselves, especially when competing for economic opportunities. *Mestizos* used the categorisation to block the access to strategic resources of those they labelled as indigenous and this, plus the overall process of ethnocide which was affecting the Quechua, forced their ethnic identity to intensify in a corresponding process of 'ethnogenesis' (1976: 281). In the process, however, the Quechua fell more definitively under the aegis of 'protective' national policy on indigenous people which was in fact rather restrictive compared to state policy encouraging the colonisation of 'undeveloped' regions through infrastructural expansion. Here, then, we saw at least three sets of actors defining the ethnic boundary: the state with its definition of the indigenous *comuna*, the colonists and the indigenous people. Indigenous people were culturally distinct, despite the fact they wore Western clothes, avoided face-painting and feather-wearing when with *mestizos* and spoke Quechua which was understood by many non-indigenous people (1976: 278). But it was not cultural difference that maintained the ethnic boundary; this was a product of political and economic relations.

Internal colonialism was not actually a vital feature of Whitten's argument and in his edited volume on Ecuador (1981a) it received only a passing mention, although many of the same ideas as before characterise the chapters in this volume. Elsewhere, the 'theory' of internal colonialism remained rather vague, liable to be applied as a metaphor to any situation of exploitation that displayed ethnic or racial dimensions and liable also to over-emphasise the internal homogeneity of colonisers and colonised and the rigidness of the boundary separating them (Stone, 1979; Wolpe, 1975). Yet it enjoyed a certain vogue precisely because of its focus on economic exploitation alongside ethnic and racial discrimination, even if the relationship between these remained rather under-theorised and ultimately reductive: ethnic identities became the mere products of economic relations; culture as a value *in its own right*, with which people might mobilise, define themselves and come into conflict, was not really embraced.

With the analysis of colonialism came the analysis of resistance. Whitten broached this in his work on the jungle Quechua – in so far as he saw the indigenous people as struggling to defend their land and interests – and similar concerns were voiced by others. Previously, there had been a tendency to see indigenous or peasant resistance as a supposedly traditional, conservative resistance to modernisation and national incorporation. Now it began to be seen as a positive thing, the resistance of an oppressed minority against political and cultural domination. In her ethnography of Chuschi, an indigenous 'closed corporate community' in the Peruvian Andes,

Billie Jean Isbell investigated 'the structural defences the indigenous population has constructed against the increasing domination of the outside world' (1978: 11). She took the idea of internal colonialism as a theoretical basis for her work (1978: 19), but it did not figure in much detail: the point was simply to emphasise political and economic inequality and to locate the village in the national context, rather than seeing it as an isolate in the old functionalist fashion.

The central conflict in the village was between 'the communal members' ideology of self-sufficiency and the increasing pressures toward cultural and economic incorporation into the nation' (1978: 11). This was expressed mainly through a division between *comuneros*, the indigenous insiders, and the *vecinos* (literally, neighbours), the *mestizo* outsiders resident in the village, who included the shopkeepers, bureaucrats, teachers and the priest. The fundamental distinction between them was not dress or language or 'outward orientation to the Peruvian nation', it was accepting or negating 'membership in the commune with all of the attendant obligations' (1978: 73) – these involved the reciprocal exchange of labour and participation in certain activities and rituals, including ones in which the insider–outsider boundary was dramatised. Ethnic boundaries were maintained by different sets of activities and by fairly rigid labelling: Isbell reported universal agreement on who belonged in which category (1978: 73).

These mechanisms of differentiation constituted a 'defence' against the outside world in the sense of a barrier rather than a positive strategy. More direct tactics were employed by the migrants from the village to Lima, and by return migrants. The migrants in Lima formed a society which intervened in village politics, organising the village's communal council, removing a disliked *mestizo* school director, trying to turn Church lands into a village cooperative and, in general, mediating between national bureaucracy and the village. The migrants had an ambivalent status in the village, since they were seen as insiders and outsiders, urban and rural, beneficial for the village, but also trying to control it for their own ends. They occupied the bureaucratic posts once held by *vecinos*, but identified themselves as *comuneros* or 'sons of *comuneros*' (1978: 193) – there must have been flexibility here in ethnic identifications that belies Isbell's more rigid depictions of the *vecino–comunero* boundary.

Both Isbell and Whitten saw indigenous people as active agents and this was an important antidote to the characterisations of them as powerless objects of change and acculturation that were part and parcel of much official *indigenismo*. In Mexico, too, social scientists at this time increasingly emphasised the historical and contemporary role of indigenous people in shaping Mexican society as a whole, giving rise to what Bonfil Batalla (1996 [1987]) would later call '*México profundo*', the deep form of the Mexican nation that underlay the 'imaginary Mexico' that had been imposed by European colonisers and that denied the day-to-day reality of most Mexicans' lives.

Images of indigenous powerlessness and forcible assimilation were being reaffirmed at the time by portrayals of indigenous Amazonians as the helpless victims of 'progress'. Studies on ethnic relations in the Amazon region were rather limited at this time: under the influence of Lévi-Straussian structuralism and North American cultural ecology, anthropologists had instead tended to examine indigenous social organisation, mythology and symbolism. When ethnic relations were dealt with it was often – not surprisingly under the circumstances – in terms of ethnocide and genocide (Davis, 1977; Jaulin, 1970; but see Barbira-Freedman, 1980) and anthropologists were often advocates for indigenous causes. The plight of Amazonian indigenous people spurred the formation of the campaigning organisation Survival International in 1969.

Seeing indigenous people as active historical agents was therefore important, but some of the difficulties of indigenous people resisting as active agents were also made evident in Isbell's and Whitten's work. The Chuschinos' strategy was to resist by blocking, but in doing so they risked becoming 'a satellite' of the urban migrants' world which, although it was not losing an indigenous identity in a straightforward manner, was less unequivocally indigenous (Isbell, 1978: 217). In contrast, the jungle Quechua were actively trying to engage with new economic opportunities, but since their struggle involved intensifying their ethnic identity, they were being blocked by *mestizo* colonists and constrained by state indigenous legislation. Thus to be 'indigenous' and to struggle for progress seemed to be, in Latin American nations, contradictory endeavours.

BLACKS: REVISIONIST HISTORIES AND BLACK CULTURE

Studies of blacks during this period continued to focus on Brazil, although other regions also began to appear, notably Ecuador and Colombia. In many cases, the influence of Marxism or, more broadly, political economy made itself felt. In contrast to the studies of indigenous people, however, there was less reconsideration of the nature of racial identifications and a continuing tendency to take for granted categories such as white, black and *pardo*, even though the contingent character of these identifications had already been made clear. One of the problems was that, increasingly, observers wanted to emphasise that racism did exist in Brazil and elsewhere and highlighting the flexibility of these categories seemed to work against this trend. The point, in my view, is to reach an understanding of how both flexibility and racism coexist. The way to grasp this was already implicit in the material on indigenous–*mestizo* relations, which showed that individuals could move from one category to another, conditional on their move being accepted by others in any given situation, without this abolishing the category of indigenous, or the racism or even the ethnocide directed at that category. However, many of the commentators on race in Brazil were wrapped up in questions of the relation between race and class and this sort of approach escaped them.

Brazil

One example of the concern with race and class was the sociologist Octavio Ianni who, sometimes in collaboration with Fernando Henrique Cardoso, had been writing about race and capitalism in southern Brazil since the 1960s (Cardoso and Ianni, 1960). His approach to this was similar to that of Fernandes in that his predominant concern was with the transition from slavery to capitalism; likewise, his conclusion that white Brazilians adopted 'an ideology of compromise', allowing social mobility for some blacks and repressing the majority (Ianni, 1966: 51), was similar to Fernandes' notion of 'accommodation'. Ianni took a highly reductionist line, however, arguing that 'the socio-economic and political importance of the labour force clarifies and explains cultural, racial and other manifestations which have been obscured ... by the analyses of some sociologists and anthropologists' (1972: 239). Thus any racial (or ethnic or cultural) identifications and dynamics could be explained in terms of the labour force in a class society; in this view, the position of indigenous people and Polish immigrants is very similar to that of blacks since both are subject to negative stereotypes that facilitate their exploitation as labour (Ianni, 1966: 54–6). There is little hint in any of this that 'black' might be a category worth investigating in its own right: this would be merely the obscurantism of anthropologists.

Historian Carl Degler made an important contribution with his book *Neither Black Nor White* (1971), an extended comparison of race relations in Brazil and the US which challenged the idea of racial democracy in the former region. Others such as Toplin (1971) and Skidmore (1972) made similar revisionist interpretations, and Toplin also pointed out that, with desegregation and positive discrimination in favour of blacks, the US itself had changed, making the comparison even less straightforward. Degler traced historical differences between Brazil and the US, disavowing the notion of benevolent slavery but focusing on the so-called 'mulatto escape hatch', which accorded people of mixed ancestry a special place (1971: 107) and allowed them to move up the social scale. This escape hatch, which had emerged for historical reasons connected with the lack of Portuguese women and Portuguese machismo, was the central difference between Brazil and the US.

Degler presented evidence of racial prejudice – much of it anecdotal and impressionistic, but overall quite convincing – and argued that the mulatto escape hatch fitted into a powerful ethos of whitening which held that black was inferior to white, but allowed some upward mobility for individual mulattoes who would then also strive to further whiten themselves by association with non-blacks and by 'marrying up' the racial hierarchy if they could, thus whitening their children even more. This whitening had been noted before by Fernandes and others (for example, Banton, 1967) and Skidmore (1974) produced a historical study tracing whitening as an ideology combining ideas of mixture and white superiority, and as a government policy on, for example, immigration. Whitening was also part of popular knowledge in Brazil – the adage that 'money whitens' was a well-known one, signifying that a wealthy black person might be labelled as non-black and, more generally, that such a person moved up the racial hierarchy in social terms. Degler simply highlighted the phenomenon of whitening and located some of its historical roots. The importance of this is that the valuing of whiteness has to be seen, in my view, as a cultural dimension in its own right; it is, of course, connected strongly to class issues, but it cannot be reduced to them. For example, the power of a whitened aesthetic – although not necessarily a completely white aesthetic – in shaping people's ideas of beauty is strong, especially for women (Burdick, 1998: ch. 1; Caldwell, 2004; Edmonds, 2007; Simpson, 1993; Wade, 2009b: ch. 5). There is recent evidence of a black bodily aesthetic gaining ground (Fry, 2002; Pinho, 2006), which complicates the dominance of whiteness, but reinforces the point that these racial dynamics need to be examined in their own right.

Degler also argued that the mulatto escape hatch created 'inner burdens of colour' in the sense that, because there was a possibility of avoiding blackness and successful blacks often did so, many blacks felt ashamed of being black. Furthermore, it was very hard to create the kind of black solidarity movement that the US had witnessed in the 1950s and 1960s, which mobilised blacks as a clear social group and challenged prevalent negative definitions of blackness. This was also the conclusion of Toplin (1971) and Skidmore (1972). Nevertheless, it should be noted that black activists were already present in Brazil when the UNESCO studies started and they were to become increasingly important (see Chapter 5). This was something that these analyses found hard to cope with since, while they recognised the existence of black activists, they assumed that black mobilisation was structurally impeded by the divisions between blacks and mixed-race people (in all the gradations that the whitening syndrome implied). Black activism could never be anything more than marginal in this view.

Winant accuses Degler of class reductionism, saying that his analysis 'saw economic mobility (and thus, integration into a class society) as the key question in Brazilian racial dynamics' (1992: 177), but I find it hard to substantiate this reading. Degler predicts that racism will become more significant and, if anything, makes a plea for greater black solidarity to combat this; he certainly does not tend to 'confirm the traditional wisdom about "whitening" as the preferred solution to Brazil's racial problem' (1992: 177) but rather sees it as part of the problem. My problem with Degler is rather that of an anthropologist with a historian: there is no detailed ethnography showing how racial identifications work in particular situations. He assumes that whitening is mainly a question of special treatment for a 'mulatto' person, allowing him or her – although Degler does not examine the gender issues involved, which are certainly relevant (see Wade, 2009b) – greater social mobility. But he does not present convincing evidence that this special treatment exists and, in fact, there may be other ways in which whitening associated with upward mobility for black people can occur. A black or brown man may make money and marry a lighter woman – which is a relatively common pattern in Brazil (Moutinho, 2004; Telles, 2004: 176). A black or more frequently a brown woman may find a wealthier white husband or lover (which may be partly due to images of dark-skinned women as sexually attractive). This type of marriage is less common in Brazil than darker man with lighter woman unions (Telles, 2004: 176); it may be that extra-marital relationships between lighter men and darker women are more common, following a long-established pattern (Goldstein, 2003: ch. 3; Wade, 2009b).

Carlos Hasenbalg entered the debate about racism in Brazil with an argument reminiscent of Bastide's earlier work (which has been too often included with that of Fernandes, but actually departed from it in significant respects). This formed part of what Winant (1992) calls the structuralist approach to race in Brazil and it sought to explain 'the perpetuation of racial inequalities in Brazil' (Hasenbalg, 1985: 27; see also Hasenbalg, 1979; Silva and Hasenbalg, 1999: 53). Like Bastide, Hasenbalg argued that racism was not an anachronistic hangover from slavery, but was an active part of capitalist society, working in favour of whites in a competitive situation; 'race as a socially elaborated attribute may be conceptualised as related mainly to the subordinate aspect of the reproduction of social classes' (1985: 27). Here is the class reductionism that Winant claims to find in Degler's approach. However, in maintaining racial inequalities 'the racist practices of the racially dominant group' included not only actual discriminatory behaviour, but also 'a racist social organisation that restrains the motivation and level of aspiration of non-white people' (Hasenbalg, 1985: 27–8). This, then, brought a level of cultural ideology into the argument and grasped aspects of the symbolism and practice of whitening; still, it was subordinated to the reproduction of a capitalist class structure.

Winant adds that both Hasenbalg and Anani Dzidzienyo focused on the 'smooth preservation of racial inequalities' – the subtitle of Hasenbalg's doctoral thesis – or the idea that the 'official Brazilian ideology of non-discrimination ... achieves *without tension* the same results as do overtly racist societies' (Dzidzienyo, 1979: 7) and he argues that this conclusion came at a time when Brazil's military regime had crushed most opposition (Winant, 1992: 180–2). In fact, as Winant goes on to argue, and as Andrews (1991, 1992, 2004) has also shown in detail, black opposition to racial inequality has a long, if uneven, history. But if Hasenbalg and Dzidzienyo overstated their case (as did Toplin and Skidmore in this respect), they were highlighting what Fernandes had called the 'accommodation' that was characteristic of the Brazilian racial order and that defused some of the tension that racial inequality generated.

Hasenbalg made a further point that contested Degler's central argument about the mulatto escape hatch. His main purpose was to supply hard data showing the degree of racial inequality in Brazil. To this end he analysed 1976 national household survey data and showed, for example, that in terms of occupation people who self-identified in the standard census categories of *preto* (black) or *pardo* (brown) got less return for a given level of education than whites did (1985: 38); rates of social mobility were higher for whites than non-whites. This was vital evidence, because much of the argument for the existence of racial discrimination had previously relied on showing that most blacks were in the lower strata (which was liable to be explained away by saying that slavery had put them there and class mechanisms maintained their place) and on anecdotes about exclusion of blacks in specific instances. Here then was irrefutable statistical evidence that blacks and browns were being systematically discriminated against. Such evidence has accumulated since this early intervention, showing unequivocally that racial inequality exists, independently of class stratification (Hasenbalg and Silva, 1999; Lovell, 1998; Telles, 2004). What was interesting was that Hasenbalg found it logical to compare non-whites to whites; *pardos* were in basically the same position as *pretos*; the 'favourable' position of the *pardo* seemed irrelevant. Later studies have often continued to use the white/non-white divide to assess racial inequality, because white/non-white economic differences are much greater than black/brown differences (Lovell, 1998; Telles, 2004: 114). Nelson do Valle Silva, working with the same household data in the 1970s, argued this even more forcefully: he found that *pardos* were discriminated against more than blacks and he specifically rejected Degler's thesis (Silva, 1985).

All this constituted a challenge to the idea that whitening was a central feature of the Brazilian racial order and it was influenced by a political desire to combat the force of whitening as an ideology that divided non-whites and by the emerging black social movement that was pushing for greater 'black' consciousness and identity. Treating *pretos* and *pardos* together statistically implied that there was an objective basis to the political solidarity of blacks and mixed-race people that black activists were trying to achieve. This struggle gained ground to the extent that in the mid 1990s, President Cardoso recommended the national statistics agency use a single *negro* category – although it has not yet done so (Telles, 2004: 86). But, in my view, the move underplayed the continuing importance of the ideology of whitening and, more important, its structural consequences in the society.

For example, both Hasenbalg and Silva ignored the situational nature of racial categorisation and took the survey categories of white (*branco*), brown (*pardo*) and black (*preto*) for granted. These were self-identifications in the survey and thus reflect how individuals categorised themselves. These categorisations are variable, however, and also differ from classifications made by others. It is known, for example, that in Brazil there has been a steady trend of 'browning' in the censuses between 1940 and 2000, with the *preto* category declining (from 15 per cent to 6 per cent), the *branco* category diminishing slightly (from 64 per cent to 54 per cent) and the *pardo* category growing (from 27 per cent to 40 per cent) – this may be due to real changes, but is very likely due to people reclassifying themselves (Telles, 2004: 30; see also Nobles, 2000). This evidence does not add up to a straightforward process of whitening, as the white category is decreasing, but it does point to a tendency to avoid blackness. This is reinforced by Telles' comparisons of classifications by self and by interviewers (2004: 90–1). He shows that for people who were classified as *pardos* by either self or interviewer, but not by both, there was a much greater tendency for the non-*pardo* classification to be white rather than black: that is, people tended to prefer a whiter categorisation – at least in these rather particular social contexts of census form-filling.

Also, both Hasenbalg and Silva showed that *pardos* were still intermediate between blacks and whites; to them the black–*pardo* difference was small enough to justify its analytical removal, but the fact remained – and has been corroborated by later studies (Telles, 2004: 114) – and it needed explanation. Why are *pardos* better off, even if not much so? Degler's error was to assume that racial discrimination was the only factor determining social mobility, such that the intermediate position of the mulatto must have been due to less discrimination. Silva argued that *pardos* suffered more discrimination, but did not explain how they achieved a better economic position than *pretos*. The intermediacy of the *pardos* is not necessarily due to them receiving favourable treatment; instead, I argue, it may be due to a structural linkage between processes of upward mobility and processes of whitening. In a system such as Brazil's, some black people make money. If they then marry (or just have children with) whiter people, then their offspring are more likely to be classified as *pardos*. These children are then likely to have the benefit of a good education and other economic opportunities, assuming the black parent transmits his or her wealth in this way. It may then be the case that these children suffer discrimination – even more than their black parent – and may not get as much return on their education as a white person, but they are already economically intermediate. This kind of marital strategy has been shown to exist for black people in Brazil, where Telles found that black men and women who married browns or whites had higher levels of education than their mates (Telles, 2004: 191). I found a similar marital strategy in Colombia (Wade, 1993a: ch. 16), as did Urrea et al. (2006: 135), who say that, in the city of Cali, 'black, mulatto and even *mestizo* people develop strategies of social ascent in their unions, which, because of the racialised hierarchy of Colombian society, are expressed as forms of "whitening"'. The point is that there are structural links between vertical mobility and whitening which create a general association between being 'whiter' and having more money, education and power.

Colombia and Ecuador

During this same period, some rather different approaches were being taken in other regions. Norman Whitten had begun his research in the town of San Lorenzo, on the Pacific coast of Ecuador, where the main complex of ethnic and racial identifications involved local blacks and incoming *mestizos* from the highlands who were exploiting local resources, especially timber. To do so they had to make use of local black labour and some blacks, especially lighter-coloured ones, acted as intermediaries in this situation. Whitten took a Weberian approach to stratification that did not assume the primacy of class. Instead he looked at the intersection of class, ethnicity, status (defined as positive orientation towards the community) and kinship as principles of social differentiation, and concluded that 'ethnic and status lines divide classes in San Lorenzo; they influence the manner of participation in the economic order and figure prominently in the dynamics of social mobility' (1965: 89). Although the *mestizos* often looked down on the blacks, they also had to adapt to the local scene and, although whites and *mestizos* were at the top of the class structure, there was a significant black middle class and blacks in general were taking increasing advantage of the expanding opportunities around them (1965: 202).

Whitten's later book, *Black Frontiersmen* (1986 [1974]), incorporating changes since his first study and encompassing the 'wet littoral' of the Pacific coast from northern Ecuador up into southern Colombia, was more definitive about the existence of racial discrimination. The book dealt primarily with black culture in the area, looking at how local blacks adapted to an 'economically marginal' niche, which went through boom and bust cycles of natural resource exploitation and which also altered the 'social demography' of the zone as outsiders came and went (1986: 4).

In terms of local ethnic relations, increasing *mestizo* immigration had resulted in black disenfranchisement (just as it had for jungle Quechua – see above). Black and mixed-race entrepreneurs and intermediaries were being tagged as 'communists' (because of their control over black labour networks), allowing immigrants to take over the best brokerage positions, and immigrants were being more exclusive in their social relations. The Catholic Church was restricting the polygyny which had been a crucial feature in black upward mobility strategies, allowing certain families to accumulate resources. Black women were becoming central figures in more autonomous families and, since they were being employed directly in shellfish gathering by whites and *mestizos*, were less able to participate in black men's upward mobility strategies (1986: ch. 8).

Whitten outlined the idea, which he and others were later to develop, that in Ecuador the overall ideology of the nation as mixed served to exclude blacks (and indigenous people). In practice:

> if access to new resources for those classed as 'negro' and 'indio' in modernising Latin American nations is blocked, then there is no reason for denying that processes of discrimination leading to *de facto* segregation are under way in the wet littoral and elsewhere. (1986: 198)

Here, having done fieldwork in San Lorenzo and among the jungle Quechua, Whitten was taking a broad view of indigenous people and blacks in the nation-state, which made a refreshing change from the usual academic separation of these two categories. He also dealt a blow to Harris's idea about the maximisation of ambiguity in racial classification: 'regardless of the various permutations and combinations occurring in racial calculations ... blackness is the opposite of whiteness and national concepts of "mixed" in Colombia and Ecuador stand opposed to "black" just as white is the opposite of black' (1986: 199). This approach was uncompromising about the existence of racism and thus fitted in with some of the statements coming out of Brazil at the same time in relation both to racism and to binary racial oppositions. In contrast to Brazil, however, the pacific coast of Ecuador and Colombia suggested an opposition between black and white/mixed, not between black/brown and white. Whitten's work also contrasted with the much more benign view of race put forward by Solaún and Kronus (1973) in their study of Cartagena, Colombia, which held that the 'miscegenation-tolerance syndrome' was a dominant trend and would abolish remaining practices of discrimination. Some people, at least, still purveyed the myth of a (potential) Latin American 'racial democracy'.

Whitten also did some collaborative work with the Colombian scholar Nina de Friedemann (Whitten and Friedemann, 1974) who had been researching aspects of black culture in the Colombian Pacific coastal region. Apart from her interest in kinship structures among blacks in this gold mining region, Friedemann, who was a central figure in the study of blacks in Colombia until her death in 1998, was mainly concerned with what she called the 'invisibility' of blacks in Colombian history (except as slaves), in Colombian anthropology and sociology, and in representations of Colombia as a country. Her concern was to expose this racism and to reinstate blacks and their African heritage as a legitimate part of the nation and of academic study (Friedemann, 1984; Friedemann and Arocha, 1986; see also Arocha, 1992). I will return to the overall approaches of Whitten and Friedemann in the next chapter, when I discuss more recent ways of locating indigenous people and blacks in the nation-state.

Michael Taussig's early work fitted in some ways into debates about race and class in the sense that he was concerned with blacks as peasant farmers, under pressure from capitalist expansion and his approach was strongly influenced by Marxism (Taussig, 1980). But he was primarily concerned with issues of cultural resistance and with the devil mythology of black peasants in the Valle region of Colombia, according to which a sugar plantation worker could make a pact with the devil to increase his income, but could only make barren money that had to be squandered in luxury consumption and could not be made productive; meanwhile, the worker's body would waste away. This Taussig interpreted as a judgement, from the perspective of people living in a pre-capitalist mode of production, on the alienating nature of capitalist social relations. The particular concern with the devil was connected by Taussig to the history of slave religion – although it was more generally related to the imposition of Christianity in a colonial regime – and the attempts by blacks to construct their own religious domain, resignifying central elements of Christian symbolism, such as the devil.

Taussig's work thus fitted into the concerns with resistance that I discussed in the previous section, but his angle on this was quite subtle and the kind of defensiveness that Isbell documented was less evident. Peasants' opposition to capitalism was ambivalent: the very myth of the devil pact recognised the desire for luxury capitalist commodities and it hardly constituted a political strategy. But Taussig asserted that their world view, as expressed in the myth of the devil pact, 'may even simulate the political action necessary to thwart or transcend [the process of commodity formation]' (1980: 17). There was a danger, however, that Taussig was being over-romantic in his depiction of a pre-capitalist mode of production and in his view that the beliefs he documented could stimulate effective political action against capitalism. It remained unclear, moreover, at what point the peasants' opposition to capitalism shaded off into a frustrated desire for its commodities.

Black Culture

The work of Whitten, Friedemann and Taussig raised the issue of black culture which had been sorely neglected in the post-war Brazilian studies of race and class, with the exception of Bastide's study of Afro-Brazilian religion, first published in 1960 (Bastide, 1978). Indigenous culture had, of course, long been a legitimate object of academic attention – even if it turned out to be not that different from *mestizo* culture – because indigenous people were a legitimate Other in the anthropological gaze. Black people, in contrast, tended to be seen in cultural terms as ordinary citizens, if often as second-class ones in economic and political terms. This was least so in Brazil where, for example, Afro-Brazilian religious practice was clearly African influenced and thus evidently 'different' in cultural terms; the same was true for Afro-Cuban religion, which had been studied by the Cuban intellectual Lydia Cabrera (Rodríguez-Mangual, 2004). Even so, Peirano (2008) classifies the study of Afro-Brazilian culture as a concern with 'nearby alterity' compared to the 'radical alterity' of indigenous people. In Colombia and elsewhere, however, blacks were rarely thought to have a culture *sui generis*.

   This is partly why the study of blacks was generally institution-alised as the study of race – with difference signalled by physical features – while the study of indigenous people was that of ethnicity – with the difference signalled by cultural features. This is also partly why, as noted in the previous chapter in relation to the UNESCO studies, blacks tended to be studied in their relations with others, while many studies of indigenous people examined them as cultures in their own right. However, it is clear that cultural features were also important in constituting differences perceived as racial: stereotypes of blacks all over Latin America commonly included ideas about their supposed laziness, happy-go-lucky attitudes, disorganised family life, taste for music and dance and so on. Even if some of these supposed attributes (sexuality, musicality) were seen as natural, it is clear that images of blacks often involved a whole way of life, not just a set of phenotypical features. Hence it is important to include the study of black culture in the study of 'race relations'.

Black culture had been studied from very early on – by Ortiz, Nina Rodrigues and Carneiro, for example – but their concerns were not with ethnic or racial identities. Melville Herskovits – who actually started off doing anthropometric studies of blacks in the US as a student of Franz Boas – took up this kind of study in the 1930s, minus the racist trappings. His main interest was in locating African survivals in the New World, although this also involved detailed ethnographic work on many aspects of black culture in Haiti, Brazil and the US (Herskovits, 1966). African survivals and adaptations was a concern that also informed Bastide's work to some extent (Bastide, 1971) and in general set the agenda for the study of black culture in the Americas.

On the question of African survivals, an influential and lasting point of departure was that adopted by Mintz and Price (1976), which held that Africans brought to the New World probably shared some basic cultural principles or orientations that underlay the great variety of languages and cultures from which they came. Thus the importance of music and dance in ritual activity was something that a variety of Africans might have had in common and that might have affected how they built up new cultural practices in a slave regime. Or a common concern with the birth of twins across a range of West African cultural contexts – whether the local reaction was to revere or to kill them – could lead to a widespread, but equally varied, interest in twins in black contexts in the Americas.

A different approach was to see black culture in the Americas more as a result of local processes of adaptation, even if such processes might have common features shaped by the history of slavery, racism, oppression, particular forms of labour (such as the plantation economy) and so on. This approach had something in common with the views of E. Franklin Frazier, who had been criticised by Herskovits, for arguing that slavery had caused African cultures to disintegrate, making US black culture a new creation (Herskovits, 1941). Later scholars of the adaptation approach, such as Whitten and Szwed (1970), by no means discounted African influences, but did not dwell on them either.

The difference in these approaches is evident in the heated debates about 'the black family'. Many scholars had noted patterns of flexibility in family organisation among blacks all over the Americas – although it was often seen pejoratively as disorganisation, since, for example, cohabitation rather than marriage was often a feature, leading to 'illegitimate' children. Some people saw in this the persistence of some features of African marriage and kinship – for example, the importance of extended families and wide kin networks – others saw it as adaptation to slavery or more generally economic marginality, especially since the same trends could be observed among non-blacks living long-term in similar conditions (see Bastide, 1971; MacDonald and MacDonald, 1978; Whitten and Szwed, 1970: 43). Undoubtedly, whatever patterns existed in the twentieth century were the result of multiple factors, but the debates concerned the exact weighting of the factors and this was almost impossible to resolve.

Something of a middle ground in this debate has been claimed by Richard and Sally Price, who have developed Mintz and Price's original idea of cultural principle in relation to Maroon cultures in Suriname and French Guiana. They show that some basic and long-standing aesthetic principles of African origin – for example, ones that value striking contrasts of colour – are expressed in many different cultural practices, such as crop-growing, textile production, house decoration. The precise form of expression is mediated by many factors, including historical contingencies such as the availability of different sorts of materials through global trade networks (Price and Price, 1999). This detailed history and ethnography brings factors of local and transnational political economy and adaptation back into relation with cultural principles.

The point of these debates is that the matter of African survivals was also a question of the construction of black culture in the Americas and this was far from being a simply academic question, but one related to racial identities and politics. Was black culture just an amalgam of European and Amerindian cultures? Was it something that emerged more or less from scratch in the New World? Did it have significant African roots which would give blacks their own cultural identity? While Candomblé religious practices in Bahia are clearly African-derived (see Chapters 5 and 6), there are no simple answers to these questions at a broader level, partly because they are so emotionally and politically charged and partly because they are very hard to assess with historical evidence – what appears to be of African origin can turn out to be European and vice versa.[2]

Thus black culture became something of a political football all over the Americas, with its status undecided, but important to the growing politicisation of racial identities in Latin America (following the US pattern to some extent). In some areas, black culture appeared to be simply peasant or working-class culture, in others it was clearly particular. For some, black culture did not really exist; for others, it was the basis for black consciousness. I will return to this question later in the context of ideas about diaspora.

CONCLUSION

The approaches examined in this chapter represented a useful advance on those of the previous decades. Many of them, in the end, despite specific efforts on the part of anthropologists and sociologists to avoid this, remained constrained by a dependency approach and by the limits of debates about the relative roles of ethnicity (or race) and class. Dependency and, more generally, a Marxist analysis were vital in producing a broad view of economic and political inequalities. They also forcefully raised the possibility of locating the social scientist as a political agent. Anthropologists had sometimes acted as advocates for 'their people' in the past, whether to defend them against charges of irrationality, savagery and backwardness or to help them against specific threats to their land and livelihood. A Marxist-oriented perspective grounded this advocacy in a powerful critique of encroaching capitalism and political inequality.

But these approaches could not account for particularities. As Bourricaud (1975: 357) said, the simple fact of Peru's dependency could not help us to understand the intricacies of its social stratification system. Such analysis tended to adopt too instrumentalist a view of ethnicity, in which ethnic and racial identities became the expression of economic determinants – even if van den Berghe (1975) assured his readers that he made no *a priori* judgement about the primacy of class over ethnicity. Of course, ethnic and racial identities can hardly be independent of economic concerns, but they can become ends and priorities in their own right alongside those concerns. The business of trying to decide which carries most weight, class or ethnicity/race, becomes then a rather fruitless exercise, trapped within a basically Marxist problematic. The emergence in the 1970s of gender as a major area of debate in the social sciences reinforces this critique – although for a while gender was simply added to the balancing exercises which then juggled three dimensions of difference instead of two. In the end, though, it is not really necessary to assign primacy, but rather to look at how race, ethnicity, class and gender (not to mention age) interact in specific circumstances. The approaches being worked out by scholars such as Whitten and Taussig, while they drew on Marxism and concepts developed in the analysis of colonialism, were moving beyond these towards a perspective that located indigenous people and blacks in the nation-state seen as a political economy *and* a cultural space, itself situated in a global world.

5
Blacks and Indigenous People in the Postmodern and Postcolonial Nation – and Beyond

During the 1980s and 1990s, the overall context for understanding race and ethnicity shifted under the influence of postmodernism and postcolonialism. It is useful to briefly examine these trends in order to grasp how they affected the study of race and ethnicity in Latin America. Postmodernism is many different things, but I think it is useful to roughly distinguish between postmodernism as a trend in philosophy and social theory, and postmodernity as a trend in social formations – it goes without saying that the two are linked in complex ways.[1]

Postmodernism is, in part, the paradoxical result of the rational search for certainty. The more systematic this search becomes, the more it reveals that certainty itself cannot be achieved. Of course, relativism is hardly a new epistemological position, but it has received new impetus since this period. In philosophy, post-structuralists such as Jacques Derrida developed the structuralist insight that any identity is constructed in relation to difference. There is no solid pre-given centre or simple presence; these exist only in relation to something else (a position that Barth had, in effect, argued for ethnic groups); therefore, the closure or completion of identification is permanently deferred by differentiation. There is no final reading of a text – and 'text' here became extended to refer to symbolism in general. The post-structuralist technique of deconstruction, in the simplest sense, thus consists of discovering how certain readings depend on hidden identifications, categories and rhetorical devices which, when looked at anew, cannot be taken for granted.

Michel Foucault argued that 'discourses' – roughly, modes of representation – construct social realities. People's ways of thinking of the world, themselves and others around them are constituted – rather than simply constrained – by discursive formations, that is, more or less coherent ways of representation of a given realm of activity and experience. Thus, for example, the discourse of psychiatry defined certain possible ways of thinking about madness. This is not a question of an external and possibly false 'ideology' influencing people's thought and behaviour; people reproduce the discourse as truth through their own thought and behaviour. It is possible to step outside given discursive formations – this was what Foucault was doing in his historical analysis of them – but it takes a critical effort and, in any case, one cannot step outside discourse itself.[2] Both Derrida and Foucault were part of a so-called 'linguistic turn' in social theory (Giddens, 1987: ch. 4) which involved focusing on language and, more broadly, representation and symbolism.

Lyotard specifically criticised the major 'metanarratives' of Western thought, the grand teleological accounts of the progress of humanity that produce totalising explanations, which seek to explain everything within the compass of one overarching schema. When science seeks after truth, it needs to legitimate its own rules and it achieves this by reference to metanarratives which, according to Lyotard, included the creation of wealth (modernisation), the emancipation of the working subject (Marxism) and of the rational subject; metanarratives enshrined central values of Western modernity as the legitimate goals of science and progress. For Lyotard, there was no inherent reason why these metanarratives should be unquestionable; they could no longer reign supreme.

Finally, alongside these challenges to the 'Enlightenment project' of rational progress towards systematic, solid knowledge based on science, there was a challenge to the assumed authority of the (mainly Western and mainly male) intelligentsia and scientific community which – the Romantics and doubters such as Nietzsche aside – had carried forward this project. This challenge came from feminism and from postcolonial intellectuals. Feminism raised the possibility of the scientific project as a specifically male project (Keller, 1986; Merchant, 1983), suggesting that knowledge was not absolute but gendered. From the perspective of the (postcolonised) periphery, postcolonial writers challenged the authority of knowledge produced from the (postcolonial) centre. Edward Said (1985), for example, dissected the discursive formation of Orientalism, showing how the East had been constructed as Other in the Western mind by a tradition of representation, and how this had affected the production of knowledge about the East. Other intellectuals, such as Homi Bhabha and Gayatri Spivak, also questioned the infallibility of Western knowledge and revealed its links to colonial systems of oppression (see Bhabha, 1994; Spivak, 1999). Postcolonial critiques also led to an interest in diaspora.

The concept literally refers to the dispersion of an ethnic group from its homeland. It has come to represent the complex movements and networks mainly of (post)colonised peoples around the world, and the identities, knowledges and cultural forms they produce in border-crossing exchanges. Diaspora is often seen as a set of unpredictable practices which undermine dominant centralised authority, challenge the taken-for-granted boundaries of the nation-state and reveal how apparently localised identities and cultural forms have in fact been formed through long-standing translocal exchanges and movements – movements which may easily escape official histories and accounts (Brah, 1996; Gilroy, 1993a, 2000; Yelvington, 2006).

Ideas of this kind have had several lasting consequences in thinking about race and ethnicity, even if the term 'postmodernism' lost some of its currency after about 2000. First, the constructedness of identity became even more important; feminism was a crucial influence here. Identity is seen as constructed through complex processes of relationality and representation; it is a process, not a thing, and is constantly under renegotiation (even if the outcome of the negotiation is often the same for particular people). Second, as mentioned in Chapter 1, the reification and essentialisation of identity was challenged more intensively – the idea is no longer acceptable that a given person or group might have a basic identity that could be characterised in terms of a core, defining essence; groups and indeed individuals are 'decentred', they have no single identity (Hall, 1992a; Landry and MacLean, 1993: ch. 7). As Wilson puts it: 'relationality must be present for identity to exist, but the very basis of meaning in difference leads to the crossing-over of signifiers and the undermining of any pretensions to boundedness' (1995b: 6). Or, to put it another way: 'identities are not just fluid, nor just multiple, they are fluidly multiple and always relational, which presents an analytical and conceptual challenge to anthropologists' (Jackson and Warren, 2005: 561). Third, multiple identities and the challenge to metanarratives both implied that the seemingly 'big question' of the primacy of race/ethnicity versus class was less of an issue, although, as noted in Chapter 1, class difference continues to be an important theme, especially in the context of globalising neoliberalism and the associated increase in social inequality. Fourth, culture, or more accurately, the politics of culture, became a central focus (although anthropologists, at least, had always been concerned with culture, even if the infrastructure of economic relations did preoccupy even them during the 1970s). But, in the wake of postmodernism, culture is not something that groups just 'have', it is a discursive construct that is lived, but is also open to different readings and political deployments.

The term 'postmodernity' refers to a generalised social condition, dominant from the late twentieth century. The term is less common now than in the 1990s and it is more common to refer to globalisation, or sometimes neoliberalisation, to talk about the set of economic and social changes that continue to shape the world. In any case, at issue is a set of processes through which the infrastructure of capitalism has penetrated more pervasively and 'shrunk' the surface of the globe with communications technology. It also involves the flexibilisation of capitalism, with globally distributed fragments of production processes being rapidly tailored to volatile market demands. Western economies have become decentralised but they remain dominant and Western polities continue to impose market and production conditions on much of the rest of the world, although rising powers, such as China, India and Brazil are increasingly able to participate in shaping the global economy. Meanwhile, people, representing both labour and capital, have become increasingly mobile, constantly crossing national boundaries and constituting transnational movements, spaces and connections (Basch et al., 1994). The theme of diaspora emerges again, without, however, erasing the nation-state as a player of continuing importance on the global scene.

Culture has become increasingly commoditised and culture – whether of the nostalgic past, the present or the future, or of Africa, Asia, the Americas or Europe – is packaged and sold to people in specific market niches who define their lifestyles by highly differentiated consumption – if they can afford to consume at all. Politically, there has been a blurring of class boundaries, the demise of organised working-class politics, centred on trade unions, and the emergence of political mobilisation around a host of issues such as sexuality and gender, ecology, animal rights, housing, the environment and other forms of consumption. National boundaries are often crossed in the practice of these social movements, even if the nation-state remains a key domain of action. Despite the emphasis on consumption and culture, some Marxist scholars have interpreted these trends as the product of capitalism in its 'late' phase (Harvey, 1989; Jameson, 1991).

These changes are crucial in the study of race and ethnicity, because of the importance of the social movements that have increasingly emerged around issues of ethnic and racial identity, in Latin America and elsewhere. Related in part to the demise of working-class politics, itself connected to the flexibilisation of capitalism and to the critique of metanarratives, this also fits in with postcolonial critiques which have opened up an intellectual space for the voices of previously marginalised minorities. In Latin America, especially, postcolonial critiques have a long history – Freyre's definition of Brazil as a mixed country and the better for it was, in effect, a challenge to the knowledge about race and modernity produced in Europe and North America – but this was mainly intellectuals speaking on behalf of their nations and, rarely, on behalf of indigenous people and blacks. In recent decades, blacks and indigenous people have increasingly been speaking for themselves, although not necessarily without such intellectuals, both Latin American and otherwise. The emergence of a politics of culture, mentioned above, is also relevant here, as minority groups give their own readings of their cultures and there are struggles to define the constitution of cultural 'spaces'. The use of spatial metaphors is not coincidental here because minorities are often engaged in a concrete struggle for land rights as part of their cultural space (see Escobar, 2008; Ng'weno, 2007b). In a globalising world, these spaces are not just local, but national and international: the arena for the constitution of identity is now recognised to be, and indeed to have been for centuries, a global one.

In the rest of this chapter, I will look first at attempts to theoretically locate black and indigenous cultures in the nation-state that emerged in the 1980s and 1990s, and then explore more recent perspectives that look beyond the nation. In the next chapter, I will examine the social movements that have grown around race and ethnicity. My treatment of blacks and indigenous people together in this chapter, as opposed to separately as in previous chapters, follows my own long-held view that such a synthesis, or at least juxtaposition, is necessary, and reflects a recent and growing tendency towards this in the literature.

BLACKS AND INDIGENOUS PEOPLE IN THE NATION

Within the overall context sketched above, there was a move from the 1980s towards locating both blacks and indigenous people more firmly within the nation-state. This was not a new concern in itself. The *indigenismo* of the 1920s and the concerns with racial whitening of the same period were all about how to integrate what were seen as problematic or exotic black and indigenous populations into the modernising nation; but this was about how to define particular nations, rather than analysing the nation or nationalism as such. Considerations of race and class in Brazil were also about the integration of blacks into a class society; this, however, took the nation for granted. A new angle emerged that can be summed up with Benedict Anderson's widely cited definition of the nation as an 'imagined community' (1983). This focused attention on the nation in its cultural and symbolic dimensions and opened the way to asking how blacks and indigenous people as categories imagined by different sets of people might fit into their 'image' of the nation. There is, of course, a danger here that concrete social relations get lost – never Anderson's intention in his analysis of nationalism – but this sort of perspective moved away from the preoccupation with race/ethnicity and class of previous decades towards a greater concern with the nation and with black and indigenous groups as participating in a space where a politics of cultural struggle was in process.

MESTIZAJE, WHITENING AND NATIONALISM

Norman Whitten had already shifted his focus of research from blacks on the Pacific coast of Ecuador to indigenous people in the jungles east of the Andes. But a concern with blacks was still present in his writings and this obeyed an attempt to grasp the Ecuadorian nation as a whole in its ethnic make-up. In his 1980s' work, he argued that Ecuadorian nationalism was based on 'an ideology of ethnic homogenization' or 'racial mixture', that is, *mestizaje* (1981b: 15; see also Whitten, 1985: 39–44, 223–41; Stutzman, 1981). This ideology could be used to exclude those considered unmixed, the more so because the ideology had 'a tacit qualifying clause which ups the price of admission [to the mixed nation] from mere "phenotypical mixture" to cultural *blanqueamiento* ("whitening", in terms of becoming more urban, more Christian, more civilised; less rural, less black, less indigenous)' (1981b: 15). People labelled as black and indigenous – using a variety of possible terms – were most apparent in peripheral areas where natural resources desired by the state and foreign nations are located. Mixed Ecuadorians, who considered themselves to be the true nationals, considered progress to consist of transforming the peripheries of the nation through development that changed both the land and the people on it in ways that conformed to 'the ideology and designs of North American industrial growth' (1981b: 14) but were at odds with the ecology of the tropical forest and its management by local people.

Local blacks and indigenous people might resist, either through explicit protest or through 'ceremonial enactment and symbolism' (1981b: 15), making use of, for example, elements of local mythology. The contradictory effect was that blacks and indigenous people in these areas seemed to be both 'assimilating to modern Ecuadorian ways, and ... developing into a militant ethnic bloc' (1985: 19); Ecuador itself seemed to 'be nationalizing and becoming more diverse at the same time' (1981b: 15). Meanwhile, local *runa* (indigenous people) in the jungles at the borders of the Andes and Amazonia contended with the contradiction between two apparently reasonable principles: 'they are *of* urban Ecuador, and ... they are *of* Amazonia' (Whitten, 1985: 252): they sought a measure of control and autonomy in both systems. There was much in Whitten's approach here that was similar to his earlier work (1986 [1974], 1976), but the presence of the nation-state as a cultural space was now more forceful. This was partly because, by 1981, the indigenous movement had grown in Ecuador to the extent that indigenousness was a concern at the highest levels of the state, not just as a 'problem', but as a political contender.

Whitten's work was an important inspiration for my own work on Colombia. The basic ideas about *mestizaje* and *blanqueamiento* that he and Stutzman (1981) elaborated are very similar to the Colombian situation (Wade, 1993a). There seem to me, however, to be certain problems with applying Whitten's ideas directly to Colombia. This is partly because, while there are important populations of black people in the remote and underdeveloped Pacific coastal region, there are also blacks in many other areas of Colombia, including its cities. Indeed, the 2005 census indicated that only about 20 per cent of Afro-Colombians live in the Pacific coastal region.[3] Whitten's primary focus on blacks (and indigenous people) in peripheral areas led him to see both categories as being stereotypically opposed to the nation; mixed people, and especially developers, classed them as 'non-nationals' (1985: 42). For Colombia, while it is true that, in certain planning and academic circles in the 1990s, Pacific coast blacks might be contrasted to *la sociedad nacional* (national society) – with all the overtones of internal colonialism that this invokes – it seems to me that the specificity of the position of blacks in Colombia, and I think elsewhere in Latin America, lies in the fact that they can be classed as both nationals *and* non-nationals (or at least not fully and properly nationals).

In my view, the location of blacks and indigenous people in the cultural space of the nation-state needs more, and more historical, analysis than Whitten gave it. As I argued in Chapter 2, black identity has never been as institutionalised as indigenous identity and blacks have been seen much more as (second-class) citizens, typically studied in relation to non-blacks in a 'class society' and often assumed not to have a 'black culture'. In this sense, they have been seen – and, in Colombia, emphatically consider themselves – as nationals; and this is a long-standing trait (Sanders, 2004). On the other hand, they are also subject to exclusion when whites and *mestizos* define them as beyond the bounds of legitimate nationality, as non-nationals, as distant from the core values of being (light-coloured) *mestizo* or white, urban(e), civilised and educated. The sliding between being included by non-blacks ('we are all brothers, we are all *mestizos*') and being excluded by them ('blacks are all animals'; 'a monkey dressed in silk is still a monkey') defines for blacks in the nation a particular space where they both appear and disappear.

I have also been interested in exploring *blanqueamiento* not just as an ideology, but as a social practice through which the hierarchical racial order of Colombia is re-created. The work on whitening discussed in previous chapters, by scholars such as Degler and Skidmore, needs to be complemented by ethnographic studies of how it works at a grassroots level and how this level links to broader ideologies and practices. Looking at blacks and non-blacks in a small frontier town and in the city of Medellín (Wade, 1993a), I argued that there were powerful structural links between non-blackness and upward mobility (see also Martinez-Alier, 1989). Successful blacks, even when success was by very local standards, ended up being dependent on and/or associating with non-blacks. Often, even if they had no personal motive to whiten themselves or their children, they were absorbed into a non-black social matrix, thus reiterating the hierarchies of the racial order. On the other hand, non-blacks continued to control most economic opportunities and blacks who were not successful were marginalised and depended heavily on family networks to survive, forming cultural and physical nuclei of blackness which, again, seemed to reiterate national hierarchies by associating blackness with poverty and working-class or rural black culture. For example, in the frontier town, a handful of blacks were relatively successful and most of them were linked in significant ways to non-blacks; some left the town and studied in the capital, Bogotá. As economic opportunities were increasingly controlled and expanded by non-blacks in the area, many blacks moved away to more clearly black, and poorer, parts of the Pacific coast region.

The links of whiteness with success and blackness with poverty were recreated. In sum, there was a balance between non-black exclusion and inclusion which was matched by a balance between black nucleation and dispersal. This is not unrelated to Fernandes' idea of a system of 'accommodation', but it is vital to understand this on the level of the cultural space of the nation, not just the social relations of a class society.

A different way of capturing these cultural dimensions is the idea of a 'transformist hegemony' elaborated by Brackette Williams, working outside Latin America, but in a context that is similar in some respects. In her research on Guyana, she argued that cultural struggles existed over the value of historical and cultural contributions made by Africans, East Indians, Amerindians and Europeans to the emerging nation, with different groups ranking contributions in different ways (1991: 166). Nationalist attempts to create cultural unity dealt with diversity 'by assimilating elements of that heterogeneity through appropriations that devalue them or that deny the source of their contribution'. This constituted a transformist hegemony – a term derived from Gramsci – in which domination worked partly by appropriation and resignification. If low-ranked groups maintained their claim to certain cultural contributions in the amalgam of national culture, these were devalued and these groups were defined as 'not "true" members of the ideologically defined nation'. Those claiming status as the real producers of the core elements of national culture had the ideological power to redefine the meaning of the elements appropriated from marginal groups (1991: 30–1). This is a useful approach to ethnicity and race in the nation-state because it directs attention towards processes of resignification by which particular cultural elements become incorporated (accommodated) into nationalist versions of the nation's culture as long as their significance is defined within the central value complex of the dominant groups – just as individual blacks may be accommodated on condition that they behave in certain 'acceptable' ways.

Mestizaje, *Inclusion and Exclusion*

The concept of transformist hegemony is illuminating because *mestizaje* is about processes of transformation (of people, of communities, of nations) in which things ('blood', appearance, culture) change in the direction of inclusion, yet other things (racialised hierarchies) remain the same and point towards exclusion. The opportunity for inclusion exists in the same time and space frame as the opportunity for exclusion. This close coexistence of inclusion and exclusion is particularly evident in the realm of kinship and the family – which is, after all, a prime site in which *mestizaje*, as a sexual encounter, may occur. Although he was writing about a particular context – the Piro of Peruvian Amazonia – Gow (1991: 257) hit upon a more general truth when he said that 'identifying a person as of a particular "race" places that person within the history of the construction of kinship'.

It has been said that the differences in racialised appearance that can exist within a single family in Latin America indicate the relative absence of racism there. However, it is also within the family that racial difference can create subtle exclusions. I found this in Medellín, Colombia, with a case in which darker and lighter sisters had very different social trajectories and networks (Wade, 1993a). The power of race to work in and on the family comes across powerfully in Moreno's work on *mestizo* women in Mexico. She looks at the relationship these women have to their racialised bodies in the context of pervasive hierarchies that value the *güera* (blonde) higher than the *morena* (brown): women sometimes felt that lighter-skinned siblings got preferential treatment and this could subtly shape their whole experience of family life (Moreno Figueroa, 2008). All over Latin America there are hierarchies of beauty that enthrone whiteness and define blackness and indigenousness as ugly – although potentially sexually desirable, when allied with youth and often when mixed with whiteness to produce a 'brown' rather than a fully black or indigenous body (the *mulata* and the *chola* are common sexualised and gendered racial images: see Kutzinski, 1993; Pravaz, 2003; Weismantel, 2001: 155–65). Beauty pageants reinforce this hierarchy and even when dark-skinned women are occasionally elected queens, they may then straighten their hair and wear light brown contact lenses (Canessa, 2008; Rahier, 1999).

Mestizaje thus appears as a key terrain for the operation of racism; and the fact that *mestizaje* often works in zones of intimacy (sex, the family, the body) means racism lodges deep in the heart of people and society, making it difficult to both see and resist (Wade, 2009b).[4] *Mestizaje* needs to be understood as a deeply gendered process. As I mentioned in Chapter 2, race mixture in both colonial and republican Latin America was mediated through gender hierarchies in which (white) men controlled women and, specifically, their sexuality and procreative power. Still in 1930s Rio de Janeiro, white men were able to 'deflower' (take the virginity of) dark-skinned women with relative impunity in the face of laws that considered this a sexual crime. The deflowering of white women by white men and especially by dark-skinned men tended to be prosecuted more vigorously, in order to defend the honour that white women were presumed to have and dark-skinned women to lack (Caulfield, 2003).

In more recent times, although the protection of honour assumes a less explicit role, sexual relations between people of different racialised identities still forms an arena for the expression and enactment of racial hierarchy. In Chapter 4, I cited data indicating that, in Brazil, darker-skinned partners often had better education than their whiter partner: education (which, in these data, stood in for 'class') was needed to 'compensate' for colour, thus reiterating the low value of blackness (Telles, 2004: 191). In Colombia, I found that the partners in interracial relationships were always at risk of being judged in terms of assumed motives connected to race – black women who 'married up' might be seen as 'racist' (that is, rejecting their own blackness); black men who married up might be accused of trying to capitalise on the status of a whiter wife (Wade, 1993a). In a similar way, Viveros found that powerful racial hierarchies and images shape sexual and emotional relationships between black and non-black people in Bogotá, and that even people in stable conjugal relationships 'find themselves obliged to position themselves continuously in relation to [sexual stereotypes]' (2008: 72; see also Fernandez, 1996; Goldstein, 2003: ch. 3; Wade, 2009b: ch. 5). The very thing that creates the image and partial reality of a society in which race is not a major axis of social stratification – *mestizaje* – is also a key mechanism for reiterating and recreating racial hierarchies in both public and intimate spheres.

Mestizaje has been presented in recent years as including a subaltern version, a '*mestizaje* from below' (Hale, 2005: 25), in which the down-trodden and darker-skinned classes implicitly or explicitly contest the value of whiteness from the perspective of their mixedness (Wade, 2005, 2006a). De la Cadena (2000), for example, describes the 'indigenous *mestizos*' who identify as *mestizos* without rejecting their indigenousness: being *mestizo* means being a successful *indígena*. Yet de la Cadena also shows that these successful *mestizos* retain racist attitudes towards *indios* they see as being inferior and unsuccessful. The hierarchies of *mestizaje* remain, even as the ultimate value of whiteness is challenged. Weismantel (2001: 173, 247–8) argues that, in the Andes, *mestizos* who act in dominating ways – for example, abusing others – become meta-phorically masculinised and whitened (or at least de-feminised and de-indigenised), thus reiterating links between power and whiteness. *Mestizaje* is an arena in which struggles over transformations take place – which transformations count as valuable and which are inferior – in which some basic values of race and power persist.

Overall, this focus on *mestizaje* within the nation moves away from the classic opposition between the US and Brazil, which anyway has been the subject of much reassessment (Daniel, 2006; Seigel, 2009; Silva, 1998; Skidmore, 1993; Toplin, 1981), and sees each region as operating a different form of racism. I think that, implicit in the classic contrast and helping to shape it, is an unstated assumption about biology. Racism in the US has often been seen as 'deep' – deeply rooted in the social fabric and based on the 'deep' biology of blood and genotype. The contrast is then made with Latin America, where racism is said to be superficial – subordinate to class and based on mere phenotype, only 'skin-deep'. This, in my view, attempts to legitimate the contrast in terms of a mistaken biology – after all, both genotype and phenotype are equally 'biological'. The surface/depth metaphor is misleading, both for biology and for society. There are, of course, real differences between racism in Latin America and the US, but these are historical and cultural, not biological; neither are they helpfully understood in terms of surface versus depth (Wade, 1993b).

ETHNOHISTORY AND THE NATION

Alongside the interest in the nation-state has come a concern with history. This had been an integral part of the work of the previous decade, since Marxism and dependency perspectives were very alive to historical change, but the emphasis tended now to be more on history from the native point of view (for example, Harris, 1995a; Hill, 1988; Hugh-Jones, 1989; Price, 1990). Over time, this ethnohistorical approach has increasingly become part of mainstream history, inspired in part by subaltern studies.[5] I will look at some examples from the Andes, where a good deal of ethnohistorical work has been done (Ramírez, 2009; Rivera Cusicanqui, 1993), although not all of it has dealt with locating indigenous people in the emerging nation-state.[6]

Harris (1995b), for example, takes a long-term perspective on how indigenous and *mestizo* identities have been related to participation in the market, with indigenous identity today being defined fundamentally by participation in collective institutions (cf. Isbell, 1978), while market activities are more individual.

The nation-state hovers in the background, since it constrains the operation of the market, but it is not a central focus.

Tristan Platt (1995), however, tackles markets in the context of nation-building. He argues that it is misguided to see indigenous communities in nineteenth-century (and indeed present-day) Bolivia as resisting the national market and only participating in it through force. While this may have happened, he contends that 'intervention in the market could represent an *Indian strategy*' (1995: 260). Resistance is thus not always as obvious as it might appear. In national debates about the pros and cons of protectionist and laissez-faire trade policies, Platt argues that indigenous people were generally on the side of protectionism and that they struggled to retain colonial-type tributary systems against the republican liberalism that was striving to construct a new nation; in addition, Inca revivalist movements used the symbols of republican nationalism (1995: 287) This is a much more nuanced vision of an ethnic minority in the nation-state than that which sees it simply as an oppressed, victimised minority or assumes the automatic 'resistance' of pre-capitalist economic activity to capitalism.

Platt (1993) argues that nineteenth-century indigenous people in Bolivia had their own 'national projects' involving a 'just' social order for them in economic terms, and that they arrived at 'a religious interpretation of the panoply of new invented traditions emerging in coins and public monuments, in heraldry, flags and civic festivals, from the creole architects of the new *Patria*' (1993: 168). For example, in their nationalist imagery, the creoles represented the indigenous people as a young woman being saved from the jaws of the Spanish by the liberating heroes, paternalist defenders and patriarchal possessors of the nation and her indigenous people. The actual indigenous people were not so helpless, and creoles saw them as backward, recalcitrant and savage, to be controlled through the possession (and rape) that was already suggested by the 'saving' of the indigenous virgin. For the indigenous people themselves, the Virgin Mary was associated with *pachamama*, the earth-mother, while Simón Bolívar, the Liberator, became her son, a Christ-like figure; both underwrote the social reproduction of indigenous life and community within the new republic. Indigenous people and creoles, then, had different ideas of what the new nation would be like and where indigenous people would fit into it: as virgins to be saved and savages to be civilised or as inhabitants of a sacred space of social reproduction and messianic renewal. As in the previous example from Platt's work, the point is that seeing things from the native point of view allows a much more nuanced and diverse perspective on issues such as 'resistance', showing how subaltern groups often deploy the ideologies and symbols associated with their oppressors to express a sense of identity and a moral purpose. This is partly because, in many of these cases, the dominant ideologies included strong values of protection and justice, whether these were phrased in terms of colonial regal duties towards vassals or liberal principles of equality and liberty.

A focus on ethnohistory is not only about seeing the past in a new way. It is also about how the past feeds into the present. In a widely cited analysis, Joanne Rappaport starts from the assumption that 'history is a question of power in the present, and not of detached reflection on the past' (1990: 15). For the Páez indigenous people of the Colombian Andes, historical consciousness 'is founded on a moral link with the past that is operationalized in the interests of achieving political goals in the present' (1990: 9). The Crown and the state have been a constant presence for these indigenous people, against which they have fought to define their autonomy, using both written and oral histories as 'a vehicle for changing the course of history' (1990: 180). The histories themselves are reshaped as changes occur in the political context in which they are articulated and today they work to create a 'textual community' (1990: 183) which acts as a basis for defining the Páez as an ethnic group, based in part on the central role of literate indigenous leaders, who can operate in both directions at the interface of the oral and the literate, but also on the history embedded in the landscape which is readable by everyone. In Rappaport's analysis, then, indigenous resistance and ethnic identity within the nation-state is built around historical consciousness; memory is a resource for the present (see also Rappaport, 1994, 2005: ch. 5).

Ethnohistory of Afro-descendants in Latin America is less well developed than for indigenous people, despite a burgeoning literature on slave life (for example, Karasch, 1987; Lauderdale Graham, 2002; Mattoso, 1986; Montejo and Barnet, 1993; Reis, 1993). The pioneering work of Richard Price on the Samaraka Maroons of Suriname is a good example of how history and memory act as a key resource for fashioning community, resistance and identity (1983, 1990, 2007; see also Price and Price, 1999). Giving a prominent, even dominant, place to Samaraka narratives in his texts, Price documents how these people have preserved oral traditions that focus on a period, roughly 1690 to 1760, when their forebears escaped from slavery and set up their own communities in the forest, waging a long war with the white colonists and finally achieving a peace treaty. These traditions serve as a symbol of continuing autonomy and independence, although not isolation. Price's work raises the issue of how 'real' oral histories are. He insists they are valid – and he triangulates them with the narratives of missionaries and colonial officials, drawn from archival sources, which also act as corroboration – but this is not the central point. More important is the role that memory plays in consciousness and imagination.

INDIGENOUS PEOPLE AND THE NATION-STATE

Seeing indigenous people in the context of the nation-state from a postmodernist perspective indicates that 'none of the terms ... *Indians, nation-states*, and *culture* are monolithic and static categories' (Urban and Sherzer, 1991b: 12). The papers in the collection by Urban and Sherzer (1991a) highlighted that indigenous ethnic identities and nation-states are highly interdependent and, in some sense, mutually constitutive.[7] Indeed, I think that some of the shift by anthropologists towards seeing indigenous people in the frame of the nation-state was due to a recognition that many indigenous people had long seen themselves as located in the nation-state (see Sanders, 2004), and were also increasingly seeing themselves as 'ethnic groups' in national contexts as a result of their historical experiences (Jackson, 1991; Turner, 1991).

Abercrombie – interestingly, a historian – writing on the K'ulta of the Oruro region of Bolivia, states:

Modern day 'indigenous ethnic groups' and 'indigenous cosmologies' are unintelligible apart from their struggle with the state: they are founded upon its existence, and they are recreated only in so far as they can maintain, and mould to their own purposes, a 'state within'. (1991: 111)

In his view, 'the gods of the oppressors ... are required for the reproduction of K'ulta society' (1991: 110–11) in that, for example, the rituals that the K'ulta use to ensure the reproduction of their society identify local ritual leaders with Jesus Christ and invest them with elements of Christian saintly power. In other words, local cosmology has adapted to Christian hegemony which is then necessary for indigenous society.

Of course, it has been widely recognised that 'indigenous culture' has for a long time been a hybrid of different elements (Friedlander,

1975; Harris, 1995b: 359): the point, however, is not to see ethnic identity as something which simply persists despite this, but rather as something that emerges in that interaction. As Abercrombie (1998: 85) says, '"indigenous culture" [has] been shaped for centuries through the collective interfaces between households or hamlets and powerful states'. It would be overstating the case, however, to imply that indigenous ethnic groups are totally dependent on the state for their very existence. Like Abercrombie, Howe shows how Kuna indigenous identity has been formed in long-term *interaction* with the Panamanian state. For a start, part of the identity of the Kuna, who live on islands off the Caribbean coast of Panama, is their dress complex, particularly for women. This complex, however, only appeared in the nineteenth century, since its nose-rings, bead leg-bindings and the famous Kuna *molas* (hand-stitched appliqué designs worn on women's blouses) were based on imported goods; it also developed partly in response to contact (Howe, 1991: 25). The drinking of *chicha* beer during parties also became an important symbol of Kuna identity, but this was partly because the Panamanian state disapproved of it and tried to stop the practice in the 1920s during a programme of forced acculturation which also targeted the wearing of leg-bindings by women.

Howe's chapter also shows that there is no simple opposition between the Kuna and the state, in this case the police: some policemen had female Kuna companions, despite the jealous guarding of Kuna women by their menfolk; some Kuna also opposed the *chicha* parties; some of the police were themselves Kuna. Furthermore, Howe demonstrates how other parties come into the interactive constitution of identity. The Kuna attracted attention in the US as possible 'white indigenous people' and there were a number of expeditions to study them. In 1925, the Kuna revolted against the acculturation programme to which they were being subjected and received support from the US, partly because some North Americans saw them as noble indigenous people being crushed by a basically black or mulatto nation-state (see also Howe, 1998). Thus identity was being constructed in an international frame.

Jackson's chapter (1991) reaffirms this: an 'ethnic' identity for the Tukanoans of Colombian Amazonia is an emergent phenomenon, in a process that elsewhere has been labelled 'ethnogenesis' (see Hill, 1996). In this case, identity emerges in a complex interaction between government agencies, national indigenous organisations, Protestant missionaries, the Church, anthropologists and different factions within the Tukanoans. The state has adopted different positions in response to indigenous organisation which emerged in Colombia in the 1960s in the Andean regions: it has varied between official repression (for example, under President Turbay, 1978–82) and official recognition (for example, with the 1991 Constitution). Indigenous organisations based on Andean indigenous experience are also active in the Amazon region and their representations of indigenous society are being adopted by Tukanoan activists: 'Tukanoans are learning how to be proper Indians from non-Tukanoan Indian images and values' (Jackson, 1991: 147). The image of an 'indigenous community' with its own culture and boundaries is especially inappropriate for the Tukanoans since the practice of language exogamy (marrying someone who speaks a different language from oneself) continuously blurs cultural boundaries, yet this is the image that both highland indigenous organisations and government agencies are used to and it is thus deployed by Tukanoan activists as well. The Catholic Church sponsors the local indigenous organisation because it wants to reassert its authority in an area where North American Protestant evangelical missionaries are active. The Tukanoans themselves divide over 'progress' or 'tradition', and anthropologists also have different agendas depending partly on institutional splits between more 'academic' and more 'applied' orientations (Wade, 1993a: 33–4). The overall result is that Tukanoan 'culture' has become a reified object, subject to representation, negotiation and attempts at preservation – in 1983, for example, the Ministry of Health established a 'shaman school' for older men to teach younger ones (Jackson, 1995).

If indigenous identity is constituted within the context of the nation-state, the opposite is also true. Howe contends that, in order 'to cast themselves as the forces of order, and state control as the only appropriate kind of order, [the Panamanian authorities] *needed* the Kuna to be anarchic' (1991: 34). To construct its order and civilisation, the nation-state needs disorder and savagery, and these may be seen as internal rather than external. On the other hand, the ideology of *indigenismo* used indigenous people to confer uniqueness on Latin American national identities in a global world (see Chapter 2) and this is still common today. Hendrickson (1991) argues that, in Guatemala, indigenous *traje* (clothing) is used by government agencies, in tourist information and in beauty contests, as both a symbol of the uniqueness of Guatemala and a symbol of its supposed unity (see also Hendrickson, 1995: ch. 3). Meanwhile, indigenous dress when worn by an indigenous in daily life is also a mark of low status. Similarly, Abercrombie argues that 'urban "non-Indians" continue to make the relationship of their culture to that of "Indians" fundamental to their own identities' (1991: 96), by defining themselves as that which is not indigenous. Thus, for example, in the city of Oruro, *mestizos* hire indigenous shamans during carnival time to make offerings in an 'indigenous' way to deities thought to be indigenous. This constructs indigenous people as ritually powerful, but at the same time as fundamentally different. 'All [the Oruro carnival dance groups] represent, in some form, an "Indian within", elevated to a high and powerful rank within urban "folk" religion, as it is within a nationalism in sore need of an anti-imperialist and legitimating identity' (1991: 119); in the view of elite nation-builders, 'indians occupy a timeless world that preserves uniquely Bolivian customs from the depredations of imperialist and transnational modernity' (Abercrombie, 1998: 318). The nation needs indigenous people to specify a unique identity; non-indigenous people need access to an identity that 'taps the wild powers apparently unattainable for ... civilised folk' (Abercrombie, 1991: 119).

BEYOND THE NATION: TRANSNATIONALISM AND DIASPORA

The examples above suggest the importance of looking beyond the confines of the nation in order to understand the constitution of indigenous identities and cultures: this points to a departure from 'methodological nationalism' (Wimmer and Glick Schiller, 2002). The Kuna were involved in complex relationships with the US; the Tukanoans, with US missionaries; highland Guatemalans, with images of themselves that are purveyed through the medium of global tourism; highland Bolivians with a nationalism that itself responded to transnational imperialism. The importance given in contemporary social and cultural theory to transnationalism and diaspora, mentioned above, draw our attention to the way indigenous and black identities are enmeshed in globalising networks, which are long-standing but also becoming more ubiquitous and intensive.[8]

The processes of migration between Latin America and the US can have important impacts on the way indigenous identities are constituted. Kearney looks at Mixtecs and Zapotecs from Oaxaca who migrate to north-western Mexico and California – Zapotecs mainly working in urban service industries and small business and Mixtecs mainly as rural farm workers. He explores the 'political, social and cultural practices whereby citizens of a nation-state construct social forms and identities that in part escape from the cultural and political hegemony of their nation-state' (2000: 174): in this case, the migrants create a space they call 'Oaxacalifornia', which is segregated to an important degree from mainstream California.[9] The migrant population is subject to pressures from the US state, in terms of control of (illegal) immigrants, and influences from the Mexican state, which sends consuls, the state governor of Oaxaca and representatives from the Instituto Nacional Indigenista to visit them. Meanwhile, the migrants themselves maintain close links with relatives back home and send significant quantities of remittances, despite their own precarious and oftentimes illegal situation. The indigenous migrants bring traditions of corporate communities and indigenous organising that are adapted to their new situation and, in the process, a new, stronger sense of a wider ethnicity emerges, which is distinct from the more localised identities that reigned in Oaxaca.

Mixtecs have experience of struggles on different terrains: first, as peasants in Oaxaca, where they are threatened and abused when they try to organise as local communities to gain land rights; second, as agro-industrial workers in the north-western Mexican state of Baja California, where many Mixtecs migrate, perhaps before going north to the US, and where they are forced to join a single official union, with other attempts at organisation being suppressed; third, as workers in US–Mexican border towns, where they are abused as *indios*. These experiences, and especially in the border areas, create a growing sense of being *indígena* and specifically Mixtec and the migrants form Mixtec organisations, even though these are repressed. When in California, Mixtecs also create organisations that address the problems found on the three terrains mentioned above and in the US. This creates and reinforces a sense of an encompassing Mixtec identity, on the basis of which claims are made to human rights for Mixtecs as a self-identified ethnic group. (The human rights discourse doubtless emerges out of the globalisation of this kind of quasi-judicial concept: see Chapter 6; see also Brysk, 2005; Sieder et al., 2005.) Mixtec ethnic identity is also partly media generated, giving it a greater public currency than grassroots organisations alone could achieve. One result of this identity formation process is that using ethnicity as a basis for solidarity reinforces the idea of the Mixtecs as different and thus potentially opens them up to even more abuse.

Transnational migration for Mixtecs creates a sense of ethnic identity that is based on a multiplicity of experiences and on constant movements of people, information and goods between Oaxaca, Baja California, US-Mexico border towns and California; it is mediated by both the US and Mexican governments, by global discourses of human rights and by communications technologies such as TV, the internet and mobile phones. Rouse (1995) questions whether transnational migration necessarily creates a clear shift towards a 'sense of identity'. He suggests that Mexican migrants may come from a context in which Western logics of 'identity' are counter-balanced by forms of reckoning of personhood that depend on one's place in a social network, rather than abstract attributes (such as being 'indigenous' or 'Mixtec'). Although a move to the US can foster a sense of identity in this abstract form, migrants may also undermine this in their daily practice, by forming non-identity-based networks across ethnic boundaries and building up patron–client networks that also cross boundaries of race, class and ethnicity. Although Rouse thought the migrants were victims of racism (as Latinos), they rarely talked in these terms and instead spoke of themselves as hard and loyal workers. However, it is significant that the migrants that Rouse studied were *mestizos*, not indigenous people: there was arguably less basis for an identity to emerge, while the kind of globalising discourse that refers to indigenous populations worldwide as victims in need of protection – as enshrined, for example, in the International Labour Organization's Convention 169 on Indigenous and Tribal Peoples (1989) – was not really available to them either.

Black identities and cultures are also mediated by long-term transnational and diasporic processes (Gordon, 1998; Sansone, 2003: ch. 1; Sansone et al., 2008; Yelvington, 2001, 2006). Earlier on, I noted that the identity of Brazil as a 'racial democracy' – and one could extend this to include some other Latin American nations – was constituted in dialogue, sometimes tacit, sometimes explicit, with the US. Seigel (2009) tracks the movements, backwards and forwards, of ideas and people between the two countries, in which these images of race relations were constructed. She examines the black press of São Paulo in the 1920s, for example, in terms of its generally cosmopolitan perspective and its particular 'Afro-diasporic communications' with Chicago newsmen: the Afro-Brazilian journalists were attempting to formulate an anti-racist strategy 'with tools drawn from every facet of their multidimensional context' (2009: 180). They did not, however, attack racism in the head-on way that US blacks did (when the latter found, for instance, that they were being refused visas to enter Brazil), but used ideas of a national racial democracy as a tool to campaign for actual racial democracy (as a universal liberal ideal), while also supporting Brazilian national identity and avoiding the appearance of disloyalty.

The Garifuna of Honduras are an interesting demonstration of the transnational shaping of identity.[10] An already diasporic people, due to their migration in the eighteenth century from the Caribbean island of St Vincent to what would become several distinct Central American nations, Garifuna have since migrated extensively to the US. They are regarded as 'autochthonous' people in Honduras, because of their pre-independence settlement and can claim land rights on that basis. Yet, in New York, where they are outsiders, they hesitate to identify as Honduran, because of the racism and marginalisation they encounter there. One way forward in these circumstances is the 'articulation of the Garifuna Nation in diaspora', that is a black transnational entity, rooted historically in the island of St Vincent (England, 2006: 226). This transnational experience shapes Garifuna identity in Central America, as well as in the United States.

The encounter of migrant Afro-Latins with the racial classification system of the US and with racial politics and racism there has shaped ideas about blackness in Latin America in recent years. Many Latin Americans who would not consider themselves 'black' find themselves classified as such when they arrive in the US; others are defined 'white' in ways which socially separate them from 'black' people, including perhaps their own relatives, in ways they were not expecting. They react in varied ways to this, depending partly on how 'black' they are or feel: some accept the identity, while also retaining a strong Latino identity (Rodríguez, 1994). There is a resistance to conforming to US racial categories and Latinos in general are well known for ticking the 'other race' box in the 'race' section of the US census form and then writing in some other designation, such as 'Dominican' (Duany, 1998; Rodríguez, 2000). A number of scholars argue for recognising the specificity of an Afro-Latino category that is neither simply African American nor simply Latino (Lao-Montes, 2007).

However, it is difficult to avoid the conclusion that one of the factors behind the move towards a more inclusive black category, evident a number of countries, is the image and experience of the US. In the Dominican Republic, where dark-skinned people have been somewhat allergic to identifying as black, often describing themselves as *indio*, 'traditional racial perceptions of Dominican "whiteness" are being challenged by a transnational population that has suffered in its own flesh the sting of racism in the United States' (Sagás, 2004: 67; see also Simmons, 2009). In Bahia, Brazil, young black people continue to participate in very long-term transnational exchanges and currently are strongly influenced by US black culture, style and music and also by US racial terms, such as 'black' and 'brother' (*brodi*), which they use frequently (Sansone, 2003: ch. 3). Young black Garifuna men in Honduras adopt a black 'bad boy' image (in speech, fashion, posture, etc.), which they have learned in the context of the intensive transnational movements that exist between Garifuna communities and the US. They use this to contest dominant images of 'peaceful Garifuna', which they associate with Honduran racial orders that cast them as humble and powerless (Anderson, 2005). Aside from illustrating that racial images need to be seen in a transnational frame, this example suggests that the experiences of black (or brown) Latin Americans in the US – despite the ambiguous position that Afro-Latins seem to occupy – can feed back into national contexts in ways that reinforce a broad (and assertive) category of 'black'.

These processes are not necessarily fed directly by migration to or experience of the US. In the Colombian town of Tumaco, on the southern Pacific coast, Agier (2002) argues that the annual carnival celebrations arranged by local intellectuals and cultural promoters involved the use of local images of the devil, a well-known local priest and a musician hero-figure (who had duelled with the devil) in ways that purveyed simplified, essentialised, dichotomised definitions of whiteness and blackness. In fact, local oral narratives portrayed these figures as racially ambiguous – the devil, for example, is portrayed as black, white and mixed race, a threat but also a teacher. Agier does not relate this process of simplification to US influences in particular, but rather to cultural activists' desire to make their productions legible to a global audiences and circuits of commoditised images of culture.

Definitions of blackness are transnationally influenced in other ways too. The Colombian census of 2005 adopted for the first time a rather broad category of black that encompassed people who defined themselves as *negro*, *mulato*, *afrocolombiano* and *afrodescendiente*. This category attempts to measure the 'black' population of Colombia, as distinct from the non-black (and the indigenous), in a way that begins to approach an inclusive US-style definition. It was decided on after lengthy negotiations between the government statistics agency, academics, black social movements and others, which took place partly in international conferences, titled 'Todos Contamos' (We All Count), supported by the World Bank and the Inter-American Development Bank. Meanwhile, both banks had been showing an increasing interest, since the mid 1990s, in 'Afro-Latins' as an object of bank policy and support (Wade, 2009a). The black social movements, which lobbied hard for the inclusive approach, wanted to include the category *moreno* in the census question, but the government balked at this as overly inclusive.[11]

These transnational processes are not as recent as these examples make it appear. They have been going on for many years, as Gilroy (1993a) shows in his delineation of the Black Atlantic and the constant movements across it that linked the Caribbean, the US and Europe. The *négritude* artistic and intellectual movement of the 1930s Caribbean was actually developed in France by the Martinican Aimé Césaire and the Senegalese Léopold Senghor, who were students in Paris; Caribbean intellectuals at the time also had strong links with key figures in the black literary and artistic movement known as the Harlem Renaissance (Irele, 2004); the influence of the Jamaican intellectual Marcus Garvey, founder of the Universal Negro Improvement Association, was felt all over the Caribbean around the same period (for example, among Nicaraguan blacks; see Gordon, 1998).

Matory's work expands Gilroy's Black Atlantic southwards a bit by mapping movements between Africa, Europe and Brazil. He argues that Brazilian Candomblé religious practices (which are often seen as a survival of 'pure African' culture in Brazil, with cult houses sometimes sending representatives to West Africa to make sure they are conforming to 'original' models) were shaped very strongly in the mid nineteenth century by Brazilian blacks who went to Africa, where they were educated in English-speaking Presbyterian schools, often became Freemasons and frequently visited England. These men were proud of their English connections and adopted Anglicised names; but they also imbibed Yoruba culture and religion in Nigeria and passed that concern on to Candomblé practices in Bahia when they returned. Meanwhile, the whole position of Yoruba culture and religion in Lagos was being shaped by returnee migrants from Brazil (some expelled from Brazil as rebels) in the mid nineteenth century, who found some shelter in the British protectorate in Lagos and were joined there by free blacks from Sierra Leone, the US and Jamaica. These people helped 'Yoruba culture' become the dominant presence in Nigeria. In general, there were hundreds of Africans and Afro-Brazilians travelling back and forth between

Bahia and Lagos between 1855 and 1930 (Matory, 1999; see also Matory, 2005, 2006).

Moving to the later twentieth century, Matory (2005: 149) argues that Brazilian nationalists took the Candomblé of north-eastern Brazil as 'a "folk" emblem of a "racially democratic" nation-state' and in so doing have, since the 1970s, 'inadvertently resurrected forms of Black transnationalism that had been in decline in Bahia since the 1940s'. Not only did Candomblé – its imagery, its gods, its lexicon – spread from the north-east across the rest of Brazil, but this avowedly transnational form, connected to Africa, was placed at the heart of the nation. During the 1940s and 1950s, links between Candomblé houses in Brazil and Africa were maintained by occasional visits of Afro-Brazilian priests and some white intellectuals to Africa. Candomblé could serve as a symbol of Brazilian folklore, but it was also controlled by the state and Candomblé priests in Bahia had to register with the police. From the mid 1960s, given the official status Candomblé was acquiring, such visits were increasingly sponsored by the Brazilian federal government and the municipal government of Salvador, Bahia. Meanwhile, the Nigerian government sent many students and academics to Brazil: some of them taught Yoruba and did research on Candomblé (Matory, 2005: 169–75). This kind of transnational black connection built on the earlier connections of the nineteenth century and formed a multivalent way for different people to think about Brazilian national identity in the twentieth century and its roots in 'Africa'.

In short, black and indigenous cultures and identities are constituted in these transnational and diasporic movements in which blackness and indigeneity become globalised images and networks. Again, the temptation is to think of this as quite recent – a product of transnational social movements and discourses of human rights (see Chapter 6). In the next section, it becomes clear that transnational images of blackness and indigenousness have been around for a long time.

THE POWER OF BLACKS AND INDIGENOUS PEOPLE

The transnational dimensions of both indigenousness and blackness link to a theme that emerged in Abercrombie's analysis – the powers imputed to black and indigenous people. To talk of 'wild powers', as Abercrombie does, may seem fanciful – hardly a central element of racial and ethnic distinctions – but Taussig's work indicates that this is far from the case. Focusing on Colombia, where indigenous people are a tiny minority, Taussig says that 'the enormity of the magic attributed to those Indians is striking' (1987: 171); the more 'savage' and remote the indigenous people, the more powerful they are said to be – even among the indigenous people themselves. The power they are said to control is sought after to solve the classic trilogy of life's problems – *amor, salud y dinero* (love, health and money). Indigenous curers work in frontier towns, but also advertise in the national newspapers. The hallucinogenic drink *yagé*, used in ritual curing, comes from the Amazon region, but is also on sale in Bogotá. This attribution of magic, argues Taussig, is 'a cunningly wrought colonial *objet d'art*' in that it stems from ideas about 'wild men' – savage yet powerful – that existed before the conquest of the Americas and were transferred onto indigenous people; it is also, however, 'third world modernism, a neocolonial reworking of primitivism' (1987: 172) in that the spread of capitalism has actually given more power to indigenous people as non-indigenous people feel more distant from the source of 'primitive' strength. Taussig is hardly unaware of the economic factors in the construction of identity, but 'to focus exclusively on the conscious economic interests of the individual is to lose sight of colonial mythopoesis working through the political unconscious' (1987: 185). There are politico-*cultural* dimensions of identity that are missed by the politico-*economic* bias of instrumentalist approaches to ethnic and racial identity. And the images of the wild man, the shaman and the indigenous healer are all located in a transnational imaginary of great historical depth.[12] Silverblatt (2004: 163–73), for example, shows how indigenous and black people were feared and sought after as healers in colonial Peru, with some white women learning indigenous ways in order to tap sources of power. Paradoxically, 'the powerless and conquered ... were viewed as having the most dangerous occult powers' (Behar, 1989: 94).

Blacks in Colombia are also attributed powers as healers and sorcerers – usually those from the isolated Pacific coastal region. In Brazil, African and Afro-Brazilian deities are worshipped and asked for help in Candomblé and Umbanda religions by all kinds of people; as we have seen, some Candomblé ritual specialists travel to West Africa and return to their religious centres back in Brazil with 'authentic' and revitalising ritual practices (Henfrey, 1981: 95; Matory, 2005). Herein, again, lies a long history of the attribution of magical power – dangerous and powerful, evil and enticing – to Africans and their descendants (Taussig, 1987: 217; Wade, 1993a: 293).

With blacks in Latin America (and elsewhere), just as important are the intertwined images of sexual, musical and dancing power. This is an underlying element in the literary trends of *negrismo* that emerged in the 1920s (see Chapter 2), as it is in the phenomenon of sun-tanning that emerged at about the same time. The ambivalent sexual attraction felt by whites for blacks is also a recurrent theme in colonial contexts (Wade, 2009b; Young, 1995). Sex and music often fit together. In Colombia, for example, definitions of national music in the early decades of this century centred on guitar-based styles associated with the white/*mestizo* Andean interior. By the late 1940s, 'tropical' styles associated with the Caribbean region of the country and with the Caribbean basin itself were all the rage, despite grumpy protests from some conservatives about 'foreign' and even 'African' music swamping 'authentic' Colombian music. The reasons for the rise of this music are complex, but one element was the 'modern', liberated sexuality it was held to embody (Wade, 2000). Styles of music associated with blacks, or as danced to by blacks, are still seen as sexually immoral and/or exciting by many people in Colombia.

This was far from a simply national phenomenon. For a start, the rise of musical styles associated with blackness did not only occur in Colombia, but was characteristic of, for example, Cuba and Brazil at slightly earlier dates (Moore, 1997; Vianna, 1999), with all three drawing on the popularity of black music in the US. In addition, the link between blackness and sexuality that was evident in all these cases was long-standing and widespread and, from the late nineteenth century was increasingly associated with modernity in a paradoxical way: a sexuality that was seen as 'natural', was therefore also 'modern' in its liberation. This was part of the international artistic current of primitivism, which valued 'primitive' traits for their 'natural' and 'uncivilised' qualities, from which 'modern' people had become alienated (Price, 2001: 45; Torgovnick, 1990; see also Barkan and Bush, 1995).

The point is that, within the cultural space of the nation, images of racialised powers – indigenous magic, black sexuality, white civilisation – are symbols competing for room, for legitimacy, in defining what the nation is and can become. Shamanism has been seen as a vital institution, internal to indigenous groups, that helps them to endure as cultural units (for example, Elsass, 1992; see also Langdon and Baer, 1992). But shamanism also works interactively in the construction of indigenous identity as part of a much broader, national and transnational cultural space. Music can also be important in underwriting black identity in specific locales, but this likewise occurs within a national and transnational – and especially a 'black Atlantic' (Gilroy, 1993a) – musical context of styles identified as more or less black (see Béhague, 1994).

This gives a different view of racial and ethnic identities in the nation-state and transnationally. This has been and still is largely analysed as a struggle over economic resources and political power, but there are important cultural, symbolic and moral dimensions as well. From this perspective, it is even more necessary to see indigenous people, blacks and the nation as mutually constituting cultural categories. To sustain itself, the nation feeds on the power of blacks and indigenous people, just as they feed on the power of the nation-state. In this process, the exchanges of symbolic elements takes place in a transnational and diasporic frame, within which national imaginaries constitute themselves.

6
Black and Indigenous Social Movements

The national and transnational context has become a vital one for understanding ethnic and racial identities partly because of the emergence of movements that seek to revitalise those identities and make indigenous people and blacks – or Afro-descendants, as recent terminology has it – into players in the politics of economy and culture. These movements often feed on symbolic and concrete links with each other and with movements outside Latin America, which is what makes the transnational context important too (Andolina et al., 2005; Brysk, 1996, 2000; Fontaine, 1981; Jackson and Warren, 2005; Radcliffe et al., 2002; Warren and Jackson, 2003).

Black and indigenous social movements have been around for a long time. Recent ethnohistorical works have highlighted the importance of slave and indigenous rebellions, how runaway slaves or *cimarrones* formed renegade communities (*palenques* and *quilombos*), the contribution of slave resistance to abolition and so on.[1] The Frente Negra Brasileira was active in the 1930s (Andrews, 1992), black organisations were around in Brazil when the UNESCO studies were being carried out in the 1950s (Fernandes, 1979: 98) and the Movimento Negro Unificado was formed there in 1978 (González, 1985). In Colombia, black organisations date from the 1970s (Wade, 1995a).[2] Indigenous rights organisations likewise sprang up all over Latin America from about the 1960s. However, it has been from the 1980s that these movements have gained strength and multiplied.[3] Also new has been the advent of official multiculturalism, since the late 1980s, in which many states across the region have recognised ethnic diversity and enshrined rights for indigenous and, in some cases, Afro-descendant people in their constitutions and legislations (Sieder, 2002; Van Cott, 2000).

'NEW' SOCIAL MOVEMENTS

The reason why black and indigenous social movements have attracted attention in the last couple of decades is partly because of their proliferation, but also because they form part of a more general phenomenon, also dating from the mid 1960s, but accelerating from the 1980s, termed 'new' social movements, although there has been debate about how 'new' they really are. They include everything from squatters' associations, Christian Base Communities, gay rights groups and animal rights campaigners to workers' cooperatives, indigenous land rights organisations and ecological groups.

They are said to be new because they seem to be different from the classic trade unions workers' protest of earlier decades: there is less of an emphasis on either modernisation or revolution as the basic options, and more on the multiplicity of political spaces that can be carved out in the nation, and the globe, in which 'politics' is no longer a separate level, but is integral to social life. There is also often less emphasis on the sphere of production (labour versus capital) and more on 'reproduction' (for example, of the environment, whether urbanised or rural). Among new social movements, a divide has also been identified between 'strategy' and 'identity' – the extent to which a movement focuses on strategic, instrumental ends (for example, obtaining land) or on asserting a right to a cultural space for its identity (Escobar, 1992b; Escobar and Alvarez, 1992; Foweraker, 1995). Alvarez et al. (1998a) contend that the two aspects should not be divided: there is always a culture of politics and a politics of culture. The point is that identity as *an end in itself*, whether it is linked to material rights or not (and it almost always is), constitutes something of a new trend.

The context for the emergence of these new movements is complex. Hall contends that the decentring of the modern subject and the dislocation of stable foci of identification by globalisation has brought about a new search for identities (Hall, 1991, 1992a). Escobar argues that, for many in Latin America, modernity itself has failed as a project and new forms of grassroots collective action have emerged (Escobar, 1992a). Such movements can propose adjustments to the process of development, which tailor the process more towards local people; they can also propose alternative modernities, which seek to promote and defend marginalised ways of life, or even radical alternatives to modernity itself, which challenge the very basis of capitalism and 'progress' (Escobar, 2008: ch. 4). In a similar vein, Kearney (1996: 8) writes that 'in this post-development moment [in Latin America] ... conditions that promote diversity appear to be deepening, creating a climate conducive to the resurgence of indigenous identities'.

Also important are two interrelated sets of factors. On the one hand, although exploitation and oppression of ethnic and racial minorities in Latin America (and elsewhere) has been long-standing, it is reasonable to suggest that changes in the global economy over the last few decades – structural adjustment, neoliberal reform – have intensified pressures on these peoples, both integrating them more strongly into national and global economies and subjecting them to exploitation. It is well known that neoliberal reforms, by opening markets to global trade and rolling back state protection for vulnerable classes, has increased impoverishment in many areas. One need only look at the process of 'development' in the Amazon basin or the Pacific coastal regions of Ecuador and Colombia to see how Afro-descendant and indigenous groups have been disadvantaged (Escobar, 2008; Fisher, 1994; Treece, 1990; see also Yashar, 2005: 67). The reaction of the largely indigenous population of Bolivia to neoliberal proposals to privatise water and gas in 2000 and 2003 was a reflection of, but also a major spur to, indigenous organising there (Lazar, 2008; Postero, 2007). Similarly, neoliberal reforms have often been cited as one of the key spurs to the emergence of the indigenous-based, armed group, Ejército Zapatista de Liberación Nacional (EZLN), in Chiapas, Mexico (Harvey, 1998; Stephen, 2002).

On the other hand, although there has long been a consciousness among indigenous and Afro-descendant groups of their location within a national and indeed international social order (see Chapter 5), it is also reasonable to suggest this consciousness has intensified and spread more widely in recent decades. This process has been spurred by increasing levels of education, especially higher education – it is no accident that early black organisers in Colombia were university students (see also Rappaport, 2005). It has also been prompted by growth of a transnational communication society, which has fostered knowledge among minorities of the worldwide context of decolonisation and of other indigenous and black movements elsewhere in the world, especially in North America. Of vital importance too has been the growth of international interest in indigenous matters, as evident, for example, in International Labour Organization's Convention 169 of 1989 and the United Nations Universal Declaration of Rights of Indigenous Peoples of 1994. Black and indigenous social movements draw symbolic and material strength from a transnational network of multilateral organisations, NGOs and other social movements, as well as globalised and often commoditised cultural representations of indigenousness and blackness (Brysk, 2000; Fontaine, 1981; Sieder, 2002). Although international conventions and declarations may have little legal binding force, they are quasi-judicial instruments that can be used to strengthen claims made both nationally and locally (Sieder et al., 2005).

In this regard, the globalisation of discourses of human rights has been significant (Cowan et al., 2001). The language of rights has penetrated into ever-growing areas of political discourse and into areas previously regarded as 'private', such as child labour, child abuse or organ trafficking (Brysk, 2005). Claims about land, culture, access to resources, education, racism and so on can be phrased as claims to human rights and this gives them international legitimacy, while also universalising their appeal. The human rights perspective reframes a claim: it is no longer a demand being made for special treatment by a culturally distinct group of people; it is a demand to be treated as human by people who just happen to be culturally distinctive. At the extreme, it is claimed that the right to have one's cultural difference recognised and respected is a human right. This universalises 'the right to difference' and makes it appear part of the natural social order: people who claim that this right has been denied them are cast as victims in need of reparation, rather than trouble-makers bent on securing special privileges.

Indigenous and black minorities' growing consciousness of their own identity and position does not take place only from the bottom up, as it were. It is a process strongly mediated by a variety of non-indigenous people and institutions, which complicate any simple divide between grassroots, ethnic social movements and 'the dominant society'. First, the Catholic Church, influenced by liberation theology and its concern for the poor, has been very important in supporting and indeed initiating both indigenous and black social movements at a local level, often through broader regional programmes such as the Pastoral Afroamericana (Burdick, 1998; Cleary and Steigenga, 2004; Wade, 1995a; Wilson, 1995a).

Second, indigenous movements depend on what Rappaport (2005) calls *colaboradores*. These non-indigenous collaborators – academics, like herself, supporters, priests and advisers – form an important part of the movement. Rappaport shows how internally heterogeneous the 'indigenous movement' is, not only in terms of non-indigenous participation, but also because of the varied positions of different indigenous activists – some well educated, other less so; some educators themselves, some not; some very local activists, others with more cosmopolitan, national and international experiences. A similar picture emerges when looking at the Zapatista movement in Mexico. This is often taken to consist of the armed group, the EZLN, but Leyva Solano (1998) argues that Zapatismo as a social movement is comprised of multiple networks connecting various sectors of civil society, including women's organisations, radical left-wing organisations and individuals, and international activists and networkers. Also vital is the globalising discourse of human rights, which the Zapatistas use to mobilise local, national and transnational networks and alliances (Speed and Leyva Solano, 2008).

Third, the state itself is a very significant interlocutor and mediator of ethnic social movements. This will become apparent throughout this chapter, so I will not enter into detail here: the point is that it is naive to think in terms of a simple opposition between the state and ethnic movements; the mere fact that many Latin American states have conceded special legal rights to indigenous and, less often, black groups complicates such a divide.

A final important factor in understanding the emergence of ethnic movements in Latin America is regional processes of democratisation and changing regimes of citizenship. Yashar (2005) argues that processes of democratisation, which were dismantling the region's dictatorships, opened spaces for political expression and participation of various kinds (see also Van Cott, 2000; Winant, 1992). At the same time, neoliberal citizenship reforms, which privileged the individual and marginalised collective or corporate identities and loyalties, undermined the spaces of autonomy that many indigenous communities had managed to establish *vis-à-vis* the state. This put them under threat and, paradoxically, spurred precisely the kind of collective identity and organisation that the reforms had aimed to undo – providing that communities had some kind of 'transcommunity network' to facilitate this process (Yashar, 2005: 55).

BLACK AND INDIGENOUS MOBILISATIONS

Yashar's particular argument applies more to indigenous than black people insofar as it refers to the (partial) autonomy of indigenous communities in the nation-state. In general it is noticeable that, despite the strides made by Afro-Colombian and Afro-Brazilian movements, among others, indigenous organisation has generally been more successful than black organisation, as shown by the example from Colombia given in Chapter 2. In my view, this is to do with the historical institutionalisation of indigenous identity, which gave indigenous people a conceptual, political and often a territorial basis – hence the importance of land rights struggles – on which to organise themselves. This is the autonomy that Yashar (2005) says was threatened by neoliberal citizenship regimes. An institution-alised identity also helped indigenous people to gain international backing. Blacks, in contrast, have not had this historical basis. Observers such as Toplin (1971), Degler (1971), Skidmore (1972) and Hasenbalg (1979) also argued that, whether due specifically to the 'special place' of the *pardo* or more generally to a system based on *mestizaje*, with the possibility of whitening, black mobilisation was inherently difficult to achieve, because of the ambiguity of the 'black' category. This is still the case to some extent (Burdick, 1992; Hanchard, 1994; Sansone, 2003: 56, 103; Wade, 1993a: ch. 17; Winant, 1994: ch. 10), but previous analyses, by treating black mobilisation as blocked by a permanent structural obstacle, found it hard to account for the evident mobilisations that have occurred. I think it is more fruitful to relate black political mobilisation to the overall political context – as others have done with indigenous mobilisations – so that, for example, in Brazil it flowered with democratic opening and in Colombia with constitutional reform (Arocha, 1992, 1998; Wade, 1995a; Winant, 1992).

It is interesting that where black groups have mobilised with a degree of success, there has been a tendency for them to adopt a stance that positions them as indigenous-like (Anderson, 2007, 2009; Hooker, 2005, 2009: 137–8; Ng'weno, 2007a; Restrepo, 2002; Wade, 1995a). This is evident in the case of Colombia and also Honduras, although in distinctive ways. In Colombia, as mentioned briefly in Chapter 2, constitutional reform in 1991 led to Law 70 of 1993, which recognised 'black communities' as an 'ethnic group' and accorded them special rights, although not as fully as for indigenous people. Notably, the law confined itself principally to rural, riverine, black communities in the Pacific coastal region, which were defined in terms of 'traditional production practices' and rooted residence on their lands. The image conveyed was of a bounded ethnic group, similar to the image of indigenous groups. This was because the state was accustomed to dealing with indige-nous-style 'ethnic groups' and thus willing to deal with black social movements in the same way; and also because really opening up legislative rights to the whole Afro-Colombian population seemed both too complex and too threatening. Afro-Colombian movements tended to adapt to this mould, focus on the Pacific coast and emphasise their cultural and historical difference, playing down issues of racism, while small, urban Afro-Colombian movements struggled to stake a claim in the process, trying to work with the small footholds in the law that could address Afro-Colombians as a wider constituency. Gradually, urban movements have gained some ground, with racism being given more attention and the state including a broad 'black' category in the 2005 census (see Chapter 5; see also Wade, 2009a). This indicates that the indigenous-style mould is not necessarily a permanent straitjacket.

In Honduras – and indeed in Guatemala and Nicaragua – Garifuna people were able to claim a position as an authentically 'autochthonous' people, equal in legal status to other indigenous peoples, because of their particular history, plus their cultural distinctiveness, especially their language.[4] The state accepted this equality, even if there have been attempts to divide ethnic activism on black/indigenous lines (Anderson, 2007; England, 2006). Anderson (2009) contends that the use of an indigenous-like stance by black groups is not necessarily negative. A discourse of rooted black (rural) indigeneity and a discourse of diasporic, cosmopolitan (urban) blackness coexist for Garifuna people and this can be politically productive: it opens up multiple options for identifying, rather than simply causing contradictions (see also England, 2006: 191–204).

Nicaragua was a front-runner in the process of recognising minority rights, with the Sandinista government in 1986 approving the Law on Autonomous Regions of the Atlantic Coast and enshrining multiculturalist policies that protected the rights of *costeños* living in the coastal region. *Costeños* actually compromised a number of indigenous groups (notably the Miskitus), two groups of Afro-descendants (Creoles and Garifunas) and *mestizos*, many of whom had migrated there after about 1900 (Hooker, 2009: ch. 4). In this case, differences between these groups were encompassed in a policy that gave rights to a previously marginalised region, but Hooker (2009: 140–6) argues that, while this put indigenous and Afro-descendant people on an equal footing and created multiracial and multiethnic spaces in which different groups had to communicate and cooperate, it ignored the racial hierarchy of Nicaragua – including the fact that the region was marginalised in the nation precisely because it was historically black and indigenous (Gordon, 1998). This was evident in the inclusion of *mestizos* as beneficiaries of the law. In fact, because they are the demographic majority, *mestizos* have attained a dominant position in the institutions of regional self-government set up by the law. In practice, communication and cooperation has occurred between indigenous and Afro-descendant groups, increasing subaltern solidarity, but not between *mestizos* and others, thus reinforcing racialised power differences between dominant and subaltern groups.

Hale et al. (2003) give an example of this subaltern cooperation and communication – not, however, without tensions and disagreements – between indigenous and Afro-descendant groups involved in making land claims in the Nicaraguan Atlantic region. Individual communities often made overlapping land claims, but in a majority of cases they negotiated agreements to make multicommunity claims, both for strategic reasons of achieving strength in numbers for particular claims and to present a more united (black and indigenous) *costeño* front to the state. Some claims reasserted a particular ethnic identity (for example, Garifuna); other claims were multiethnic. Like the Honduran case, the Nicaraguan example suggests that potentially productive alliances can form between indigenous and black groups when they are positioned on an equal footing: for blacks to be seen as 'indigenous' in some way is not necessarily a problem.

Brazil is analogous in some ways to the Colombian case. In the 1988 constitutional reform land rights were opened to *remanescentes das comunidades dos quilombos* (remnants of *quilombo* communities), seen as historically rooted communities – indigenous style. Meanwhile, other rights, aimed at addressing racial inequality – the most notable having been special access to university places, implemented from 2003 – have been accorded to the Afro-Brazilian population as a whole in a controversial programme of affirmative action (see below; see also Htun, 2004; Skidmore, 2003). A particularly interesting aspect of Brazil is the re-emergence of indigenous communities in the country (Warren, 2001) and particularly in the north-east of Brazil, an area apparently occupied mostly by Afro-descendant peasant farmers. This is a process of 're-Indianization' (French, 2004: 665). Or rather, in this area, some communities have asserted an indigenous identity and made land claims based on this, while others have affirmed their identity as *quilombolas*, claiming land as residents on 'remnants' of old *quilombos* (Arruti, 1997; French, 2009). Some individuals identify as both indigenous and black (French, 2009: 90; Pinheiro, 2009). The things that prompt a community to go in one direction rather than another often seem, to the outside eye, rather contingent: particular bits of historical information, stories and memories; the role of outside mediators, such as priests, who have their own ideas about local history. People within a given community might disagree on whether to identify as *quilombolas* or not (French, 2009: ch. 4).

French also shows that legal categories (not only of 'indian' and '*quilombo* remnant' but also 'land owner', share-cropper', etc.) and legal processes (through which land may be claimed) are important mediators in the process; they constrain and facilitate options for local people.

This re-emergence of indigenous communities raises the question – by no means confined to the Brazilian case, but common all over Latin America and indeed elsewhere – of authenticity: are these people 'real indians'? Are they 'real blacks'? – although that question seems to be less often asked, perhaps because black groups have far fewer opportunities to claim land rights. In the Brazilian north-east, 'real' indigenous people are said to have disappeared many years ago, assimilated by *mestiçagem*; so the sudden appearance of people claiming to be indigenous must, it is said, be a fraud. The cultural traditions they lay claim to must be 'invented' traditions and therefore fake.

This is a highly complex and ambiguous area, in which contradictory stances are common among anthropologists, the state and social movement activists. Anthropologists, for example, may well try to support specific land claims with historical evidence and data showing hidden indigenous (or Afro-descendant) histories and practices, in part because legal processes often require such 'proofs' and, in Brazil and elsewhere, anthropologists are contracted by the state to investigate and validate land claims by indigenous (and Afro-descendant) communities. In effect, the anthropologists try to show these are 'real' *quilombola* or indigenous communities. On the other hand, at a more general level, most anthropologists contest arguments about authenticity and try to avoid ideas of invention understood as artificiality (Clifford, 1988, 2001). All culture is 'invented' in some sense. Culture, tradition, identity and land claims are emergent phenomena which should not be validated only by their historical rootedness.

Agents of the state, for their part, often require that indigenous people 'prove' their indigeneity in legal terms in order to access entitlements defined in law. Around Lake Titicaca, for example, the definition of 'customary territories' for indigenous people has emerged in conflicts between National Reserve authorities and Uros leaders. What were once flexible, ill-defined boundaries have become fixed as part of the way the state and the Uros relate to each other in legal procedures (Kent, 2008). On the other hand, states do not always take an inflexible line. The Brazilian state has been rather accommodating in terms of defining people and their lands, allowing legal recognition of indigeneity for groups previously considered non-indigenous, not just very recently but over a number of decades (French, 2009: 69–70). The same goes for the category *quilombo*, which has also been subject to ongoing processes of negotiation and redefinition in law (French, 2009: 92). In Colombia, too, the legal category of 'black community' – the entity able to make a land claim – was originally restricted to the rural Pacific coastal region, but, in a few cases, has been recognised by the state outside that region and even in an urban area.[5]

The people who are making land claims, for their part, may choose to emphasise deep roots and even ancestries of 'blood' in order to validate their status as 'true indians' or blacks. On the other hand, in Nicaragua, indigenous and black land claimants adopted a discourse of collective memory, collective residence and collective struggle – all more short-term and less essentialist – to legitimate their claims and their identities (Hale et al., 2003: 378). As noted above, in the Brazilian north-east, some people identify as both indigenous and black at the same time (French, 2009: 90).

These contradictory stances indicate that the matter of authenticity is a terrain of struggle and negotiation, not a question of simple definition – just as one would expect of an important cultural value. I return to the question of authenticity in Chapter 7: the point I wish to make here is that, while there is still a significant difference between the categories 'indian' and 'black', which has important political consequences, the category 'indian' does not carry any guarantees of authenticity. The Brazilian north-east case shows particularly well that these two categories share a common ground, in terms of contested and negotiated political and cultural processes of identity formation, even if they continue to occupy different imaginary spaces in the structures of alterity.

INTERSECTING DIMENSIONS OF DIFFERENCE

A key characteristic of black and indigenous movements is the intertwining of different axes of identification and action: ethnicity, race, gender, class, sexual orientation, religion, music and so on. For example, in Brazil an early if amorphous black movement was the 1960s 'Black Soul' movement, which emulated some of the ideology and trappings of the US black power movement and took US black soul music as a focal point (Hanchard, 1994: ch. 5). Then, in the 1970s, Winant (1992) argues that blacks were active in the strengthening of democratic political opposition to military rule, later going on to organise as blacks; class and racial identities were continuously overlapping and intersecting here and, for example, a Black Commission was created within the Partido Trabalhador. Winant also mentions the *afoxés*, groups rooted in Afro-Brazilian religious practice which are active in carnival as dance and musical groups, but which also act as community associations with political and self-help ends. This combination of music and dance with politics and community uplift is also characteristic of some of the *blocos afros* (black carnival associations), such as Ilê Aiyê (Agier, 1995; Barcelos, 1999: 161; Kraay, 1998: 22). Within all these organisations and groups, there is great debate about what weight to give class, race, gender and so on as organising, mobilising principles – should blacks seek to participate in national political structures along class lines, or work against these through socialism, or focus on reaffirming black identity above all else? Should men and women organise separately or together? Should movements focus on local issues or transnational networks and agendas? Such issues equally affect indigenous movements. These questions – which are familiar enough to a European or North American reader – are not easily resolved, but the point is that they indicate the increasing importance of the politics of identity, difference and culture in issues of race and ethnicity in Latin America.

Ethnicity, Race and Class

Although black and indigenous social movements are concerned with culture, language, violence and political representation, class remains a vital concern in the broad sense that most of these movements include a struggle for material goals, especially land. With Colombia's Law 70 of 1993, which opened the way for land claims by 'black communities', the issue of land became central to black identity, but one in which urban black groups had little stake. They did, however, have a strong interest in class issues linked to the urban labour and housing markets: goals of achieving access to material resources were integral to their interest in promoting the visibility of black culture, as the latter aim implied the former. In the city of Cali, for example, black movements focused on music and dance, particularly hip-hop and rap, but also 'folkloric' styles such as *currulao*, from the Pacific coastal region. Local activists spent a lot of time generating resources to pursue the promotion of these activities, seen as a way of life involving subsistence and lifestyle (Wade, 1999). More generally, their cultural project clearly implied an explicit stance on racism and the racial segregation that they felt subject to. The idea that they lived in a 'ghetto' was constantly reiterated (even if indices of segregation were not comparable to US racial ghettos – see Barbary and Urrea, 2004).

For black movements in Colombia, issues of racism, displaced for a time by an overriding concern with land for rural black communities, have been returning to centre stage. There is 'a reorientation of the ethnic debate towards the anti-discrimination struggle' (Hoffmann, 2004: 221, my translation) and a focus on dimensions of racial inequality that are easier to assess nowadays thanks to survey work (for example, Barbary and Urrea, 2004) and, particularly, the 2005 census, which counted Afro-Colombians in a contested but more or less effective way for the first time since 1912. The report of the government's Inter-Sectoral Commission for the Advancement of the Afro-Colombian, Palenquero and Raizal Population, published in May 2009, deployed data of this kind and recommended a national strategy against racism.[6] In Brazil, too, while land may be important to *remanescentes dos quilombos*, the vast majority of Afro-Brazilians live in cities and are more concerned with police harassment, the labour market, racism and violence. In Brazil, as we have seen, a concern with racial inequality has a long history: issues of class have always been central to race in that country – indeed, the problem there has been more to show that race is not *only* about class, but has its own dynamic.

For rural indigenous and black people, however, land continues to be of the greatest importance. While it may be true that peasant studies and the category of peasants – both of which have land at their very heart – have 'diminished dramatically in importance in the discourse of policy-makers and scholars of Latin America alike in the last decade of the twentieth, and the early twenty-first century' (Seligmann, 2008: 325), the struggle for land is central to indigenous mobilisation and, in some cases, to black mobilisation as well.

The importance of land insistently brings class issues into ethnicity and race for blacks and indigenous people alike. Schryer shows how, in the region of Huejutla in central Mexico, 'militant peasants identified their struggle [over land] in terms of an ethnic conflict between Indians and non-Indians' (1990: 4). Because conflicts over land cut across ethnic boundaries, however, there were divisive disputes among indigenous people about whether to join land invasions, and about the meaning and function of central indigenous cultural institutions such as the civic-religious hierarchy and communal land tenure. The Ejército Zapatista de Liberación Nacional in Chiapas, although it took a patriotic line with statements that 'There is in us, as in Our Great Mexican Nation, indigenous and *mestizo* blood', also clearly has a basically indigenous identity: 'we believe that if thousands of indigenous people rise up in struggle, then it is a matter of indigenous insurrection'.[7] The causes of the rebellion are connected to land, neoliberal reform, the impact of liberation theology and so on, but also to the racism that indigenous people have for centuries experienced at the hands of local *mestizos*. Harvey argues that the political message of Zapatismo required 'a new language' which was 'found in the convergence of Zapatistas' critical interpretation of Mexican history and the indigenous people's own stories of humiliation, exploitation and racism' (1998: 166). Questions of class and 'land' as an abstract category of political analysis become entangled in issues of identity, culture and 'land' as the basis for a cultural way of life. This is also seen in the division that exists in the southern Peruvian Andes between indigenous peasants, who produce directly from the land with collective labour, and *mestizos*, who use private labour and appropriation. This class division, however, is expressed through Andean cultural categories with participation in collective ritual and adherence to an ideology of egalitarianism being central to indigenous identity (Gose, 1994). Also in Peru, around Lake Titicaca, the 'customary territories' of the Uros people – albeit their recent emergence belies their 'customary' status – are central to Uros organisation, but land (and, in this case, water) is not a simple resource for subsistence production. Instead the whole struggle to define these territories and give them clear and defensible boundaries has also been linked to issues about who controls the lucrative trade in tourists who come to visit the famous floating reed islands of the Uros, with the aim of preventing non-Uros from cashing in on this opportunity (Kent, 2008). Again, issues of identity are inseparable from material resources and control over them.

In Colombia, black organisations emerged in the 1970s, taking inspiration from the US Black Power and civil rights movements. The use of North American black symbolism continues, especially in urban areas, but it was supplemented in the 1980s by the more recognisably Caribbean and Latin American imagery of the *cimarrón* (runaway slave) and the *palenque* (runaway slave community), particularly with the national organisation Cimarrón – which continues to be a relatively small affair, compared to the national indigenous organisation. The principal concern here was black identity and consciousness-raising among urban blacks. During the 1980s, the Church formed many 'peasant organisations' (as well as indigenous organisations) in the Pacific coastal area and these were mainly for local blacks. The chief concerns were land, farming and infrastructure, but black history and identity were also promoted by Church personnel – some of whom were members of Cimarrón. In the early 1990s, with constitutional reform going on, opening a forum for blacks and indigenous people to voice their concerns, black organisations multiplied and debates about race and class, culture and material factors (although less about gender) took place, dividing black groups. Cimarrón began to work with peasant associations, making class issues a more important part of its agenda, but still linking them to issues of black identity (Wade, 1995a).

Overall, the Colombian example indicates that land does not emerge on its own as an issue, but is always mediated by questions of identity and culture; this is partly because land is seen as a foundation for cultural identity. As French (2006: 353) says in relation to *quilombola* land claims in north-east Brazil, the temptation is to 'place the greatest emphasis on the land grant as instrumental in identity formation', but in fact, 'land should not overshadow the role of cultural forms and practices [especially assuming a black identity, linked to "Africa"] in the formation of new ethnoracial identities and self-identifications made possible by legal provisions'. The juggling of race/ethnicity and class thus goes on in a very practical way in all these regions, as concerns of land and identity overlap and interweave. Scholars analysing the process differ and some retain a basically Marxist approach against what they see as the abandonment of political economy by postmodernists, but even they accord cultural dimensions a good deal of autonomy (Kearney, 1996). Generally, however, the debate is now less about the primacy of race/ethnicity versus class and more about how they interact with each other – and with other dimensions of difference.

The Uros case and the Colombian material point to a dimension that has assumed particular importance recently in Latin America as a whole: 'territory' has taken over from 'land' as the key issue. Black communities in Colombia were insistent on defining 'collective territories', which were not just plots of land for subsistence purposes, but whole areas designed, in theory, to support a cultural way of life. Allowance had to be made for hunting, fishing, collection of forest materials and so on (Ng'weno, 2007b). Activists in the Proceso de Comunidades Negras, one of the main black organisations in Colombia, developed the concept of *territorios de vida* (territories of life) to describe a whole project of sustaining localities, a region, and cultural, ecological and social difference *vis-à-vis* the nation and global capitalism (Escobar, 2008: 25). This acquires particular significance in the face of the devastating violence that has afflicted the Pacific coastal region since the 1990s, displacing – deterritorialising – local Afro-Colombians (and indigenous people), destroying their life-ways and opening up the region to increasing capitalist penetration. Something similar can be seen in the establishment by the Zapatistas of autonomous municipalities, a policy declared by the EZLN in 1994 and which led to dozens of such municipalities being established – and subjected to harassment and intimidation by the state. Their purpose is to control health, education, land, housing and food locally, but also to promote indigenous languages and cultural traditions (Stephen, 2002).

Territory, Ecology and Biodiversity

Linked to questions of land and territories is the emergence of ecological concerns, which has shifted the balance away from the simple ownership of land towards the reproduction of the environment, seen as an integral aspect of the reproduction of cultural life-ways and identities (Blauert and Guidi, 1992; Collinson, 1996; Escobar, 2008). The demand for land by indigenous people, and indeed the ceding of land to indigenous communities by the state, often has the explicit aim of 'protecting the environment'. Fisher observes that the Kayapó of the Brazilian Amazon purvey the image of them as resisting the threat of environmental degradation because it is in their 'nature' to do so. In their case, however, this image is manipulated by them in their strategic engagement with the state aimed at obtaining resources, and they do not, according to Fisher, have an 'environmental consciousness' as such (1994: 229–30).

In Colombia, black movements based in the Pacific coastal region have developed complex positions in relation to 'political ecology', the politics of ecological distributions (Escobar, 2008: 6; see also Asher, 2009). In 1992, the Global Environment Facility (GEF) initiated Proyecto Biopacífico, a project for the conservation of biodiversity in the Colombian Pacific. This started as a conventional attempt to map and conserve biological resources, part of a global trend towards conserving biodiversity. As Escobar argues (2008: 105), it is possible to think in terms of a gradual shift from capitalist exploitation as simply destructive of the environment towards a situation in which, while destruction and degradation certainly continue and may predominate, there is an increasing awareness of the economic promise that biodiversity holds for the future: this can lead to a conservationist form of capitalism, often sponsored by NGOs, such as the United Nations (UN) or the World Bank (which funded GEF), and underwritten by nation-states. In the Proyecto Biopacífico, there was a concerted attempt to include and engage local black and indigenous communities, but, given the emphasis on conservation, there was a double risk. Either these people would be seen as a threat to biodiversity, if they engaged in practices seen as destructive, such as the logging and open-cast mining that many black communities were involved in, with the increasing use of mechanised technologies of extraction. Or they would be cast in the role of guardians of the environment, either 'naturally' disposed to be 'at one' with nature, in a global primitivist discourse of the 'noble savage' particularly deployed in relation to, and in some cases by, indigenous communities (Conklin and Graham, 1995; Ellen, 1986; Varese, 1996), or needing education and legal constraints to persuade them to use only non-destructive production practices.

By 1995, however, the increasing mobilisation of the black movement, and in particular the Proceso de Comunidades Negras (PCN), which were pushing forward land claims under Law 70 of 1993, was increasing pressure within the Proyecto Biopacífico to take black and indigenous community participation more seriously. The whole process of biodiversity conservation was recast as a mechanism for allowing these communities to appropriate and defend *espacios de vida* (life spaces) in which nature and culture, territory and identity, were intrinsically related. Local people became increasingly involved in the Proyecto itself in a way that, in Escobar's view, made it into a 'counterwork' aimed at creating an 'alternative modernity' (2008: 145–53, 185–97). Asher, while recognising the struggle of local black communities and the 'anti-institutional stance' of the PCN, is critical of the idea that a 'counterwork' was under construction. She emphasises that black movements and the state were both using similar discourses – of sustainability, biodiversity, participation, etc. – to 'construct their understandings of culture, nature and development'. Black resistance was thus 'at least partially shaped by the very discourses of political and economic modernity they opposed' (Asher, 2009: 20). By 2000, however, the Proyecto Biopacífico had been largely dismantled and its work passed on to a number of more mainstream institutes.

Whatever the fate of the Colombian project, the point is that ecological concerns have become integrated into black and indigenous social movements in ways that, as with the discourse of human rights, speak to a broad and transnational constituency. The interest of transnational corporations, especially the pharmaceutical and agro-industrial companies, in bioprospecting – biopiracy, as it seems to some – or in selling genetically modified crop seeds, has provoked resistance from various quarters, including from indigenous communities. For example, a US company patent on the Amazonian vine, *B. caapi*, used to make a hallucinogenic drink for shamanic purposes, was overturned in 1999 by an alliance of indigenous organisations and other campaigners (Hayden, 2003: 200).

The problem with harnessing ethnic social movements to these kinds of ecological concerns is that, while the alliance may prove very fruitful in some ways – including economically, as in the case of the Body Shop's contract with the Kayapó of Brazil for the supply of raw materials – it may also prove constraining (Conklin and Graham, 1995). Indigenous and black people may remain dependent, albeit on more socially conscious capitalist companies. More importantly, they may lock themselves into a role as the 'noble ecological savage', reinforcing widespread stereotypes and potentially closing off other kinds of opportunities. Black communities receiving land titles in the Colombian Pacific region, for example, are constrained to use only ecologically sustainable production practices. This may suit their purposes – indeed may even be an active choice – but it also implies a restriction on the community's autonomy to decide its own way forward, while other people in the same region may be using all kinds of non-sustainable practices. That is, the black and indigenous communities are the ones who get saddled with the tasks of ecological conservation.

Ethnicity, Race and Religion

Earlier on, I mentioned the important role of the Catholic Church in mediating the emergence of black and indigenous social movements. The Church has been active, for example, in educating black and indigenous people who become leaders; it has also started a large number of community organisations. Liberation theology was a vital inspiration for non-indigenous clergy to grasp and promote indigenous and black rights and identities; it also gave rise to a *teología india*, driven in part by indigenous clergy, which attempted to formulate a Christian theology that responded to indigenous perspectives (Brysk, 2000: 194; Cleary and Steigenga, 2004; Renard, 1994). Among the Guatemalan Q'echi', Catholicism provided in the past and still furnishes 'the organisational structure and discursive medium binding communities together in political action' (Wilson,

1995a: 307). In Chiapas, pastoral workers of the diocese of San Cristóbal de las Casas 'served as an ally in indigenous struggles for human rights', by introducing indigenous communities to the notion of human rights and facilitating the development of indigenous perspectives on rights (Kovic, 2008: 258). Norget (2004), however, takes a more cautious line, emphasising that relations between the Catholic Church and indigenous communities may also represent the persistence of a paternalist and authoritarian stance on the part of the clergy.

It is also the case that Protestant evangelical churches, which have had huge success among indigenous (and black) communities in Latin America, have been seen as having a double edge (Canessa, 2000). Often, evangelical movements are seen as opposed to indigenous movements, even if they both draw their clientele from the same ranks of society. They are often politically conservative and seen by indigenous activists as the religious face of Yankee imperialism. They tend to repress aspects of indigenous practices, as 'pagan' and 'sinful', which are generally seen as central to indigenous identity and culture (the consumption of alcohol, the chewing of coca, the ritual kinship of godparenthood); they encourage indigenous people to abandon these practices and embrace 'modern' behaviours, generally seen as 'Western'. They often cause severe dissension within indigenous communities. On the other hand, they have promoted education and provided the kind of social networks and resources that often sustain social movements; and they often have a radically egalitarian theology that inspires movements against inequalities and social injustice of any sort. In Ecuador in the 1980s, Protestantism 'reconstituted new spaces for cultural (re)production. Politically, the regional indigenous Evangelical organization emerged "as a representative of indigenous people before the state"' (Lucero, 2006: 37, citing Blanca Muratorio).

Given the importance of Afro-Brazilian religion in Brazil, it is not surprising that this has formed a focus of identification. There is a tremendous variety of religious practice from different types of Candomblé, involving worship of and possession of the devotee by African deities (who may be symbolically paired with Christian saints), through Umbanda, a more recent and eclectic religion combining elements of what may be termed *macumba* (similar to Candomblé, but also pejoratively used to mean 'witchcraft') and European spiritism, to Catholicism and varieties of evangelical Protestantism. There has been a good deal of debate about the political character of different groups and the extent to which they reinforce or challenge the status quo. Brown (1986), for example, argued that Umbanda groups generally reproduced relations of patronage and inequality, but Henfrey (1981) showed how, *within* working-class Candomblé in Bahía, subtle differences between groups in terms of religious practice and symbolism (conscious African orthodoxy about deities and 'serious' behaviour versus a more eclectic attitude to deities and a more 'fun' approach) fitted into different class relations (old-style proletariat working in paternalistic relations for white masters who patronised 'African-style' Candomblé versus new-style proletariat working in factories whose more eclectic religious activities were not controlled by this patronage). Therefore, religious symbolism and practice are open to a wide variety of interpretations and Brown's conclusions may have been largely due to the middle-class focus of her study (see also Ireland, 1992; Rostas and Droogers, 1993).

Thus, while the emergence of Umbanda may have involved the whitening of *macumba*, by removing certain elements seen as African and savage (Brown, 1986), when it is practised in a low-income settlement in Rio, where most people are black and brown, it can take on a much 'blacker' and working-class feel. Hale (1997) shows how white, middle-class Umbanda mediums, although they might become possessed by the spirit of a *preto velho* spirit (an old black slave), tended towards a more whitened version of Umbanda, with the *pretos velhos* as submissive figures, redeeming themselves spiritually through long suffering. The poorer, darker-skinned mediums adopted a more Africanised approach and their *pretos velhos* were physically battered old men and women, their bodies a mute denunciation of slavery and racism, their moral and spiritual redemption a kind of victory over white oppressors.

In Bahia, the religious panorama reinforces this sense that, while politics and religion are closely entangled, it is difficult to predict exactly how this will occur. Selka (2007) argues that the Catholic Church may promote black culture through its 'inculturated masses', which incorporate elements deemed black or African, but that many black activists in Bahia see the Church as essentially conservative. There is a strong symbolic connection between Candomblé and black identity. However, many Candomblé initiates are white, while only a minority are Afro-Brazilians and many of these are not active in the black movement. On the other hand, many black people participate in evangelical churches, many of which are politically conservative and avoid a critique of racism, while they are also well known for demonising Candomblé as a savage practice. But some evangelical movements adopt a more progressive approach, in which issues of race are addressed.

Even if race is not addressed directly, other effects can ensue. Burdick (1998), for example, reports that in Rio de Janeiro a Christian Base Community, drawing on liberation theology, had a light-skinned leadership and failed to disturb racism in its midst. In contrast, the Pentecostal Assembly of God, with its discourse of radical personal transformation, the spiritual empowerment of the humble and universal human equality, not only attracted many blacks and treated them equally, but placed some of them in positions of leadership, thus undermining racism, even if the matter was not necessarily discussed openly and there was 'a deep antagonism' between the organised black movement and the Pentecostal movement (1998: 147). Burdick found that many black evangelical women identified self-consciously as black and suggests that the evangelical emphasis on inner beauty helps black women to counter the powerful Brazilian aesthetic that values whiteness or a certain kind of exotic or highly sexed brownness (1998: 131, 147). Later, Burdick (2005: 316) found some 30 named Protestant groups dedicated to fighting racism and nurturing Afro-Brazilian identity. Their rise is partly due to the state's formal admission in 1995 that racism is a problem; to the conversion to evangelism of some black activists; to the theological support given by key evangelical leaders to anti-racism, often phrased as a matter of (divine) human rights; and to the participation in evangelical churches of a growing black middle class.

Just as participation in evangelical Christianity can have informal effects, Burdick (1998: ch. 5) says the same is true of popular Catholicism. Women who worship Anastácia – one of the slave figures who can possess Umbanda mediums, but who is also a popular Catholic icon – may be viewed by black activists as incompatible with the need to develop a strong, anti-racist political black identity, because Anastácia is depicted as light-skinned, blue-eyed, long-suffering and not rebellious. But the women develop an everyday sense of blackness, inspired by the story of Anastácia's suffering as a slave, her strength and fortitude in the face of racial abuse and her refusal to submit to her master's sexual predation. These women also develop practices – black beauty salons, informal conversation groups, small organisations, such as literacy schools – that have material effects in the social world.

In sum, to grasp the significance of religion to ethnic and racial mobilisations, it is important to abandon a simple split between 'culture' and 'politics'. Although religious movements are sometimes apparently at odds with organised political ethnic movements, they may coincide in a formal sense and, more importantly, they become entangled in less obvious, more everyday ways, for example, through nourishing a sense of self, of entitlement, of social justice and of the possibility of transformation. Religious practices also build social networks and senses of community that facilitate indigenous and black social movements.

Ethnicity, Race, Gender and Sexuality

Perhaps the most important departure from the race/ethnicity and class theme has been that involving gender and sexuality (Wade, 2009b). Only in the 1980s and 1990s did gender and sexuality really become an issue in studies of race and ethnicity in Latin America. It did not occur to, say, van den Berghe to ask whether being male or female made any difference to indigenous or *mestizo* identity in 1970s San Jerónimo, even though feminism was flowering in social science at the time. The way that women (although not necessarily gender inequality) did enter debates was mainly through studies of the family, particularly the black family. Women as well as men were also inevitably involved in discussions of race mixture, although it is striking how, for example, Mörner (1967) managed a history of race mixture which ignored the issue of gender inequality and sexism (cf. Powers, 2005; Smith, 1997).

In the 1980s and 1990s, gender emerged as an important axis of critical analysis for understanding colonialism, the nation and the transnational – all of which, as we have seen, are important contexts for race and ethnic identities. Gender and sexuality are not the same thing, but since gender difference is often seen in terms of sexual difference and since gender inequality often involves control over sexuality, the two are closely connected. This is perhaps most evident in relation to colonialism and race. As hooks says: 'Sexuality has always provided gendered metaphors for colonisation' (1991: 57). Colonisation, whether within or beyond national boundaries has often been seen as the male domination of feminised space, construed variously as wild, unruly, seductive, submissive or threatened. In colonial contexts, the boundaries of colonial domination have frequently been sexual boundaries as well, with important material and symbolic dimensions whether or not they were crossed (McClintock, 1995). And crossed they usually were, because, as Young says: 'Colonialism ... was not only a machine of war and administration, it was also a desiring machine' (1995: 98) – and the object of desire was the power of black sexuality. Hence: 'Sex is at the very heart of racism' (Hyam, 1990: 203; see also Nagel, 2003; Wade, 2009b).

Nationalism is 'constituted from the very beginning as a gendered discourse, and cannot be understood without a theory of gender power' (McClintock, 1993: 3). Nationalist discourses and practices call on women in various ways: as reproducers of biological offspring which swell the nation's population, as producers of cultural offspring who will know where they belong, as symbols of national boundaries and national identities, as participants in national struggles, and as workers in the national labour market (Anthias and Yuval-Davis, 1992: 115). They may be seen positively in any of these roles, but as Guy (1991) shows in her study of prostitution in Argentina, they may also be seen as a threat, polluting the nation with their sexuality.[8]

Gender has also been seen as vital to understanding the formation of diaspora and transnationalism. Early formulations of black nationalism in the Caribbean and the Americas – actually an intrinsically transnational phenomenon – have been seen as reflecting the patriarchal assumptions of the mainly male protagonists of the movements, such as Aimé Césaire, Frantz Fanon and Marcus Garvey, which were later contested by feminist writers (Stephens, 2005; Wright, 2004).

In relation to race and ethnicity in Latin America, a pioneering study of gender and race was first published in 1974, prefiguring the later interest in these issues. Martinez-Alier's study of colonial Cuba (1989) showed that upper-class men could have covert (or even overt informal) relations with women lower down the racial ranking without this threatening their status – even marriage was less dangerous – because their position as men allowed this. White women, in contrast, would dishonour themselves and their families, because their sexuality was seen as a male possession. Thus white dominance was effected in a crucial sense by white male control over white women, in terms of 'protecting' their sexuality and marriage choices, whether they liked it or not; and by white male control over black and brown women, in terms of having privileged access to their sexuality, again like it or not. Black and brown women could be mediators of social mobility in the sense that, whether they planned this or it was forced on them, having a sexual relationship with white(r) man could spell economic advantages for them and any resulting offspring. But the racial difference often meant an informal union which could label the woman, but not the man, as sexually immoral. Bastide (1961) recognised many of the same processes for contemporary Brazil, but he spoke about white men 'defending' white women's honour and thus glossed over gender inequality. Indeed, it was not until Martinez-Alier's preface to the second edition of her book that she wrote: 'In nineteenth-century Cuba the reproduction and reinforcement of class inequality [took place] through the interplay of racial discrimination and gender hierarchy' (1989: xv).

Following this cue, I argued in Chapter 5 that *mestizaje* is a gendered process which creates both racial inclusion and racial exclusion. As a stark example, one could look today at patterns of sexual tourism, in which mostly white men (and some women) from Europe and North America seek out brown-skinned Latin women and men (for both homosexual and heterosexual encounters). The gendered and racialised inequalities involved here show particularly clearly the reiteration of hierarchy through interracial sex, with inclusion being severely reduced, due to the commercial nature of the transaction. Even then, however, a sense of inclusion, partly fictive, is produced by the tendency of the sex tourists to repress the commercial aspect and think of the encounters as inclusive, voluntary and even desired by their partners. Some encounters do turn into longer-term connections, maintained precariously across the Caribbean or the Atlantic. The sex workers, for their part, may also build on their encounters to create spaces of autonomy and opportunity for themselves, leading in some cases to migration to North America or Europe (Brennan, 2004; Kempadoo, 1999; Wade, 2009b: 191–9).

The importance of gender for understanding racial and ethnic identities also arose in a different context: the formation of social movements. Here, the issue of gender emerged from the dissatisfaction of black feminists with, on the one hand, the patriarchal attitudes of black male activists (hooks, 1981) and, on the other, with the ethnocentrism of white feminists (Amos and Parmar, 1984; Carby, 1982). Feminism tended to use either a notion of patriarchy that opposed all men to all women as rather homogeneous categories sharing an essential interest, or a political economy approach that focused on the exploitation of women's labour in domestic and work contexts. All in all, existing approaches seemed to ignore that black women might have a particular perspective and position (Anthias and Yuval-Davis, 1992: ch. 4; Collins, 2000). For example, radical feminism had targeted rape as a male instrument for the oppression of women. But in the US the accusation of raping a white woman had typically prompted the lynching of black men, so its meaning was different for black women. Or again, Marxist-feminist explanations of women's low wages often pointed to the real or supposed dependence of women on men. But black (African-American and African-Caribbean) women in Britain and the US, while they still receive low wages, tend to be less dependent on a male wage than white women. Therefore, it would seem that racial discrimination is creating a specific problem for black women, who may deal with it partly through reciprocity within extended family networks that permits them to continue working full-time despite low wages. The answer to these analytical problems is to avoid reducing varied empirical situations to the determinations of one or two underlying factors (patriarchy, class), and instead to look at the intersection of various factors, assessing their relative roles in specific cases and the way in which they make new formations which are more than the sum of their respective parts (Collins, 2000; Crenshaw, 1991; Nash, 2008; Wade, 2009b: ch. 2).

An example of this intersection is in recent programmes that target the sexual health of young people. In Brazil and Colombia, sexual health clinics and campaigns focus on youth and to some extent class rather than race: they aim at influencing the sexual behaviour and health risks of young and vulnerable people. Their clientele may be *de facto* largely black and brown – as in Bahia – or it may be racially and culturally diverse – as in Bogotá – but this is not the subject of explicit comment: everyone is to be treated equally. Nevertheless, clinic staff tend to stereotype working-class, young black women (and men) as uncontrolled in their sexual behaviour – promiscuous, unwilling to use condoms, *machista* (the men), perhaps more likely to suffer from HIV/AIDS (Fry et al., 2007b; McCallum, 2008; Viveros, 2006). Race, class and gender work together here to construct an image of the irresponsible, young, black, uneducated woman, in which each aspect of the image reinforces the other to create a whole that is more than the sum of its parts – an image that is also deeply rooted in historical images of the black female as sexual victim and sexual temptress.

Because gender and sexuality are so integral to the construction of racial and ethnic identities, the movements that form around these identities are inevitably affected by this. Thus, for example, when one female black activist in Colombia was told by a black male colleague that it 'looked bad for a woman in her position' that she was going out with a non-black man, a whole tangled history of sexualised, racialised relations was conjured up. The idea that white men sexually exploited black women under slavery, that some black women had relations with ('sold themselves to') white(r) men to move themselves and their children up the social hierarchy, that black men did not have the same access to this channel of social mobility – all this was invoked in the implicit charge that this particular black women was betraying her 'race', betraying the racial solidarity that was expected of 'a woman in her position'. Here, to use Gilroy's words, 'racial sameness [was experienced] through particular definitions of gender and sexuality' (1993a: 85).

The intersection of race, sex and gender generates specific effects here. Any working-class person on an upward social trajectory might experience accusations of betrayal; in a country where most black people are poor, a black person has to contend with the visibility of his/her upward mobility and expectations of racial solidarity; a black woman has to cope with the weight of the particular history of white male sexual relations with black women. Although these are listed here in additive fashion, the net result is more than the simple sum of these factors: a whole complex imaginary of 'the black woman' takes on a life of its own. This imaginary can shape black women's movements themselves: some Afro-Latin women's organisations in Honduras, the Dominican Republic and Brazil promote and celebrate black culture in ways which cast black women as dancers, singers, performers, providers of food, often quite sexualised (Curiel, 2008; see also Wade, 2009b: 219).

The black social movement in Colombia also confronts the problem that ethnic-racial solidarity can gloss over problems of gender inequality and sexism within the movement. In the Pacific coastal region, women are active participants in local black social movements and in local development initiatives, promoted by the state and by NGOs (Asher, 2009; Wade, 1995). Asher argues that black women act in unpredictable and contradictory ways. They reproduce state and NGO agendas, acting in accordance with objectives of increasing female income-earning capacity (a gender-aware development objective) or claiming black land rights (an ethnic mobilisation objective). But they also undermine such agendas by introducing ethnic-racial dimensions into development agendas that tend to sideline issues of racism and structural inequality; and by introducing gender dimensions into ethnic agendas that tend to marginalise gender difference in pursuit of political solidarity (Asher, 2009: ch. 4).

Gender differences may also mean that black political mobilisation has to take different forms in different contexts. Black women and black men may well be located in urban labour markets in ways that are different from each other and from non-black women and men. Black women migrants from the Pacific coastal region to the big cities of Colombia tend to concentrate in domestic service, to a greater extent than non-black migrant women. This is due partly to the stereotype of black women as servants, which makes it hard for them to get jobs doing anything else. They can carry on with this work, even after they have children, partly by sending their children back to live in extended family networks in the Pacific coastal region (Wade, 1993a: 186–93). Thus 'black activism' in these cities consists partly of mobilising and defending the particular labour rights of these women. Black social movements are structured by both the gender and sexual aspects of black identity and experience.

For indigenous movements, the issue of gender is also of vital importance. It has been noted that indigenous women seem to be more 'traditional' than men and this seems to be because they have less contact with the urban or outside world. Marisol de la Cadena (1995) indicates how changing gender hierarchies create this phenomenon. In Chitapampa, near Cuzco, villagers distinguish each other as 'indigenous people' and '*mestizos*'. Even though they all seem like indigenous people to people from Cuzco, those who have more experience of urban environments and hold a dominant economic position in the community are '*mestizos*'. Most 'indigenous people' are women and this is partly because they have little experience of the type of urban work that helps to define a *mestizo*. This in turn is because, as land-holding has lost its material and ideological value, women have found themselves inheriting plots of land previously controlled by men who are more interested in commerce and urban work. Women work these plots in order to underwrite men's urban ventures, supplying a rural safety net. Hence 'household strategies of survival confine women to the ideological sphere of rural Indianness' (1995: 337). Many women do begin to move away from a 'traditional' indigenous identity in the village, marketing produce in Cuzco, or working as domestic servants, but this work is still seen as inferior to men's work. Although this is only one case, it indicates that if part of the perceived inferiority of indigenousness is linked in a self-reinforcing cycle to the perceived inferiority of women, then mobilising around indigenousness will have to address issues of gender inequality at the same time as those of ethnic inequality.

In Ecuador, there are real difficulties around balancing race and gender (Radcliffe, 2008). Indigenous female leaders often foreground their status as indigenous over their status as women; yet they suffer sexism on the part of indigenous men, often in their own families, who may become jealous, accuse them of sexual promiscuity and beat them when they travel alone or with other men as part of their leadership duties. Their sexuality and honour is still seen to be under male control. Meanwhile, in state-run programmes aimed at reproductive health, indigenous women are doubly marginalised, either seen as a sideline to gender-aware development programmes, or as the junior partner to indigenous men in programmes directed at the nation's ethnic diversity. Indigenous women end up figuring as reproducers of ethnic boundaries, when they may conceive of themselves not only in relation to indigenous communities, but also as national citizens actively engaging with the concept of the nation and thereby challenging the dominant definitions of them as subordinate reproducers, on which both nationalist and indigenous movement ideologies seem to agree (Canessa, 2005).

In sum, gender and sex have figured in several ways in the study of race and ethnicity in Latin America: *mestizaje*, and the inclusions and exclusions that it orchestrates, is a powerfully gendered process: its effects operate partly through this gendering. The black and indigenous movements that contest the exclusions of *mestizaje* also contend with this gendering and the masculinism that casts black and indigenous women as subordinates, bearers of ethnic identity and ethnic offspring.

OFFICIAL MULTICULTURALISM

As we have seen, many states in Latin America have passed new legislation – including constitutions – that recognise multicultural-ity or special rights for ethnic groups: for example, Bolivia (1994), Brazil (1988), Colombia (1991), Ecuador (1998), Mexico (1992), Nicaragua (1986), Paraguay (1992), Peru (1993) and Venezuela (1999) (Sieder, 2002; Van Cott, 2000). There is an official acceptance of postmodern celebrations of diversity – what one might call a postmodern nationalism that defines the nation in terms of its mul-ticulturality, rather than an ideally homogeneous culture.

However, in making an assessment of these apparently radical changes, it is necessary to grasp that such strategies often seem to obey motives of political control, and this indicates that these new trends are still subject to the play of power and resources that were so important to the dependency and Marxist perspectives of the preceding decades. In that sense, postmodern nationalism is not a radical rupture with previous social relations: there are strong continuities with the past. In addition, there is not such a complete break between ideologies of *mestizaje* and multiculturalism as may appear at first sight. Insofar as the image of the *mestizo* nation generally made room for a highly controlled and often marginalised sort of blackness and indigenousness, there are continuities with an official multiculturalism that also seeks to control diversity. In Asad's words: 'To secure its unity – to make its own history – dominant power has worked best through differentiating and classifying practices' (1993: 17). Let us look at a couple of examples.

In the Nicaraguan case, referred to above, the Sandinista government passed the 1986 Law on Autonomous Regions of the Atlantic Coast which gave a good deal of local power to various groups there and instituted bilingual and bicultural education programmes. But Scherrer (1994: 121–2) noted that the way the law was drafted meant that in the early 1990s there was 'continuous usurpation of control over eastern Nicaragua's resources and over the budgets of the regional governments by central authorities'. Under the Chamorro government, which succeeded the Sandinistas, black creoles were 'unable to advance either regional or ethnic rights' due to recalcitrance on the part of the central state (Freeland, 1995: 190) and they resented the encroachment onto the local job market of *mestizos* and other outsiders foisted on them by the central government (Gordon, 1998). As we have seen, Hooker (2009) contends that the whole policy of recognising ethnic and racial minority rights has been undermined by a refusal to address basic issues of racial inequality.

In Colombia, the state has historically been rather weak, especially in peripheral areas of the country. Indigenous organisation, which began as a 'peasant' struggle for land and became a self-consciously indigenous one, has been a thorn in the side of the state and landowners since the 1970s. Indigenous people also participated in armed guerrilla insurrection in the form of the Quintín Lame movement. At different times, the state attempted to repress indigenous people and co-opt them, and as part of the latter tactic, land grants were made, creating *resguardos* or reserves. The 1991 constitution – in the drafting of which indigenous organisations played a significant role, even though reform was more part of the demobilisation of (non-indigenous) guerrilla groups than co-opting indigenous groups – gave important land and cultural rights to indigenous ethnic groups; more limited land rights were outlined for black communities, mainly in the Pacific coastal region, plus some rights for blacks in general

(Rappaport and Dover, 1996; Van Cott, 2000: ch. 4; Wade, 2002b). As of 2005, this has resulted in the indigenous population (3.4 per cent of the total) owning 710 reserves, amounting to 30 per cent of the country's land surface. Black community collective land titles, as of 2005, numbered 132, representing about 4 per cent of the national territory (DANE, 2006).

As in the Nicaraguan case, real progress has been made in terms of raising the public profile of indigenous and black people and granting an official space to them, but again, there are limitations – more severe in a country where violence rules. Gros writes of the state's 'desire to instrumentalise an ethnic identity with the aim of negotiating its articulation with the dominant society' and a 'desire for modernisation and integration' (1994: 61, my translation). More to the point, for all the concessions they have on paper, indigenous people now march for the 'right to life', as well as the right to land, because their leaders are being displaced, terrorised and sometimes murdered by a combination of the army and paramilitary death squads, a pattern that continues despite the state's attempt to demobilise paramilitary forces (Sanford, 2004). Meanwhile, in the Pacific coastal region, 'development' proceeds regardless, with plans for roads and ports as well as colonisation on a more individual basis, alongside displacement, terrorisation and killing. This kind of violence and displacement – which seem intrinsically linked to processes of 'development' – appears to have the remarkably strategic effect of clearing large areas of land, which are then available for the expansion of existing capitalist operations of shrimp-farming and African palm cultivation in the region (Escobar, 2008; Oslender, 2008). In this context, the protections and opportunities of Law 70 and official multicultural-ism seem very weak.

An interesting aspect of the Colombian case, which is evident elsewhere, is the participation of indigenous and black leaders in formal electoral politics. Constitutional reform resulted, in December 1992, in three indigenous delegates being elected to Senate by a special indigenous constituency. Other indigenous leaders have also formed political parties, such as ASI (Alianza Social Indígena), which does not limit its support to indigenous candidates alone. Black communities were only allowed to elect delegates to the Chamber of Representatives. In Ecuador in 1996, Luís Macas, the president of CONAIE (Confederación de Nacionalidades Indígenas del Ecuador) gained a seat as a Deputy in the National Congress and in 2003 he ran, unsuccessfully, for President. He saw his participation as a historic break with traditional politics, representing a truly grass-roots-driven democratic change and bringing together workers, Afro-Ecuadorians, women, youth, human rights workers and grassroots Christian communities.[9] In Bolivia, the first indigenous president in Latin America, Evo Morales, was elected in 2005, bringing to power his party Movimiento al Socialismo (MAS), which despite its class-inflected name, has a strong indigenous base and combines ethnic and class issues in its agenda.

The impact of this political participation is not entirely clear as yet, but so far it seems from Colombia's experience that the enthusiasm of Macas and the rejoicings that followed Morales' election may need to be tempered a good deal. The process of co-option into the machine of 'politics as normal' is a powerful danger as indigenous senators and representatives get sucked into the power play of dispensing patronage in exchange for votes. There is also the related threat of fragmentation as factions divide over control of votes and resources and over alliances with mainstream political parties (Agudelo, 2005). Indigenous leaders in Colombia, soon after the election of indigenous senators, talked of 'ethnicity getting out of control', as various indigenous groups manoeuvred for power.[10] By 2000, Colombia's indigenous movement was 'struggling to harmonise three competing social movement models': grassroots networks, national lobbying organisations and indigenous political parties (Van Cott, 2000: 102). Perhaps most importantly, although these political leaders act as a powerful antidote to standard images of blacks and indigenous people, they are often rather isolated in government and have little effective power. This has been particularly the case for Colombia's black delegates in the Chamber of Repre-sentatives, who have been able to achieve little. The outstanding exception to this is, of course, Morales and his MAS party, on which more, below.

The idea that official multiculturalism is really all about political control and governance in an era of political democratisation and changing notions of citizenship underlies the influential concept of 'neoliberal multiculturalism', associated with Charles Hale (2002, 2005, 2006). He argues that neoliberal reforms – both economic policies that open markets, reduce state intervention and foster individual consumption, and political reforms that privilege the individual citizen and undercut collectivities and communities – are not necessarily as incompatible with collective identities as it may appear. On the contrary, neoliberalism also involves a cultural project, which fosters a controllable form of multiculturalism, sponsoring diversity and collective identities, as long as these remain within certain bounds – what Hale (2005: 24) calls the '*indio permitido*' (the permissible indian). Indeed, multiculturalism in this mode 'can be used purposely to thwart the sovereign status of indigenous nations' (Arnold, 2008: 170).

It is indeed possible to see how multiculturalism suits state projects of governance. Multiculturalist policies actively produce and manage blackness and indigenousness, bringing ethnic communities into direct relationship with the state (for example, via land reform agencies and a variety of other state departments, such as those for planning, statistics, culture, etc.), bureaucratising them and instituting them as collective citizens, charged with administering themselves under the aegis of the state. In Colombia, for example, black communities in the Pacific region had to organise themselves in a form amenable to the state's agencies in order to make a land claim. Communities that had little contact with the state, except at the very local level or at most regional levels were suddenly drawn into direct relationships with central state agencies, as well as a variety of other actors, such as NGOs (Hoffmann, 2004; Ng'weno, 2007b). In the context of state plans to open up the Pacific coastal region to development – and yet also preserve biodiversity there – one can see how it made sense to recognise and formalise some communities in a controlled way.

Yet it is too simple to see multiculturalism as only about state agendas of governance. Escobar (2008: 209–16) argues for Colombia that this obscures the real impact of the social movements, which fought long and hard for recognition and rights and which took an active role in negotiating the detail of the policies that emerged. Also 'the state' is not a coherent entity and its different instances may operate in contradictory ways: the agencies charged with issuing collective land titles and conserving biodiversity are not the same as the arms of the state that send the army in to flush out 'subversives' or 'narco-terrorists', or that support the paramilitaries who act as the proxies of the state to the same ends. So it can be misleading to think in terms of the agenda of 'the state'.

In addition, it is more productive to see multiculturalism as a terrain of struggle and contestation. Speed (2005) argues that, for Mexico, the ideology of multiculturalism can be controlling, when in the hands of state agents, but more progressive and empowering when in the hands of groups, such as the Zapatistas, which challenge state projects of neoliberal development. In Bolivia, too, indigenous and working-class people react to neoliberal multiculturalism in varied and unpredictable ways. They take advantage of the openings offered by Bolivia's Law of Popular Participation (LPP, 1994), which made indigenous peoples significant actors in political processes, and they assume some of the rationalities of neoliberalism, such as the duty of citizenly participation, in order to 'pose challenges to the workings of global capitalism' (Postero, 2007: 17). For example, local groups formed under the aegis of the LPP were a key force in the protests and uprisings against neoliberal projects to privatise water and gas that ultimately led to the installation of Evo Morales.

Morales himself and his party have clearly had to make some compromises in taking the reins of power. The coca leaf, formerly a key symbol for the coca-growers and their unions, which formed an important MAS power base, has had to be downplayed a bit in the context of the US 'war on drugs', despite Morales' promises to legalise the leaf. Although the vigorous eradication policies of the pre-Morales era have been relaxed, there are still some restrictions imposed on the coca-growers and some areas previously free of eradication have been subjected to it under Morales (Grisaffi, 2009: 110–11, 237). The radical ideas about educational reform espoused by Félix Patzi Paco, who became minister of education under Morales, quickly became bogged down in practical conflicts with the Church and teachers (Arnold, 2008: 173).

Another 'problem' is the increasing regional divisions within the country, with the eastern, lowland regions – whiter, wealthier and less indigenous, and also home to important economic resources – resisting Morales' policies and threatening regional secession. This may not be a problem from the perspective that sees such a reaction as the inevitable backlash caused by subaltern groups taking power; but it has the power to undermine the national project of the MAS government. Still, there can be no doubt that grassroots democracy and indigenous rights and identity have received a massive boost from the election of Morales (Postero, 2007: 230).

The operation of grassroots democracy among street trader unions in Bolivia – which are *de facto* indigenous organisations – involves the adaptation of traditional indigenous practices of consensus (which does not mean non-conflictive) politics to the urban union context. The increasing entry of indigenous actors into politics at all levels, which has been a corollary of official multiculturalism and the rise of indigenous political power as a national force, with Morales and MAS, has provided new means by which identities that are both indigenous and working class at the same time can claim rights and defend livelihoods (Lazar,

2008: ch. 8). This means that multiculturalist policies, whatever their strategic intention, worked at a very local, grassroots level to foment democratic practices – which were traditional, but also new in the context of urban unions – and that these in turn fostered the political structures and identities that helped bring about a very significant shift in power structures in the country.

Some scholars also argue that the very provision of legal instruments that multiculturalist reform often entails provides subordinate groups with new tools with which to gain ground in what is still a struggle with the state, albeit a complex and multifaceted struggle: there is an ongoing process of the judicialisation of ethnic politics, which allows black and indigenous communities and movements to gain some ground (Sieder et al., 2005). As mentioned briefly above, in Colombia, a 1996 Constitutional Court decision overrode the Supreme Court and recognised a 'black community' as existing in the city of Santa Marta, on the Caribbean coast: this was a result of a black activist organisation deploying specific legal instruments at their disposal, while also invoking the broad recognition given to black communities in Law 70 of 1993 (Wade, 2002b). This decision, indeed, invoked a conception of blackness as an encompassing racial category, which merited affirmative actions in recompense for historical racism: such a vision undermined the spirit of Law 70, which conceived of blackness as something confined to specific rural communities in the Pacific region (Ng'weno, 2007a). At the same time, individual citizens make use of the *tutela* (a legal instrument for claiming redress for the abuse of a citizen's constitutional rights) to bring cases of racial discrimination to court – for example, alleging exclusion from a night club on racial grounds (Meertens, 2009). As I mentioned earlier, there has been a shift in Colombia towards a concern with racism as it affects all Afro-Colombians (and indigenous people), not just those who live in the Pacific region: in part this is because black and indigenous movements have been able to build on the legal footholds provided by earlier legislation, which did not really address racism.

One of the most controversial attempts to provide individual citizens with special legal rights based on racial or ethnic status has been the affirmative action programmes in Brazil aimed at increasing the participation of Afro-Brazilian students in higher education (Htun, 2004; Schwartzman, 2009). This has been done by means of admissions quotas for these students in some federal universities, a measure which provoked a storm of controversy. The details are complex, but they boil down to two central debates, which are worth reviewing as they raise issues of general relevance to black and indigenous movements.

First, there is the general question of whether a society based on liberal principles of equality should allocate special rights to certain kinds of individuals or groups (Barry, 2000; Modood, 2007; Young, 1990). This is clearly an ethical issue that frames the entire shift towards multiculturalism in Latin America and elsewhere, but it arises with particular force in the case of quotas, because specific individuals see themselves as being included in a competitive system (university entrance) based on intellectual merit not, or not only, because of their merit but because of their colour or race. Conversely, other individuals see themselves as being excluded from the system, despite their merit, because they have been usurped by others who are at an advantage because of their colour or race. While other affirmative action measures – such as land grants to ethnic groups – can provoke the same kind of questions, in the sense that more land for indigenous people means less land for others, quotas present the dilemma in a forceful way. The larger ethical issue behind quotas addresses the questions of whether affirmative actions are necessary to compensate for past discriminations; whether the departure from egalitarian principles of meritocracy is ethically justifiable because it will lead to a fairer society in the longer term; whether the measures will create greater racial divisions, when the end goal is said to be the elimination of such divisions; whether the measure will create not just more racial divisions, but also more racism, when the aim is to get rid of racism; whether it would be better to address wider issues of social inequality for everyone, irrespective of race and ethnicity.

Second, there is the more specifically Brazilian question of whether affirmative actions is right for a country in which race mixture has been a foundation of national identity. This debate addresses the question of how one is to know who is 'black', and thus a legitimate beneficiary of the actions, when there is such ambiguity of racial identification in the country. In one case, two brothers applied for a quota place and one was admitted as black, while the other was denied a place. The issue also raises the question of whether these measures are in fact a US-style import, which will create US-style racial politics in a country that has traditionally not had them; whether this is seen as a good or bad thing is, of course, a matter for debate as well (Fry et al., 2007a).

My own view is that affirmative action is conflictive but worthwhile. It can have valuable transformative effects by, for example, changing the racial profile of entire university courses – such as law or medicine – at a stroke and creating new atmospheres in universities. The black students who benefit from the quotas are launched on to a social trajectory that they might otherwise not have been able to achieve. The quotas force a public debate on race in a country where open discussion of the issue is rather rare. The affirmative actions in Colombia, although not quota-based, have had a similar effect in raising the public awareness of racism. This is valuable because, as the case of Cuba shows us, to tackle social inequality in a race-blind way, while it has very important positive consequences for the poor, black population, does not resolve issues of racism. In Cuba these never went away, despite government rhetoric, and indeed have re-emerged in the context of economic crisis of the 'special period' (after the collapse of Soviet Union support), the privatisation of parts of the economy and the increasing importance of the tourist trade, which tends to favour non-blacks or cast Afro-Cubans in specific roles such as sex workers and performers of Afro-Cuban culture (Cabezas, 2006; de la Fuente, 2001; Hagedorn, 2001).

There are significant downsides to affirmative actions, of course. Beneficiaries of black quota places in universities may feel stigmatised, feeling they were admitted 'unfairly'; indeed, many such students in Rio preferred to apply via the parallel system of quotas for public school – that is poor, students – in order to avoid this stigma (Cicalò, 2008). Also, dynamics of racial segregation may continue to play themselves out within the classroom itself.[11] Yet in terms of promoting social mobility among a specific sector of the population, affirmative action seems a worthwhile move in the medium term. And fears that the system will lead to a racial polarisation, in which 'blacks' and 'whites' face off against each other, seem exaggerated in view of the persistence of typically Brazilian ambiguity about racial classification in everyday student life (Schwartzman, 2009).

Overall, the point is that the provision of legal measures such as quotas can lead to effects that, while not simple or an unalloyed good, may be productive of positive change.[12] It may well be that affirmative actions that avoid the apparent 'unfairness' of quotas work better. Directing resources and opportunities towards specific sectors of the population, deemed deserving, is an established tactic: it has not been uncommon in a number of Western countries to give special benefits for demobilised soldiers returning after a major conflict. But this can be done in a way that does not blatantly exclude identifiable individuals from particular opportunities. In Colombia, Afro-Colombian students can access special bursaries for university places, but this way of doing things *looks* less exclusive of other non-black students than a quota system does.

In societies based on principles of equality of citizens, there will always be a tension between sameness and difference. People want equality of opportunity, but realise that this is denied them by racism, sexism, heterosexism, ageism, nationalism and so on, which target the differences that people want to enact and live out. It does not work to plough on regardless of difference, as if blindness to it neutralises discriminations based on it. On the other hand, insistent attention to difference can fragment society and produce what Gilroy (2000) calls 'camp thinking', splitting people up into segregated camps. It is therefore a question of fighting oppressions based on difference – and this means making normative judgements about what oppression consists of – but simultaneously being alive to possible alliances across, and mediations of, differences, as seen in the linking of black and indigenous social movements that I have documented in this chapter.

CONCLUSION

This and the previous chapters have covered a wide variety of issues and this is indicative of the direction the study of racial and ethnic identities is going. My intention has not been to give a comprehensive review, but to indicate the kinds of approaches and issues that have been adopted by scholars of race and ethnicity in Latin America in recent years. No longer is it just a question of race *versus* class, or ethnicity and internal colonialism – although these basic issues have not gone away by any means and the issues of political economy and class that they imply are addressed now through a focus on neoliberalism and globalisation. Now racial and ethnic identities must also be seen in transnational and national contexts, as shifting, decentred, relational constructions, subject to a politics of identity, culture and difference that is entangled with class, gender, sexuality, religion, and idioms of human rights, democracy and citizenship. These identities and the movements that form around them are seen as being shaped, not in simple oppositions between dominant and subaltern sectors, but in complex networks of relationships and mediations, involving a host of different actors. In this unstable world, I wish to sound two notes of warning. The first is to do with resistance, the second with relationality and cultural continuity.

Imagining resistance

With the emergence of black and indigenous social movements, resistance has become a buzzword in anthropology and cultural studies. Interest in resistance goes back a long way, especially with Marxist perspectives on exploitation, but today, in keeping with the importance of investigating cultural politics, it has a broader meaning. It is no longer simply a question of organised political protest or even spontaneous but explicit protest. Gramscian concepts of hegemony posited that people might be persuaded to collude in their own domination, although not entirely: resistance thus became harder to pin down (Smith, 2007). Foucault emphasised the connection of knowing to power and the ability of power to construct people as subjects, rather than just govern them. Power was, in his view, pervasive, rather than just concentrated in the hands of governors. Therefore, resistance could be found wherever power operates. The influence of this approach, combined with the impact of postcolonial subaltern studies has encouraged scholars to discover resistance – 'everyday resistance' – in many activities not previously associated with this (see Abu-Lughod, 1990; Gledhill, 2000: 80–93; Mitchell, 1990; Scott, 1985; Smith, 1999: ch. 3). Any behaviour that seems not to fit in with dominant definitions of what is right and proper can be termed resistance and given political significance. The problem with this is that resistance becomes virtually independent of the intentions not only of the resistors, who may not think of things in this way, but also of the perceptions of the oppressors: if no one except the analyst can detect the resistance, then it is hard to see what real political or even academic significance it has.

This is tricky ground, because to demand conscious awareness of resistance is to ignore the subtleties of the exercise of power that Foucault was precisely trying to uncover. Perhaps we can take our lead from Foucault himself who used to give parts of his work on the history of Western notions of discipline and punishment to French prisoners with the idea of promoting their own resistance. My point is that the acid test of relevance may be the reaction of the people studied to the information constructed by the observer about their resistance. If there is no recognition, either spontaneous or emergent, then perhaps the resistance is only in the imagination of the academic. This raises the difficult question of the political relation between the observer and the observed, and this I will tackle in the next chapter.

Relational identities

I have shown how over several decades the concept of identity has become more fluid and flexible. There are those, however, who question whether a completely relational approach over-emphasises this fluidity at the expense of real historical continuities. This is not a question of denying relationality and returning to a pre-Barthian primordialist approach to ethnicity and identity; it is simply a challenge to the idea that identity is simply a matter of a boundary constituted by difference and that the cultural and material stuff invoked by identities is irrelevant. Focusing on the cultural stuff of identity, however, can lead to essentialism – the idea that a given identity is fundamentally defined by a particular set of cultural traits. The problem, as Wilson puts it for ethnic identities, is 'how to trace the history of the cultural dimension of ethnicity without relapsing into essentialism' (1995a: 10). The answer in his view – and my own – is supplied by Comaroff and Comaroff: the aim is to show how essences are constructed, 'how realities become real, how essences become essential' (1992: 20, cited by Wilson, 1995a: 10). For example, in Chapter 5's section about the power of blacks and indigenous people, it is clear that the cultural stuff about the sexuality of blacks constitutes what Gilroy – who is concerned with the same problem – calls a 'changing same' (1993a: 101), that is, a cultural complex that varies over time, but that shows real historical continuities that are relevant in the construction of relational identities (see also Wade, 2006b; Eriksen, 1991; Sahlins, 1999).

Of course, one of the features of new social movements is that they often take their own identity and their own culture very seriously. In fact, they may have a rather essentialist view of their own culture which, according to them, traces its roots continuously back through history and has an inner core which defines their identity. Now, those scholars with doubts about a radically relational approach to ethnic identity, which casts it as endlessly fluid, would doubtless be sympathetic to historical continuities which temper that fluidity. But this is subject to research, rather than imagination: scholars want to find evidence of the continuities, rather than just invoke them. Thus, as an observer, one can find oneself at odds with the people whose history and identity one is representing: they are not necessarily interested in showing how their essence became essential, but in rallying around that essence. If an anthropologist or historian shows that this essence is actually a rather variable thing, or does not have the characteristics it is supposed to have – in short, deconstructs it – then s/he may find him or herself at odds with the people to whom such an essentialism may be an important basis for their identity. This, again, raises the question of the political relation between observer and observed and it is to this that I now turn.

7
Studying Race and Ethnicity in a Postcolonial and Reflexive World

Postmodernist and postcolonial approaches, and perspectives that highlight transnational, diasporic and multilateral movements and exchanges, have made a great impact and have involved important challenges to the claims scholars – and especially Western scholars – can make to authoritative certainty, especially on behalf of others (including black and indigenous people in Latin America). They have also emphasised the tendencies that already existed to see racial and ethnic identities as relational and shifting, rather than as reified objects. But with the insistence on relationality and the abandonment of metanarratives came a strong measure of relativism and, at times, too great an emphasis on the process by which one person (usually the academic) represents another. This led away from the invigorating attention to broad political and economic inequalities that was emblematic of the 1970s towards a more fragmented analysis that, while full of attention to power, tended to focus on the politics of poetics and representation (for example, the politics of how texts are constructed and people represented in them – see, for example, Beverley, 1999), on the constant shiftings of cultural constructions and identities and on the micro-politics of the resistance detected – at times somewhat arbitrarily – in everyday behaviour. The politics of identity cannot be ignored – partly because it is important to black and indigenous people in Latin America – but too exclusive a concentration on it seemed to lead to an over-privileging of matters of discourse and representation, with issues of political economy (that is, how the product of society is created and distributed within it) being overwhelmed, despite their over-riding importance for the many people who occupy a subordinate position in global and national society.

It should be obvious from my presentation in the preceding chapter that a recognition of the flexibility of racial and ethnic identities, and of the importance of various dimensions of difference does not necessarily lead away from central concerns with land, environment and power over resources: these remained important to most of the studies I cited from the 1990s. In more recent years, too, as I traced in Chapters 5 and 6, there has been a welcome shift towards issues around transnational networks, the impacts of neoliberalism, regimes and practices of citizenship, the reform of judicial and constitutional orders, violence and human rights – in short, a shift towards politics and economics – that has corrected previous bias towards discourse and representation. But the trick is to retain both emphases and this has been a central theme of this book. This is not a question of combining 'culture' and 'economics'. These are not two separate realms that need to be balanced or combined; they are inseparable in that economics and politics and social life in general are lived *through* the medium of culture (Wade, 1999). It is a question of seeing economics, politics, race, ethnicity and gender as mutually influencing each other, rather than privileging one or two of these as determinative.

The early functionalist studies took social life seriously as an integrated whole – religion was as important as economics in constituting the 'identity' of the people concerned (although that word was not used) – but they assumed that each society was a neat whole and failed to question how communities (and identities) were constituted relationally; such relations were only really dealt with in terms of an imagined progression towards modernity. The UNESCO studies of race in Brazil and the later dependency and Marxist-oriented studies of the 1970s gave a good and necessary grip on the economics and politics of inequality – and, because capitalism was such a central focus, they did so in a way that vitally opened up the global and historical dimensions of inequality. But these studies subordinated race and ethnicity to class, as if race was super-structural 'culture', while class was infrastructural 'economics'. The mistake of subordinating race and ethnicity to class was a result of the mistake of equating race/ethnicity with culture and class with economics, as if race, ethnicity and class were not all lived through culture. Marxist approaches typically failed to see that capitalist economics are constituted through culture, not overlain by it.

Postmodernist and postcolonial approaches helped here in that, for example, power is understood as constituted through discourse, rather than discourse simply being a representation of power, but this central insight sometimes became submerged in, ironically, an over-emphasis on representation since, in practice, this becomes the images and texts through which discourse is most easily studied by academics. At the same time, the idea that discourses (and hence cultures) can be invented and that all culture is subject to constant reinvention is a useful insight into the flexibility of culture, but comes dangerously close to denying real historical continuities (Sahlins, 1993). The point is then to keep in view the basic concerns that racial and ethnic identities are involved with – resources, power, livelihood, autonomy and interdependence, knowledge of oneself and others, a sense of the past and the future – to see how these concerns are culturally constituted in a historical process and in relation to differences of power.

In recent years, in anthropology and more widely, there has been increased interest in the lived materiality of the world – in part, a reaction to previous emphases on discourse. There is an interest in phenomenology (the lived experience of being in the world), in embodiment (the lived experience of being, rather than having, a body) and in the material objects and environments which surround us. This has been spurred in part by trends in science studies, derived from actor-network theory (or material semiotics, as it is sometimes known) that paid attention to the role that physical objects play in the networks that link people. It has also derived from a growing interest across the humanities in ethnography, as a method that allows insight into the everyday, lived, embodied practices of people. Perspectives that emphasise lived materiality have yet to have a major impact on research into race and ethnicity in Latin America – although Escobar (2008) shows the influence of science studies and phenomenology, while Wade (2000) and Chasteen (2004) both address dance in a way that shows an interest in embodiment, as does some of the work on race and beauty (for example, Moreno Figueroa, 2008). But something of a concern with material, everyday practices comes through in the ethnographic attention given by Lazar (2008) to grassroots practices of democracy in union meetings in Bolivia or by French (2009) to the way legal categories and processes operate in the concrete everydayness of particular cultural settings – to cite just two examples.

In getting the balance between different approaches, it may help to give an example from my own work on blacks in Colombia. The small-scale study (after the functionalist style) of black communities is necessary to understand how they operate internally and to grasp the cultural modes through which their inhabitants live their lives. But it is not enough on its own. It is also fundamental to study (after the political economist's style) how black slaves underwrote the colonial economy, how blacks today act as labour in the cities and in rural areas, and how the regions they inhabit act as 'internal colonies'; this permits us to grasp how they are located in the long-term distribution of power and resources (that is, dimensions of racial inequality). But this only tells half the story, seeing blackness as laid over by, or derivative of this underlying history. A postmodernist approach shows how blackness has been constructed discursively in different, changing ways by different sets of people (for example, whites, blacks, women, men), and how discourse involves power relations. But the danger lies in submerging oneself in discourse alone and the politics of competing representations. Black culture becomes subject to constant reinvention and negotiation, and one loses sight of historical continuities.

The aim, then, is to see – and this can only be done through ethnographic fieldwork – that the discursive construct of blackness is constantly recreated in social and material practices of colonisation and migration, of displacement and violence, of development plans and political processes of constitutional and legal reform, of sex and marriage, of music, dance and sport, of the consumption of transnational images of blackness. The aim is to see that blackness, whiteness and mixedness (and indigenousness) are values in their own right that form goals and enter into people's social interactions; that they are connected to, but not simply derivative of, issues of economics and politics; and that historical continuity is constituted through constant change, as the same kinds of relations and expressions are remade with ever-changing cultural resources (Sahlins, 1993).

To give just one concrete and specific example: the image that black people are 'naturally' good at dancing is long-standing and widespread, and can be subjected to a postmodern and postcolonial critique about how (racist) representation and discourse constructs this image. But ethnographic attention to the practice of dance, and its material embodiedness, reveals how that image enters into the self-conception of many black people in Colombia, who embrace the image and embody it, and how it has the power to shape social interactions and define social spaces so that whether and how you dance becomes part of a process of the formation and enactment of identity (Wade, 2000).

In sum, it is not a question of returning to pre-postmodernist perspectives, but of encompassing the useful insights of postmodernist perspectives while avoiding a headlong rush into the arms of total relativism, into the endlessly shifting sands of a radical cultural constructionism that undoes historical continuity, or into the realms where discourse ceases to be a social practice that engages people in a real world.

BEING REFLEXIVE

The foregoing discussion deals with a problem of balance. A different problem of balance, which has been raised forcefully by postmodernist and postcolonial critiques, is that between the person carrying out a study and those s/he is studying.

One of the features of a postmodern and globalising world has been the increasing reflexivity of social life. This is the way that society 'feeds back' on itself so that changes produced in one place spread quickly in a global fashion. Specifically, it includes the way knowledge produced by specialists or 'experts' feeds back into the contexts from which they derived that knowledge. Thus, for example, sociological theories about marriage or political behaviour inform – usually via the media – people's decisions about how to behave in those domains. This means that social 'scientists' can hardly hope to arrive at law-like generalisations about human behaviour, since their generalisations change the thing they were generalising about (Giddens, 1990). It also means that their studying and theorising can have important political effects. In the study of blacks and indigenous people, it involves the fact that the people being studied are increasingly able to access, evaluate and be influenced (or not) by the work produced about them. Radio and television are pervasive and, for example, Kayapó indigenous people in Brazilian Amazonia both view and make films about themselves (Turner, 1992). More than a few black and indigenous leaders in Latin America have studied anthropology and ethnolinguistics and, for example: 'Guatemalan Maya intellectuals and professionals ... have begun demanding the return of their heritage, their history and their identity – from anthropologists [and] ... from their own country' (Watanabe, 1995; see also Warren, 1998).

In a world that is not only postmodern but postcolonial, the authority of the work produced by, say, anthropologists about others ('natives') is doubly questioned: not only do the 'natives' have increasing access to the work, but the status of knowledge in general is less certain and its ties to the social location of the people producing it more evident. The 'natives' may well be producing knowledge about themselves or their own social contexts that may compete as 'expert' knowledge with the accounts of non-native observers, whether because the 'natives' have themselves trained in anthropology or because they contend that 'traditional' knowledge is as valid as 'academic' knowledge. In all, the relationship of academics to the people they study becomes a lot more complex than was realised in previous decades (Rappaport, 2005).

In the 1980s, anthropologists worried over this by analysing their ethnographic practice – fieldwork and writing up. Indeed, 'reflexivity' came to mean anthropologists reflecting on ethnographic texts, leading to an excess of navel-gazing that distracted attention from the more general meaning of reflexivity, that is, the reflexive social relation between the anthropologist and the anthropologised. In this anxious self-examination, ethnographic writing could be seen, like the work of fiction, to be laden with particular rhetorical 'devices', in this case, ones of distancing and authorisation which subtly gave the anthropologist narrative authority. Part of the answer to this was, then, to write in different ways, particularly to write 'multivocal' ethnographies in which the people being studied 'spoke for themselves'. This has some real advantages in conveying a sense of the people studied as active agents (see for example Whitten, 1985), but of course it was still the anthropologist who decided what was included and excluded from the final text (Clifford and Marcus, 1986; Marcus and Fischer, 1986; Watanabe, 1995). This inequality of control is ultimately predicated on much deeper structures, that is, the uneven global distribution of control over the means of production of knowledge (research funding, universities, publishing) and therefore cannot be easily cast aside.

So the problem remains of the political relationship between observer and observed. One approach to this is to engage in advocacy – a well-established anthropological tactic. This is narrowly defined as speaking on behalf of others, who by definition are less able to do so for themselves in particular contexts (such as legal proceedings, or in official circles). More broadly, it involves promoting the cause of particular groups through publicity and campaigning. More generally still, it can include the promotion of certain basic principles – of anti-racism, respect for cultural difference – through writing, teaching, film-making and so on.

Advocacy is full of problems. Some think it is at odds with anthropology (or social science) as an enterprise, since the latter seeks to grasp an overall context, while advocacy seeks to promote one particular set of interests. There are also endless problems of *whose* interests one represents – an 'indigenous community' is rarely unified in this respect (Hastrup and Elsass, 1990; Paine, 1985).

However, I do not think these problems mean that advocacy should be abandoned. Any political engagement is bound to be conflictive and unclear; one has to make decisions, about what to advocate for, on whose behalf, which are basically value judgements, even if these are informed by anthropological knowledge. In practice, of course, advocacy in its various forms is widespread, whether through groups such as Survival International (which was inspired by the plight of Amazonian indigenous people) or the International Working Group for Indigenous Affairs (IWGIA), through the participation of anthropologists as advisers/campaigners in constitutional reform in Colombia or Nicaragua (Arocha, 1992; Scherrer, 1994: 115), or through video projects among the Kayapó (Turner, 1992).

Another set of problems arises when representations produced by an anthropologist or a historian about a particular group and its culture come into conflict with representations produced by that group, or more likely a literate elite of the group. A clear example of this comes from outside the Latin American context. One US scholar of the New Zealand Maori showed that the cultural history of the Maori purveyed by Maori intellectuals depended on certain versions of that history produced by Western scholars in the nineteenth century which were actually 'wrong'; thus Maori identity depended partly on an 'invented tradition', a term made famous by Hobsbawm and Ranger (1983). The press snapped up his academic article, ran headlines saying 'US Scholar Says Maori Culture Is Invented' and Maori cultural activists got very annoyed (Hanson, 1989, 1991). For Mayan ethnic revivalist movements, in contrast to 'many recent "constructionist" studies of Maya ethnicity … many pan-Mayanists explore the possibilities of an "essentialist" Maya identity' (Watanabe, 1995: 37; see also Warren, 1998: 77).

These examples raise questions of authenticity, to which I alluded in Chapter 6. 'Authentic' means simply 'true', but it also means original, good and wholesome. The traditions at stake in cases like these are not just factually accurate or inaccurate, they underwrite people's identities – and perhaps land claims. Identities are often represented by cultural activists in an essentialist way that may be based on history: 'Essentialism is the affirmation of common style, quality, and culture – the oneness of a people – that revitalises a sense of historical depth' (Whitten, 1985: 230). The indigenist revivalism evident in Guatemala is a good example of essentialist representations with its 'radical view of ethnicity' that 'encourages the renovation of aspects of traditional religion and culture, and … asserts the superiority of indigenous peoples over nonindigenous'

(Wilson, 1995a: 260). When academics deconstruct these historical traditions, or more generally when they show how 'essentialisms become essential', they may be weakening those identities and claims. As black sociologist Paul Gilroy says: 'some of us … are just beginning to formulate our own big narratives precisely as narratives of redemption and emancipation', and the deconstruction of history and metanarratives would seem to be at odds with this (cited in Keith and Cross, 1993: 23).

So how should anthropologists and historians react in these cases? First, I think it is necessary to maintain some qualified notion of 'truth' – or rather falsity. We do want to be able to say that certain ideas about Maori culture are factually incorrect, according to the normal canons of historical investigation (which does not mean such canons can generate unalloyed and absolute truth). Equally, I do want to be able to contest the representation of Latin American blacks as indomitable resisters that is invoked in ideologies of *cimarronismo*, which hold up the image of the runaway slave and the runaway slave community as the true essence of Colombian, or Brazilian, black history and black identity. There is another side to black history in which freed blacks owned black slaves and *cimarrones* worked on nearby haciendas and asked for Catholic priests to visit (Wade, 1993a: 87–8).

Second, it is necessary to be critical about just how essentialist black and indigenous activists are about their own history and identity. There can be a certain patronising quality to the idea that 'they' (the activists) essentialise, while 'we' (the academics) avoid this, true to our sophisticated postmodern sensibilities. Third, there is the idea that activists may engage in 'strategic essentialism' – a term coined by postcolonial critic Gayatri Spivak. They may produce essentialist descriptions for particular purposes of political struggle and this justifies the essentialism (in the eyes of the postmodern academic). Warren (1998: 37) contends that Mayan activists deploy an essentialism that is 'tactical and situational', in order to 'undermine the authoritativeness' of non-Mayan accounts of the Maya. Even this idea, however, may have patronising overtones: the essentialism is justified as long as it is deployed in the pursuit of aims that 'we', as academics, find legitimate. The activists might well ask why academics should define what is and is not legitimate in this way.

A slightly different approach is to bring out the very varied way in which activists talk about identity and history – partly a reflection of the fact that 'activists' covers a very wide range of people. Rappaport

(2005), for example, emphasises the heterogeneity of the indigenous movements in south-west Colombia and shows that, overall, indigenous representations of culture are fluid and contextual; that they point towards a (utopian) future as much as a rooted history; that they are self-consciously emergent and in process; and that they seek to establish indigenous people as national citizens as well as culturally distinctive. Nasa ideas about Nasa people are open and dynamic; they embrace and give new meaning to outside concepts from fields as varied as law and cosmology and they adapt native concepts in innovative ways. Views that are essentialist certainly appear – not only from indigenous activists, but also the state and NGOs – but they are not the only ones.

More broadly, the answer, or part of an answer, to the dilemma of how scholars and activists can deal with their knowledges is precisely to engage in the reflexivity that uncovered the whole problem in the first place. Essentialist representations are political statements, as are the deconstructions of them; so it is possible to have a dialogue between them. It is probably unhelpful to talk the language of 'invention', because all human culture is invented in some sense and there is no effective distinction between 'genuine' and 'spurious' culture (Jackson, 1995). But it is possible to juxtapose and discuss different versions of events and identities and to take those versions as political agendas with political effects that can be debated. Thus to represent indigenous people as the 'natural' guardians of the earth – an image which can be deployed by indigenous people and non-indigenous people alike – may have the effect of locking them into conservation, while many of them may want development.

A dialogue along these lines is not easy. Black activists in Colombia read some of the material I produce about blacks in that country (since some of it I write in Spanish) and sometimes we have discussions about it. The question of Africanisms often comes up, because one current of black activism and indeed of anthropology in Colombia seeks to discover the African roots of black culture, not just as a historical investigation, but as a political endeavour. I take a less Herskovitsian line, by no means denying Africanisms, but pointing out that undue emphasis on them can act to exclude the large parts of black culture which are evidently not African-derived. For Guatemala, Watanabe notes that 'Maya ... ask ethnographers how to better anthropologise themselves for their own ends'; they want advice on how to study themselves to achieve 'some kind of Maya anthropology by Maya for Maya' which is not, however, independent of non-Maya anthropologists (1995: 40, 39). Turner (1991) notes that the interest of anthropologists in Kayapó culture helped draw the attention of the Kapayó themselves to their own culture and the possibility of representing and objectifying it. So there can be debate and dialogue.

Escobar takes this a step further in his work with the Proceso de Comunidades Negras in south-west Colombia (see Escobar, 2008). His long-term work with this organisation there has resulted in co-publications with black activists who are also scholars in their own right; some of his ideas come from the conceptual debates activists have in trying to work out their own practices of political struggle (Rappaport, 2005, shows a similar trajectory). This is all part of a project called 'other anthropologies and anthropology otherwise' (Restrepo and Escobar, 2005), which takes a 'decolonial' perspective, critiquing the colonial difference which is at the heart of modernity, and which suppresses the subordinated cultures and knowledges that can become 'sites of articulation of alternative projects' (Escobar, 2008: 12). The entire structure of Western knowledge production is questioned from a perspective from 'the South'.[1] Although some of this decolonial production comes out of the US academic publishing industry, it also points to the very large academy that exists in Latin America and that has, for some time, questioned its subordinate relationship to the dominant 'metropolitan' academic world of the North (see Beverley et al., 1995; Mignolo, 2000; Richard, 1997). The question of dialogue and debate between anthropologists and anthropologised takes on a rather different aspect when the anthropologist is, say, a Brazilian in Bahia studying the black movement in Bahia (an aspect that sociologists have, of course, long had to contend with). Issues of accountability and of who has the authority to represent whom take on sharper edges when the social contexts of studier and studied overlap more closely, even if differences of class, race and professional expertise continue to divide.

There is no point being romantic about dialogues between the Northern observers and the Southern observed and pretending that the power relations that have traditionally differentiated the studiers from the studied are about to be overturned, even if those power relations are not a simple divide and much less so when considered within Latin America. My anthropological dialogue with black activists in Colombia is very limited: by the small number of black intellectuals and their restricted access to libraries, by my own location in a (distant) academic environment that does not give much value to such dialogue and so on. Others, such as Escobar and Rappaport, have managed more intensive dialogues. Latin American anthropologists almost inevitably are drawn into long-standing and complex dialogues when they work with people closer to 'home'. Still, while it is *de rigueur* nowadays to pay homage to reflexivity, real inequalities of power persist and militate against it.

Nevertheless, the future for the study of race and ethnicity in Latin America will perforce be one of increasing reflexivity, of blacks and indigenous people producing their own versions of their history and identity and engaging in debates with academics, as well as government officials, about these. This, I think, is not wishful thinking, but a simple fact. The process would be facilitated by a more equal distribution of the means of production of knowledge – a process in which the Internet is playing an important role. Here Latin America has a head-start on, say, Africa, in that it has well-established academy and better access to and distribution of information technologies. This is not to say, by any means, that the means of production of knowledge are equally distributed within Latin American nations, but there is a greater chance for dialogue between Latin American academics and black and indigenous social movements, just as there is some chance for blacks and indigenous people – albeit not many – to enter the academy if they want to and can get to its gates.

In an environment in which those who traditionally have been the 'objects' of enquiry begin to study themselves in academic mode, the boundaries between different kinds of knowledge may become less clear and indeed what counts as (social scientific) knowledge at all may be questioned. Whitten recounts a revealing encounter between Sicuanga, a Quechua indigenous, and a local schoolteacher, in discussions about local land conflicts. At one point, the former began telling mythical stories, 'seemingly out of context', about the doings of ancestors. The teacher 'had glimmers of what Sicuanga's message meant, and he knew that there was something profound there if he could only grasp it' (1985: 251). Part of that message was that there might be other ways of approaching the future than 'development' and 'modernisation', of owning the land as property and subjecting it to ever-increasing productivity. In that sense, these other kinds of knowledge constitute a critique of Western modernity (Escobar, 2008; Zanotta Machado, 1994), even if the critique is not always phrased in the language of modernity. Part of anthropology's task has always been the translation between cultures, opening to outsiders the mythical discourse of people like Sicuanga by translating it into social scientific and/or popular terminology. In this task, the relativism of postmodernity does not serve us well: anthropology may point up cultural difference but it has lost its purpose if it ceases to also mediate and translate across that difference.

Notes

INTRODUCTION

1. I would like to thank Jenny Pearce and Françoise Barbira-Freedman for their helpful comments during the process of writing the first edition of this book.

1 THE MEANING OF 'RACE' AND 'ETHNICITY'

1. There is, of course, a parallel here with the 'observer effect' in natural sciences, in which the process of observation disturbs the thing being observed. In the social sciences, however, this takes on a different, less predictable dimension. For a discussion of all these themes, see Kuhn's classic text (Kuhn, 1970); see also Giddens (1976).
2. There are many sources on the history of the concept of race. See, for example, Anderson (2006), Banton (1987), Barkan (1992), Reynolds and Lieberman (1996), Smedley (1993), Stepan (1982).
3. In fact, Jordan (1977: 18–19) says that the Bible itself gave no grounds for linking Africans with the sons of Ham; these grounds came from Talmudic and Midrashic scriptural sources.
4. Between 1802 and 1820, slave trading was abolished by Denmark, Britain, the US, Sweden, Holland and France. Illegal slave trading by some of these countries nevertheless continued thereafter. Although there were prohibitions on slave trading enacted by or forced on Spain and Portugal during this period, Brazil, Puerto Rico and Cuba continued to import slaves until about the 1870s. Slavery itself was abolished in the Spanish ex-colonies between 1824 and 1854 (except in Puerto Rico and Cuba where it persisted until 1873 and 1886, respectively), although many countries had previously enacted 'free womb laws' that freed children subsequently born to slave mothers. Slavery ceased in Brazil in 1888, while between 1838 and 1863 it ended in Britain, France, Denmark, the US and finally Holland (see Curtin, 1969).
5. Recent work in genomics has re-ignited debate about whether race is a biologically useful category, as some scientists contend that some genetic variation corresponds to continental biogeographical population categories (such as African, European, Amerindian, etc. – that is, the classic 'racial' categories) and relates to medically meaningful differences in disease suscepti-bility and drug metabolisation (see Koenig et al., 2008).
6. I will not always put the term in inverted commas in this book, but it should be borne in mind that it is nothing more than a shorthand term of reference for a variable category, as are other racial labels, such as indian, white, *mestizo*, etc.
7. Frankenberg (1993) finds that many white Americans do not consider themselves to have a 'racial identity' – for them, this is something only 'others' have. But Bernstein (2003) reports that Anglo-American teenagers in California actively claim a minority racial identity (Hispanic, black), based on dress and music styles.

8. This may seem to ignore that ideas about 'race' also exist in Japan – closely connected to its own imperial history – and also in China. In both cases, however, the impact of European writings from the nineteenth century onwards was influential in affecting the way Japanese and Chinese thinkers conceived of human difference (Dikötter, 1991; Weiner, 1995). This is not to say, however, that thinking in terms of 'blood' and other bodily essences as defining differences is uniquely European. The point is that it is primarily in Europe (and the US) that the whole ideology of race was most elaborated.

9. This raises the problem of how national identities relate to ethnic ones (see Eriksen, 1993). Briefly, a nation is an ethnic group that seeks political sovereignty over the territory of which it claims cultural ownership and control; a nation-state exists when that sovereignty is achieved. Of course, such a claim to ownership and control on the part of one group may be contested by other groups who see themselves as different but occupy, or wish to control, parts of the same territory.

10. In the previous edition of this book, I used the term 'indian' to refer to the indigenous peoples of the Americas. Many people avoid this term, since the Spanish and Portuguese term *indio* is often used pejoratively in Latin America. I continued to use the term 'indian', because I thought it did not have the same pejorative connotation in English. I also did not capitalise the word in order to put the terms 'black' and 'indian' on the same footing where I still believe they belong. Neither term indicates a national grouping, both are culturally constructed and vary over space and time. However, I now think that it is more appropriate to use the term 'indigenous people', as *indígena* is the term most used by indigenous people themselves. When I use the term 'indian', I do so in quotation marks. I continue to use the word 'black' because *negro*, while it may be used offensively in Latin America, is also reclaimed as an identity by black social movements in the region. However, terms such as Afro-Latino and Afro-descendant are increasingly common and I use these too.

3   EARLY APPROACHES TO BLACKS AND INDIGENOUS PEOPLE, 1920s–1960s

1. For more details, see the website of a 2004 conference dedicated to the UNESCO project, 'O Projeto UNESCO no Brasil: una volta crítica ao campo 50 anos depois', URL: www.ceao.ufba.br/unesco/welcome.htm
2. For summaries of the UNESCO studies, see Bastide (1957), Banton (1967), Daniel (2006: ch. 7), Graham (1970) and Fontaine (1980).
3. This survey is reported in Turra and Venturi (1995).

4   INEQUALITY AND SITUATIONAL IDENTITY: THE 1970s

1. The term '*cholo*' is a complex one, the meaning of which varies according to context. It is often used to imply a person seen as a mixture of indigenous and non-indigenous traits, typically, an indigenous person who has adopted non-indigenous practices, but the meaning attached to the term is varied (de la Cadena, 2000; van den Berghe, 1974a).

2. See also Brandon (1993), Gilroy (1993a), Palmié (1995), Price (1979) and Whitten and Szwed (1970) for different discussions of the problems involved in ideas of African 'traditions'.

5   BLACKS AND INDIGENOUS PEOPLE IN THE POSTMODERN AND POSTCOLONIAL NATION – AND BEYOND

1. Useful introductions to postmodernism, postmodernity and postcolonialism include Giddens (1990), Hall et al. (1992), Harvey (1989), Turner (1990), Spivak (1999). For Latin America, see Beverley et al. (1995), Mignolo (2000).
2. Both Derrida and Foucault actually wrote many of their works in the 1960s. Much of this was not translated into English until the 1970s and 1980s, however, and their impact on social science has been mainly from the 1980s.
3. See Dane (2006) and the Excel file at: www.dane.gov.co/files/etnicos/taller/ terri_colectivos_cnegras.xls (accessed 26 August 2009).
4. See Stoler (2002) on race, power and intimacy.
5. The Subaltern Studies Group was a group of South Asian and South Asianist scholars who focused on writing revisionist histories from the perspective of the colonised and the oppressed (Guha, 1997). For an example of how a grassroots perspective has entered into mainstream history, see *The Cambridge History of the Native Peoples of the Americas*, 3 vols, published from 1996. Two good examples of specific studies are Silverblatt (2004) and Stern (1995).
6. See Kizca (1995) for a review of ethnohistorical work on Mexico.
7. See also Assies et al. (2000), Rappaport (2005), Smith (1990), Stavenhagen (1996).
8. See, for example, England (2006), Greenbaum (2002), Sagás and Molina (2004). The last two are in the New World Diaspora series, edited by Kevin Yelvington and published by the University Press of Florida, which is a good indication of the growing interest in diaspora and transnationalism.
9. See, for example, http://www.oaxacalifornia.com/
10. Garifuna (also known as Garinagu and Black Caribs) are the descendants of a process of mixture between Africans and Carib indigenous populations exiled in the eighteenth century from St Vincent, a British colony in the eastern Caribbean, to islands off the coast of Honduras, whence they spread along the coasts of Honduras, Guatemala, Belize and Nicaragua.
11. Personal communications from Fernando Urrea Giraldo, Universidad del Valle, one of the academics involved in the discussions.
12. On the wild man, see, for example, Dudley and Novak (1972).

6   BLACK AND INDIGENOUS SOCIAL MOVEMENTS

1. For black resistance, see Andrews (2004: 22–40), Davis (1995), Heuman (1986), Klein and Vinson (2007: ch. 9), Landers and Robinson (2006), Price (1979, 1983, 1990), Reis (1993), Schwartz (2002), Taussig (1980), Thompson (2006), Whitten and Torres (1992, 1998). For indigenous resistance, see Gosner and Ouweneel (1996), Kizca (1999), Restall (2004), Rivera Cusicanqui (1993), Stern (1987). Larson et al. (1995) also have many references to the ethnohistorical work on Andean resistance. See also Kizca (1995), Hill (1996). There are

many country-specific studies, for example, Clendinnen (2003), Lewis (2003), Rappaport (1990), Stern (1993).

2. For recent overviews, see also Andrews (2009), Wade (2006a).

3. For Latin America generally, Alvarez et al. (1998b), Assies et al. (2000), Field (1994), Kearney (1996), Mallon (1992), Postero and Zamosc (2004), Sieder (2002), Van Cott (2000), Warren and Jackson (2003), Yashar (2005). For Colombia, see Findji (1992), Gros (1991), Jackson (1995), Rappaport (2005). For Guatemala, see Hale (2006), Warren (1998), Watanabe (1995), Wilson (1995a). For Mexico, see Campbell (1995), Hernández Castillo (2006), Nash (1995, 2001). For Ecuador, see Selverston-Scher (2001), Whitten (1985: ch. 6), Zamosc (1994). For Bolivia, see Postero (2007). For Brazil, see Branford and Glock (1985: ch. 5), Fisher (1994), Ramos (1998), Turner (1991), Warren (2001).

4. See footnote 10, in Chapter 5.

5. The Constitutional Court recognised a 'black community' – although not a land claim – in the Caribbean coastal city of Santa Marta (Wade, 2002b). A few land titles have been allocated to black communities outside the Pacific coastal region: see the territories listed for the province of Antioquia in the Excel document at: http://www.dane.gov.co/files/etnicos/taller/terri_colectivos_cnegras.xls

6. The term *palenquero* refers to Afro-Colombian people from the village of Palenque de San Basilio near the Caribbean coast. The term *raizal* refers to Afro-Colombians from the Colombian Caribbean island archipelago of San Andrés and Providencia.

7. The first quotation is from a communiqué issued by the EZLN on its twelfth anniversary in November 1995, circulated on the Internet by Acción Zapatista, a group at the University of Texas (now defunct). The second is from a communiqué of January 1994, cited in Renard (1994: 13). See also Nash (1995).

8. See also Briggs (2002), Findlay (1998), Parker et al. (1992), Stepan (1991), Yuval-Davis and Anthias (1989).

9. See the interview with Luís Macas in the journal of the South and Meso-American Indigenous Rights Center, *Abya Yala News* 10(2), summer 1996, published online at http://saiic.nativeweb.org/ayn/macas.html. Volume 8(3), fall 1994, of this journal is a special issue on 'Indigenous Movements and the Electoral Process'. On CONAIE, see Zamosc (1994).

10. Leon Zamosc, personal communication, based on interviews with indigenous leaders in Colombia in 1993.

11. I am indebted to Andre Cicalò, a PhD student at the University of Manchester, for this information.

12. In May 2009, a judicial decision in the state of Rio de Janeiro suspended the racial quota system, with effect from 2010.

7   STUDYING RACE AND ETHNICITY IN A POSTMODERN AND REFLEXIVE WORLD

1. See also Krotz (1997) and the website for Worlds and Knowledges Otherwise, http://jhfc.duke.edu/wko/welcome.php

References

Abercrombie, Thomas (1991) To be Indian, to be Bolivian: 'ethnic' and 'national' discourses of identity. In *Nation-States and Indians in Latin America*, Greg Urban and Joel Sherzer (eds), pp. 95–130 (Austin: University of Texas Press).

Abercrombie, Thomas (1998) *Pathways of Memory and Power: Ethnography and History among an Andean People* (Madison: University of Wisconsin Press).

Abu-Lughod, Lila (1990) The romance of resistance: tracing transformations of power through Bedouin women, *American Ethnologist* 17(1): 41–55.

Agier, Michel (1995) Racism, culture and black identity in Brazil, *Bulletin of Latin American Research* 14(3): 245–64.

Agier, Michel (2002) From local legends into globalized identities: the devil, the priest and the musician in Tumaco, *Journal of Latin American Anthropology* 7(2): 140–67.

Agudelo, Carlos E. (2005) *Multiculturalismo en Colombia: política, inclusión y exclusión de poblaciones negras* (Medellín: Carreta Editores, Institut de recherche pour le développment, Universidad Nacional de Colombia, Instituto Colombiano de Antropología e Historia).

Aguirre Beltrán, Gonzalo (1979) *Regions of Refuge* (Washington: Society for Applied Anthropology).

Alden, Dauril (1987) Late colonial Brazil, 1750–1808. In *Colonial Brazil*, Leslie Bethell (ed.), pp. 283–343. (Cambridge: Cambridge University Press).

Alvarez, Sonia, Evelina Dagnino and Arturo Escobar (1998a) Introduction: the cultural and the political in Latin American social movements. In *Cultures of Politics, Politics of Cultures: Re-visioning Latin American Social Movements*, Sonia Alvarez, Evelina Dagnino and Arturo Escobar (eds), pp. 1–29 (Boulder, CO: Westview Press).

Alvarez, Sonia, Evelina Dagnino and Arturo Escobar (eds) (1998b) *Cultures of Politics, Politics of Cultures: Re-visioning Latin American Social Movements* (Boulder, CO: Westview Press).

Amos, Valerie and Pratibha Parmar (1984) Challenging imperial feminism, *Feminist Review* 17: 3–19.

Anderson, Benedict (1983) *Imagined Communities: Reflections on the Origin and Spread of Nationalism* (London: Verso).

Anderson, Kay (2006) *Race and the Crisis of Humanism* (London: Routledge).

Anderson, Mark (2005) Bad boys and peaceful Garifuna: transnational encounters between racial stereotypes of Honduras and the United States. In *Neither Enemies nor Friends: Latinos, Blacks, Afro-Latinos*, Anani Dzidzienyo and Suzanne Oboler (eds), pp. 101–16 (New York: Palgrave Macmillan).

Anderson, Mark (2007) When Afro becomes (like) indigenous: Garifuna and Afro-indigenous politics in Honduras, *Journal of Latin American and Caribbean Anthropology* 12(2): 384–413.

Anderson, Mark (2009) *Black and Indigenous: Garifuna Activism and Consumer Culture in Honduras* (Minneapolis: University of Minnesota Press).

Andolina, Robert, Sarah Radcliffe and Nina Laurie (2005) Development and culture: transnational identity making in Bolivia, *Political Geography* 24(6): 678–702.

Andrews, George Reid (1991) *Blacks and Whites in São Paulo, Brazil, 1888–1988*. (Madison: University of Wisconsin Press).

Andrews, George Reid (1992) Black political protest in São Paulo, 1888–1988, *Journal of Latin American Studies* 24: 147–71.

Andrews, George Reid (2004) *Afro-Latin America, 1800–2000* (Oxford: Oxford University Press).

Andrews, George Reid (2009) Afro-Latin America: five questions, *Latin American and Caribbean Ethnic Studies* 4(2): 191–210.

Anthias, Floya and Nira Yuval-Davis (1992) *Racialized Boundaries: Race, Nation, Gender, Colour and Class and the Anti-Racist Struggle* (London: Routledge).

Appelbaum, Nancy P., Anne S. Macpherson and Karin A. Rosenblatt (eds) (2003) *Race and Nation in Modern Latin America* (Chapel Hill: University of North Carolina Press).

Arnold, Denise Y. (2008) New cartographies of the Bolivian state in the context of the Constituent Assembly, 2006–2007. In *Race, Colonialism, and Social Transformation in Latin America and the Caribbean*, Jerome Branche (ed.), pp. 149–92 (Gainesville: University Press of Florida).

Arocha, Jaime (1992) Afro-Colombia denied, *NACLA Report on the Americas* 25(4): 28–31.

Arocha, Jaime (1998) Inclusion of Afro-Colombians: an unreachable goal, *Latin American Perspectives* 25(3): 70–89.

Arruti, José Mauricio Andion (1997) A emergência dos 'remanescentes': notas para o diálogo entre indígenas e quilombolas, *Mana. Estudos de Antropología Social* 3(2): 7–38.

Asad, Talal (1993) *Genealogies of Religion: Discipline and Reasons of Power in Christianity and Islam* (Baltimore, MD: Johns Hopkins University Press).

Asher, Kiran (2009) *Black and Green: Afro-Colombians, Development, and Nature in the Pacific Lowlands* (Durham, NC: Duke University Press).

Assies, Willem, Gemma van der Haar and André Hoekema (eds) (2000) *The Challenge of Diversity: Indigenous Peoples and Reform of the State in Latin America* (Amsterdam: Thela-Thesis).

Azevedo, Thales de (1953) *Les Élites de couleur dans une ville brésilienne* (Paris: UNESCO).

Bailey, Stanley R. (2004) Group dominance and the myth of racial democracy: antiracism attitudes in Brazil, *American Sociological Review* 69(5): 728–47.

Banks, Marcus (1996) *Ethnicity: Anthropological Constructions* (London: Routledge).

Banton, Michael (1967) *Race Relations* (London: Tavistock).

Banton, Michael (1983) *Racial and Ethnic Competition* (Cambridge: Cambridge University Press).

Banton, Michael (1987) *Racial Theories* (Cambridge: Cambridge University Press).

Barbary, Olivier and Fernando Urrea (eds) (2004) *Gente negra en Colombia, dinámicas sociopolíticas en Cali y el Pacífico* (Cali, Paris: CIDSE/Univalle, IRD, Colciencias).

Barbira-Freedman, Françoise (ed.) (1980) *Land, People and Planning in Contemporary Amazonia* (Cambridge: Centre of Latin American Studies, University of Cambridge).

Barcelos, Luiz Claudio (1999) Struggling in paradise: racial mobilization and the contemporary black movement in Brazil. In *Race in Contemporary Brazil: From Indifference to Inequality*, Rebecca Reichmann (ed.), pp. 155–66 (University Park: Pennsylvania State University Press).

Barkan, Elazar (1992) *The Retreat of Scientific Racism: Changing Concepts of Race in Britain and the United States between the World Wars* (Cambridge: Cambridge University Press).

Barkan, Elazar (1996) The politics of the science of race: Ashley Montagu and UNESCO's anti-racist declarations. In *Race and Other Misadventures: Essays in Honor of Ashley Montagu in his Ninetieth Year*, Larry T. Reynolds and Leonard Lieberman (eds), pp. 96–105 (Dix Hills, N.Y.: General Hall Inc.).

Barkan, Elazar, and Ronald Bush (eds) (1995) *Prehistories of the Future: The Primitivist Project and the Culture of Modernism* (Stanford, CA: Stanford University Press).

Barker, Martin (1981) *The New Racism* (London: Junction Books).

Barry, Brian (2000) *Culture and Equality: An Egalitarian Critique of Multiculturalism* (Cambridge: Polity Press).

Barth, Frederick (ed.) (1969) *Ethnic Groups and Boundaries: The Social Organisation of Cultural Difference* (London: George Allen and Unwin).

Basch, Linda G., Nina Glick Schiller and Cristina Blanc-Szanton (eds) (1994) *Nations Unbound: Transnational Projects, Postcolonial Predicaments, and Deterritorialized Nation-states* (Newark, NJ: Gordon and Breach).

Bastide, Roger (1957) Race relations in Brazil, *International Social Science Bulletin* 9: 495–512.

Bastide, Roger (1961) Dusky Venus, black Apollo, *Race* 3: 10–19.

Bastide, Roger (1971) *African Civilizations in the New World* (London: C. Hurst).

Bastide, Roger (1978) *African Religions of Brazil: Towards a Sociology of the Interpenetration of Civilizations* (Baltimore, MD: Johns Hopkins University Press).

Bastide, Roger and Florestan Fernandes (1955) *Relações raciais entre negroes e brancos em São Paulo* (São Paulo: Editora Anhembí).

Bauer, Arnold (1984) Rural Spanish America, 1870–1930. In *The Cambridge History of Latin America*, vol. 4, Leslie Bethell (ed.), pp. 151–86 (Cambridge: Cambridge University Press).

Béhague, Gerard (ed.) (1994) *Music and Black Ethnicity: The Caribbean and South America* (New Brunswick, NJ: Transaction Publishers).

Behar, Ruth (1989) Sexual witchcraft, colonialism and women's powers: views from the Mexican Inquisition. In *Sexuality and Marriage in Colonial Latin America*, Asunción Lavrin (ed.), pp. 178–206 (Lincoln: University of Nebraska Press).

Bernstein, Nell (2003) Goin' gangsta, choosin' cholita. In *Signs of Life in the U.S.A.: Readings on Popular Culture for Writers*, Sonia Maasik and Jack Solomon (eds), pp. 599–604 (Boston, MA: Bedford Books, St Martin's Press).

Beverley, John (1999) *Subalternity and Representation: Arguments in Cultural Theory* (Durham, NC: Duke University Press).

Beverley, John, José Oviedo and Michael Aronna (eds) (1995) *The Postmodernism Debate in Latin America* (Durham, NC: Duke University Press).

Bhabha, Homi (1994) *The Location of Culture* (London: Routledge).

Bigenho, Michelle (2006) Embodied matters: *Bolivian Fantasy* and indigenismo, *Journal of Latin American Anthropology* 11(2): 267–93.

Blauert, Jutta and Marta Guidi (1992) Strategies for autochthonous development: two initiatives in rural Oaxaca, Mexico. In *Grassroots Environmental Action:*

People's Participation in Sustainable Development, Dhoram Ghai and Jessica Vivian (eds), pp. 188–220 (London: Routledge).

Bonfil Batalla, Guillermo (1996 [1987]) *México Profundo: Reclaiming a Civilization*, trans. Philip A. Dennis (Austin: University of Texas Press).

Bourricaud, François (1975) Indian, mestizo and cholo as symbols in the Peruvian system of stratification. In *Ethnicity: Theory and Experience*, Nathan Glazier and Daniel Moynihan (eds), pp. 350–87 (Cambridge, MA: Harvard University Press).

Bowser, Frederick (1972) Colonial Spanish America. In *Neither Slave nor Free: Freedmen of African Descent in the Slave Societies of the New World*, David Cohen and Jack Greene (eds), pp. 19–58 (Baltimore, MD: Johns Hopkins University Press).

Brading, David (1988) Manuel Gamio and official *indigenismo*, *Bulletin of Latin American Research* 7(1): 75–90.

Brah, Avtar (1996) *Cartographies of Diaspora: Contesting Identities* (London: Routledge).

Branche, Jerome (ed.) (2008) *Race, Colonialism, and Social Transformation in Latin America and the Caribbean* (Gainesville: University Press of Florida).

Brandon, George (1993) *Santería from Africa to the New World: The Dead Sell Memories* (Bloomington: Indiana University Press).

Branford, Sue and Oriel Glock (1985) *The Last Frontier: Fighting over Land in the Amazon* (London: Zed Books).

Brennan, Denise (2004) *What's Love Got to Do with It? Transnational Desires and Sex Tourism in the Dominican Republic* (Durham, NC: Duke University Press).

Briggs, Laura (2002) *Reproducing Empire: Race, Sex, Science, and U.S. Imperialism in Puerto Rico* (Berkeley: University of California Press).

Brown, Diana (1986) *Umbanda: Religion and Politics in Brazil* (Ann Arbor: UMI Research Press).

Brysk, Alison (1996) Turning weakness into strength: the internationalization of Indian rights, *Latin American Perspectives*, special issue on Ethnicity and Class in Latin America, 23(2): 38–57.

Brysk, Alison (2000) *From Tribal Village to Global Village: Indian Rights and International Relations in Latin America* (Stanford, CA: Stanford University Press).

Brysk, Alison (2005) *Human Rights and Private Wrongs: Constructing Global Civil Society* (London: Routledge).

Bueno, Salvador (1993) The black and white in the narrative of Alejo Carpentier. In *Afro-Cuba: An Anthology of Cuban Writing on Race, Politics and Culture*, Pedro Pérez Sarduy and Jean Stubbs (eds), pp. 214–21 (London: Latin America Bureau).

Burdick, John (1992) Brazil's black consciousness movement, *NACLA Report on the Americas* 25(4): 23–7.

Burdick, John (1998) *Blessed Anastácia: Women, Race, and Popular Christianity in Brazil* (London: Routledge).

Burdick, John (2005) Why is the black Evangelical movement growing in Brazil? *Journal of Latin American Studies* 37(2): 311–32.

Cabezas, Amalia L. (2006) The eroticization of labor in Cuba's all-inclusive resorts: performing race, class and gender in the new tourist economy, *Social Identities: Journal for the Study of Race, Nation and Culture* 12(5): 507–21.

Caldwell, Kia Lilly (2004) 'Look at her hair': the body politics of black womanhood in Brazil, *Transforming Anthropology* 11(2): 18–29.

Campbell, Howard (1995) *Zapotec Renaissance: Ethnic Politics and Cultural Revivalism in Southern Mexico* (Albuquerque: University of New Mexico Press).

Canessa, Andrew (2000) Contesting hybridity: *evangelistas* and *kataristas* in highland Bolivia, *Journal of Latin American Studies* 32(01): 115–44.

Canessa, Andrew (ed.) (2005) *Natives Making Nation: Gender, Indigeneity and the State in the Andes* (Tucson: University of Arizona Press).

Canessa, Andrew (2008) Sex and the citizen: Barbies and beauty queens in the age of Evo Morales, *Journal of Latin American Cultural Studies* 17(1): 41–64.

Carby, Hazel (1982) White women listen! Black feminists and the boundaries of sisterhood. In *The Empire Strikes Back: Race and Racism in 70s Britain*, Centre for Contemporary Cultural Studies (ed.), pp. 212–36 (London: Hutchinson and CCCS, Birmingham University).

Cardoso, Fernado Henrique and Octavio Ianni (1960) *Côr e mobilidade social em Florianópolis* (São Paulo: Companhia Editora Nacional).

Carroll, Patrick (1991) *Blacks in Colonial Veracruz: Race, Ethnicity and Regional Development* (Austin: University of Texas Press).

Caulfield, Sueann (2003) Interracial courtship in the Rio de Janeiro courts, 1918–1940. In *Race and Nation in Modern Latin America*, Nancy P. Appelbaum, Anne S. Macpherson and Karin A. Rosemblatt (eds), pp. 163–86 (Chapel Hill: University of North Carolina Press).

Chance, John (1978) *Race and Class in Colonial Oaxaca* (Stanford, CA: Stanford University Press).

Chasteen, John Charles (2004) *National Rhythms, African Roots: The Deep History of Latin American Popular Dance* (Albuquerque: University of New Mexico Press).

Chevalier, François (1970) Official *indigenismo* in Peru in 1920: origins, significance and socioeconomic scope. In *Race and Class in Latin America*, Magnus Mörner (ed.), pp. 184–96 (New York: Columbia University Press).

Cicaló, Andre (2008) What do we know about quotas? Data and considerations about the implementation of the quota system in the State University of Rio de Janeiro (UERJ), *Universitas Humanística* 65: 216–78.

Cleary, Edward L. and Timothy J. Steigenga (eds) (2004) *Resurgent Voices in Latin America: Indigenous Peoples, Political Mobilization, and Religious Change* (New Brunswick, NJ: Rutgers University Press).

Clendinnen, Inga (2003) *Ambivalent Conquests: Maya and Spaniard in Yucatan, 1517–1570*, 2nd edn (Cambridge: Cambridge University Press).

Clifford, James (1988) Identity in Mashpee. In *The Predicament of Culture: Twentieth-century Ethnography, Literature, and Art*, James Clifford (ed.), pp. 277–348 (Cambridge, MA: Harvard University Press).

Clifford, James (2001) Indigenous articulations, *Contemporary Pacific* 13(2): 468–90.

Clifford, James and George Marcus (eds) (1986) *Writing Culture: The Poetics and Politics of Ethnography* (Berkeley: University of California Press).

Cohen, Abner (1969) *Custom and Politics in Urban Africa: A Study of Hausa Migrants in Yoruba Towns* (London: Routledge and Kegan Paul).

Cohen, Abner (ed.) (1974) *Urban Ethnicity* (London: Tavistock).

Colby, Benjamin and Pierre van den Berghe (1961) Ethnic relations in southeastern Mexico, *American Anthropologist* 63: 772–92.

Colby, Benjamin and Pierre van den Berghe (1969) *Ixil Country: A Plural Society in Highland Guatemala* (Berkeley: University of California Press).

Collins, Patricia Hill (2000) *Black Feminist Thought: Knowledge, Consciousness and the Politics of Empowerment*, 2nd edn (New York: Routledge).

Collinson, Helen (ed.) (1996) *Green Guerrillas: Environmental Conflicts and Initiatives in Latin America and the Caribbean* (London: Latin America Bureau).

Comaroff, John and Jean Comaroff (1992) *Ethnography and the Historical Imagination* (Boulder, CO: Westview Press).

Conklin, Beth A. and Laura R. Graham (1995) The shifting middle ground: Amazonian Indians and eco-politics, *American Anthropologist* 97(4): 695–710.

Cope, R. Douglas (1994) *The Limits of Racial Domination: Plebeian Society in Colonial Mexico City, 1660–1720* (Madison: University of Wisconsin Press).

Cowan, Jane K., Marie-Bénédicte Dembour and Richard A. Wilson (eds) (2001) *Culture and Rights: Anthropological Perspectives* (Cambridge: Cambridge University Press).

Crenshaw, Kimberlé (1991) Mapping the margins: intersectionality, identity politics, and violence against women of color, *Stanford Law Review* 43(6): 1241–99.

Curiel, Ochy (2008) Superando la interseccionalidad de categorías por la construcción de un proyecto político feminista radical. Reflexiones en torno a las estrategias políticas de las mujeres afrodescendientes. In *Raza, etnicidad y sexualidades: ciudadanía y multiculturalismo en América latina*, Peter Wade, Fernando Urrea Giraldo and Mara Viveros Vigoya (eds), pp. 461–84 (Bogotá: Instituto CES, Facultad de Ciencias Humanas, Universidad Nacional de Colombia).

Curtin, Philip (1969) *The Atlantic Slave Trade: A Census* (Madison: University of Wisconsin Press).

DANE (2006) *Colombia una nación multicultural: su diversidad étnica* (Bogotá: Departamento Administrativo Nacional de Estadística).

Daniel, G. Reginald (2006) *Race and Multiraciality in Brazil and the United States: Converging Paths?* (University Park: Pennsylvania State University Press).

Davis, Darién J. (ed.) (1995) *Slavery and Beyond: The African Impact on Latin America and the Caribbean* (Lanham, MD: Rowman and Littlefield).

Davis, Darién J. (ed.) (2007) *Beyond Slavery: The Multilayered Legacy of Africans in Latin America and the Caribbean* (Lanham, MD: Rowman and Littlefield).

Davis, David Brion (1969) A comparison of British America and Latin America. In *Slavery in the New World: A Reader in Comparative History*, Laura Foner and Eugene Genovese (eds), pp. 69–83 (Englewood Cliffs, NJ: Prentice Hall).

Davis, Shelton (1977) *Victims of the Miracle: Development and the Indians of Brazil* (Cambridge: Cambridge University Press).

Dawson, Alexander S. (2004) *Indian and Nation in Revolutionary Mexico* (Tucson: University of Arizona Press).

de la Cadena, Marisol (1995) 'Women are more Indian': ethnicity and gender in a community near Cuzco. In *Ethnicity, Markets and Migration in the Andes: At the Crossroads of History and Anthropology*, Brooke Larson, Olivia Harris and Enrique Tandeter (eds), pp. 329–48 (Durham, NC: Duke University Press).

de la Cadena, Marisol (2000) *Indigenous Mestizos: The Politics of Race and Culture in Cuzco, 1919–1991* (Durham, NC: Duke University Press).

de la Fuente, Alejandro (2001) *A Nation for All: Race, Inequality, and Politics in Twentieth Century Cuba* (Chapel Hill: University of North Carolina Press).

de la Fuente, Julio (1965) *Relaciones interétnicas* (Mexico: Instituto Nacional Indigenista).

Degler, Carl (1971) *Neither Black nor White: Slavery and Race Relations in Brazil and the United States* (New York: Macmillan).

Degregori, Carlos Iván and Pablo Sandoval (2008) Peru: from otherness to a shared diversity. In *A Companion to Latin American Anthropology*, Deborah Poole (ed.), pp. 150–74 (Oxford: Blackwell).

Díaz Ayala, Cristobal (1981) *La música cubana: del Areyto a la nueva trova* (San Juan, Puerto Rico: Ediciones Cubanacan).

Dikötter, Frank (1991) *The Discourse of Race in Modern China* (London: Hurst).

Doughty, Paul (1972) Peruvian migrant identity in the urban milieu. In *The Anthropology of Urban Environments*, Thomas Weaver and Douglas White (eds), pp. 39–50 (Washington: Society for Applied Anthropology).

Duany, Jorge (1998) Reconstructing racial identity: ethnicity, color and class among Dominicans in the United States and Puerto Rico. *Latin American Perspectives* 25(3): 147–72.

Dudley, Edward and Maximillian E. Novak (eds) (1972) *The Wild Man Within: An Image in Western Thought from the Renaissance to Romanticism* (Pittsburgh, PA: University of Pittsburgh Press).

Dzidzienyo, Anani (1979) The position of blacks in Brazilian society. In *The Position of Blacks in Brazilian and Cuban Society*, Anani Dzidzienyo and Lourdes Casal, pp. 2–11 (London: Minority Rights Group).

Dzidzienyo, Anani and Suzanne Oboler (eds) (2005) *Neither Enemies nor Friends: Latinos, Blacks, Afro-Latinos* (New York: Palgrave Macmillan).

Edmonds, Alexander (2007) Triumphant miscegenation: reflections on beauty and race in Brazil, *Journal of Intercultural Studies* 28(1): 83–97.

Ellen, Roy (1986) What Black Elk left unsaid: on the illusory images of Green primitivism, *Anthropology Today* 2(6): 8–13.

Elsass, Peter (1992) *Strategies for Survival: The Psychology of Cultural Resilience in Ethnic Minorities* (New York: New York University Press).

Eltis, David (1987) *Economic Growth and the Ending of the Transatlantic Slave Trade* (Oxford: Oxford University Press).

England, Sarah (2006) *Afro Central Americans in New York City: Garifuna Tales of Transnational Movements in Racialized Space* (Gainesville: University Press of Florida).

Epstein, Arnold L. (1978) *Ethos and Identity: Three Studies in Ethnicity* (London: Tavistock).

Eriksen, Thomas Hylland (1991) The cultural contexts of ethnic differences, *Man* 26(1): 127–44.

Eriksen, Thomas Hylland (1993) *Ethnicity and Nationalism: Anthropological Perspectives* (London: Pluto Press).

Escobar, Arturo (1992a) Culture, economics, and politics in Latin American social movements theory and research. In *The Making of Social Movements in Latin America: Identity, Strategy and Democracy*, Arturo Escobar and Sonia Alvarez (eds), pp. 62–85 (Boulder, CO: Westview Press).

Escobar, Arturo (1992b) Culture, practice and politics: anthropology and the study of social movements, *Critique of Anthropology* 12(4): 395–432.

Escobar, Arturo (2008) *Territories of Difference: Place, Movements, Life* (Durham, NC: Duke University Press).

Escobar, Arturo and Sonia E. Alvarez (eds) (1992) *The Making of Social Movements in Latin America: Identity, Strategy, and Democracy* (Boulder, CO: Westview Press).

Fernandes, Florestan (1969) *The Negro in Brazilian Society,* translated from the Portuguese by J.D. Skiles, A. Brunel and A. Rothwell and edited by Phyllis Eveleth (New York: Colombia University Press).

Fernandes, Florestan (1979) The Negro in Brazil: twenty-five years later. In *Brazil: Anthropological Perspectives*, M. Margolies and W. Carter (eds), pp. 96–114 (New York: Columbia University Press).

Fernandez, Nadine T. (1996) The color of love: young interracial couples in Cuba, *Latin American Perspectives* 23(1): 99–117.

Field, Les W. (1994) Who are the Indians? Reconceptualizing indigenous identity, resistance and the role of social science in Latin America, *Latin American Research Review* 29(3): 237–48.

Findji, María Teresa (1992) From resistance to social movement: the Indigenous Authorities Movement in Colombia. In *The Making of Social Movements in Latin America: Identity, Strategy and Democracy*, Arturo Escobar and Sonia Alvarez (eds), pp. 112–33 (Boulder, CO: Westview Press).

Findlay, Eileen J. Suárez (1998) *Imposing Decency: The Politics of Sexuality and Race in Puerto Rico, 1870–1920* (Durham, NC: Duke University Press).

Fisher, Andrew and Matthew D. O'Hara (eds) (2009) *Imperial Subjects: Race and Identity in Colonial Latin America* (Durham, NC: Duke University Press).

Fisher, William H. (1994) Megadevelopment, environmentalism, and resistance: the institutional context of Kayapó indigenous politics in central Brazil, *Human Organization* 53(3): 220–32.

Foner, Laura and Eugene Genovese (eds) (1969) *Slavery in the New World: A Reader in Comparative History* (Englewood Cliffs, NJ: Prentice Hall Inc.).

Fontaine, Pierre-Michel (1980) The political economy of Afro-Latin America, *Latin American Research Review* 15(2): 111–41.

Fontaine, Pierre-Michel (1981) Transnational relations and racial mobilisation: emerging black movements in Brazil. In *Ethnic Identities in a Transnational World*, John F. Stack (ed.), pp. 141–62 (Westport, CT: Greenwood Press).

Foster, George (1967) *Tzintzuntzan: Mexican Peasants in a Changing World* (Boston, MA: Little, Brown and Company).

Foweraker, Joe (1995) *Theorising Social Movements* (London: Pluto Press).

Franco, Jean (1967) *The Modern Culture of Latin America: Society and the Artist* (London: Pall Mall Press).

Frankenberg, Ruth (1993) *White Women, Race Matters: The Social Construction of Whiteness* (London: Routledge).

Freeland, Jane (1995) Nicaragua. In *No Longer Invisible: Afro-Latin Americans Today*, Minority Rights Group (ed.), pp. 181–201 (London: Minority Rights Group).

French, Jan Hoffman (2004) *Mestizaje* and law-making in indigenous identity formation in northeastern Brazil: 'After the conflict came the history', *American Anthropologist* 106(4): 663–74.

French, Jan Hoffman (2006) Buried alive: imagining Africa in the Brazilian Northeast, *American Ethnologist* 33(3): 340–60.

French, Jan Hoffman (2009) *Legalizing Identities: Becoming Black or Indian in Brazil's Northeast* (Chapel Hill: University of North Carolina Press).

Freyre, Gilberto (1951) *Brazil: An Interpretation* (New York: Alfred Knopf).

Freyre, Gilberto (1959) *New World in the Tropics: The Culture of Modern Brazil* (New York: Alfred Knopf).

Friedemann, Nina de (1984) Estudios de negros en la antropología colombiana. In *Un siglo de investigación social: antropología en Colombia*, Jaime Arocha and Nina de Friedemann (eds), pp. 507–72 (Bogotá: Etno).

Friedemann, Nina de and Jaime Arocha (1986) *De sol a sol: génesis, transformación y presencia de los negros en Colombia* (Bogotá: Planeta).

Friedemann, Nina de and Jaime Arocha (1995) Colombia. In *No Longer Invisible: Afro-Latin Americans Today*, Minority Rights Group (ed.), pp. 47–76 (London: Minority Rights Group).

Friedlander, Judith (1975) *Being Indian in Hueyapan: A Study of Forced Identity in Contemporary Mexico* (New York: St Martin's Press).

Fry, Peter (2002) Estética e política: relações entre 'raça', publicidade e produção da beleza no Brasil. In *Nu e vestido: dez antropólogos revelam a cultura do corpo carioca*, Mirian Goldenberg (ed.), pp. 303–26 (Rio de Janeiro: Record).

Fry, Peter, Yvonne Maggie, Simone Monteiro and Ricardo Ventura Santos (eds) (2007a) *Divisões perigosas: políticas raciais no Brasil contemporâneo* (Rio de Janeiro: Civilização Brasileira).

Fry, Peter, Simone Monteiro, Marcos Chor Maio, Francisco I. Bastos and Ricardo Ventura Santos (2007b) Aids tem cor ou raça? Interpretação de dados e formulação de políticas de saúde no Brasil, *Cadernos de Saúde Pública* 23(3): 497–523.

García, María Elena (2008) Introduction: indigenous encounters in contemporary Peru, *Latin American and Caribbean Ethnic Studies* 3(3): 217–26.

García Canclini, Néstor (1989) *Culturas híbridas: estrategias para entrar y salir de la modernidad* (Mexico: Grijalbo).

Giddens, Anthony (1976) *New Rules of Sociological Method: A Positive Critique of Interpretative Sociologies* (London: Hutchinson).

Giddens, Anthony (1987) *Social Theory and Modern Society* (Cambridge: Polity Press).

Giddens, Anthony (1990) *The Consequences of Modernity* (Cambridge: Polity Press).

Gillin, John (1951) *The Culture of Security in San Carlos: A Study of a Guatemalan Community of Indians and Ladinos* (New Orleans: Middle American Research Institute, Tulane University).

Gilroy, Paul (1982) Steppin' out of Babylon: race, class and autonomy. In *The Empire Strikes Back: Race and Racism in 70s Britain*, Centre for Contemporary Cultural Studies (ed.), pp. 276–314 (London: Hutchinson and CCCS, Birmingham University).

Gilroy, Paul (1993a) *The Black Atlantic: Modernity and Double Consciousness* (London: Verso).

Gilroy, Paul (1993b) *Small Acts: Thoughts on the Politics of Black Cultures* (London: Serpent's Tail).

Gilroy, Paul (2000) *Between Camps: Nations, Cultures and the Allure of Race* (London: Penguin Books).

Glazer, Nathan and Daniel Moynihan (eds) (1975) *Ethnicity: Theory and Experience* (Cambridge, MA: Harvard University Press).

Gledhill, John (2000) *Power and Its Disguises: Anthropological Perspectives on Politics*, 2nd edn (London: Pluto Press).

Goldberg, David Theo (1993) *Racist Culture: Philosophy and the Politics of Meaning* (Oxford: Blackwell).

Goldberg, David Theo (2008) *The Threat of Race: Reflections on Racial Neoliberalism* (Malden, MA: Wiley-Blackwell).

Goldstein, Donna M. (2003) *Laughter Out of Place: Race, Class, Violence and Sexuality in a Rio Shantytown* (Berkeley: University of California Press).

González Casanova, Pablo (1965) Internal colonialism and national development, *Studies in Comparative International Development* 1(4): 27–37.

González Casanova, Pablo (1971) *La sociología de la explotación* (Mexico: Siglo XXI).

González, Lélia (1985) The Unified Black Movement: a new stage in black political mobilization. In *Race, Class and Power in Brazil,* Pierre-Michel Fontaine (ed.), pp. 120–34 (Los Angeles: Center for Afro-American Studies, University of California).

Gordon, Edmund T. (1998) *Disparate Diasporas: Identity and Politics in an African-Nicaraguan Community* (Austin: University of Texas Press).

Gose, Peter (1994) *Deathly Waters and Hungry Mountains: Agrarian Ritual and Class Formation in an Andean Town* (Toronto: University of Toronto Press).

Gosner, Kevin and Arij Ouweneel (eds) (1996) *Indigenous Revolts in Chiapas and the Andean Highlands* (Amsterdam: CEDLA).

Gow, Peter (1991) *Of Mixed Blood: Kinship and History in Peruvian Amazonia* (Oxford: Clarendon Press).

Graham, Richard (1970) Brazilian slavery: a review, *Journal of Social History* 3: 431–53.

Graham, Richard (ed.) (1990) *The Idea of Race in Latin America, 1870–1940* (Austin: University of Texas Press).

Greenbaum, Susan D. (2002) *More than Black: Afro-Cubans in Tampa* (Gainesville: University Press of Florida).

Grieshaber, Erwin P. (1979) Hacienda–Indian community relations and Indian acculturation: an historiographical essay, *Latin American Research Review* 14(3): 107–28.

Grisaffi, Thomas (2009) Radio Soberanía: the sovereign voice of the Bolivian *cocalero?* PhD thesis, University of Manchester.

Gros, Christian (1991) *Colombia indígena: identidad cultural y cambio social* (Bogotá: CEREC).

Gros, Christian (1994) Noirs, indiennes, créoles en Amérique Latine et aux Antilles, *Cahiers des Amériques Latines* 17: 53–64.

Guha, Ranajit (ed.) (1997) *A Subaltern Studies Reader, 1986–1995* (Minneapolis: University of Minnesota Press).

Guss, David M. (2006) The Gran Poder and the reconquest of La Paz, *Journal of Latin American Anthropology* 11(2): 294–328.

Gutiérrez, Ramón (1991) *When Jesus Came, the Corn Mothers Went Away: Marriage, Sexuality and Power in New Mexico, 1500–1846* (Stanford, CA: Stanford University Press).

Guy, Donna (1991) *Sex and Danger in Buenos Aires: Prostitution, Family, and Nation in Argentina* (Lincoln: University of Nebraska Press).

Hagedorn, Katherine J. (2001) *Divine Utterances: The Performance of Afro-Cuban Santería* (Washington, DC: Smithsonian Institution Press).

Hale, Charles A. (1984) Political and social ideas in Latin America. In *The Cambridge History of Latin America*, vol. 4, Leslie Bethell (ed.), pp. 367–442 (Cambridge: Cambridge University Press).

Hale, Charles R. (2002) Does multiculturalism menace? Governance, cultural rights and the politics of identity in Guatemala, *Journal of Latin American Studies* 34: 485–524.

Hale, Charles R. (2005) Neoliberal multiculturalism: the remaking of cultural rights and racial dominance in Central America, *PoLAR: Political and Legal Anthropology Review* 28(1): 10–28.

Hale, Charles R. (2006) *Más Que un Indio (More than an Indian): Racial Ambivalence and Neoliberal Multiculturalism in Guatemala* (Santa Fe, NM: School of American Research Press).

Hale, Charles R., Galio C. Gurdián and Edmund T. Gordon (2003) Rights, resources and the social memory of struggle: reflections on a study of indigenous and black community land rights on Nicaragua's Atlantic coast, *Human Organization* 62(4): 369–81.

Hale, Lindsay L. (1997) Preto velho: resistance, redemption, and engendered representations of slavery in a Brazilian possession-trance religion, *American Ethnologist* 24(2): 392–414.

Hall, Stuart (1980) Race, articulation and societies structured in dominance. In *Sociological Theories: Race and Colonialism*, UNESCO (ed.), pp. 305–46 (Paris: UNESCO).

Hall, Stuart (1991) The local and the global: globalization and ethnicity. In *Culture, Globalization and the World-System*, Anthony King (ed.), pp. 19–40 (London: Macmillan).

Hall, Stuart (1992a) The question of cultural identity. In *Modernity and Its Futures*, Stuart Hall, David Held and Tony McGrew (eds), pp. 273–325 (Cambridge: Polity Press).

Hall, Stuart (1992b) The West and the Rest: discourse and power. In Stuart Hall and Bram Gieben (eds), *Formations of Modernity*, pp. 275–332 (Milton Keynes: Open University Press).

Hall, Stuart, David Held and Tony McGrew (eds) (1992) *Modernity and Its Futures* (Cambridge: Polity Press).

Halperín Donghi, Tulio (1987) Economy and society. In *Spanish America after Independence, c. 1820–c. 1870*, Leslie Bethell (ed.), pp. 1–47 (Cambridge: Cambridge University Press).

Hanchard, Michael (1994) *Orpheus and Power: the* Movimento Negro *of Rio de Janeiro and São Paulo, Brazil, 1945–1988* (Princeton, NJ: Princeton University Press).

Hannerz, Ulf (1980) *Exploring the City: Enquiries toward an Urban Anthropology* (New York: Columbia University Press).

Hanson, Allan (1989) The Making of the Maori: Culture Invention and its Logic, *American Anthropologist* 91(4): 890–902.

Hanson, Allan (1991) Reply to Langdon, Levine and Linnekin, *American Anthropologist* 93(2): 449–50.

Harris, Marvin (1952) Race and class in Minas Velhas, a community in the mountain region of Central Brazil. In *Race and Class in Rural Brazil*, Charles Wagley (ed.), pp. 47–81 (Paris: UNESCO).

Harris, Marvin (1970) Referential ambiguity in the calculus of Brazilian racial terms, *Southwestern Journal of Anthropology* 27: 1–14.

Harris, Marvin (1974) *Patterns of Race in the Americas.* (New York: Norton Library).

Harris, Olivia (1995a) The coming of the white people: reflections on the mythologisation of history in Latin America, *Bulletin of Latin American Research* 14(1): 9–24.

Harris, Olivia (1995b) Ethnic identity and market relations: Indians and mestizos in the Andes. In *Ethnicity, Markets and Migration in the Andes: At the Crossroads of History and Anthropology*, Brooke Larson, Olivia Harris and Enrique Tandeter (eds), pp. 351–90 (Durham, NC: Duke University Press).

Harvey, David (1989) *The Condition of Postmodernity* (Oxford: Blackwell).

Harvey, Neil (1998) *The Chiapas Rebellion: The Struggle for Land and Democracy* (Durham, NC: Duke University Press).

Hasenbalg, Carlos (1979) *Discriminação e desigualdades raciais no Brazil*. Translated from the English PhD thesis by Patrick Burglin (Rio de Janeiro: Graal).

Hasenbalg, Carlos (1985) Race and socioeconomic inequalities in Brazil. In *Race, Class and Power in Brazil*, Pierre-Michel Fontaine (ed.), pp. 25–41 (Los Angeles: Center for Afro-American Studies, University of Califonia).

Hasenbalg, Carlos and Nelson do Valle Silva (1999) Notes on racial and political inequality in Brazil. In *Racial Politics in Contemporary Brazil*, Michael Hanchard (ed.), pp. 154–78 (Durham, NC: Duke University Press).

Hastrup, Kirsten and Peter Elsass (1990) Anthropological advocacy: a contradiction in terms, *Current Anthropology* 31(3): 301–11.

Hayden, Corinne P. (2003) Suspended animation: a brine shrimp essay. In *Remaking Life and Death: Toward an Anthropology of the Biosciences*, Sarah Franklin and Margaret Lock (eds), pp. 193–225 (Santa Fe, NM: SAR Press).

Hechter, Michael (1975) *Internal Colonialism: The Celtic Fringe in British National Development, 1536–1966* (London: Routledge and Kegan Paul).

Helg, Aline (1995) *Our Rightful Share: The Afro-Cuban Struggle for Equality, 1886–1912* (Chapel Hill: University of North Carolina Press).

Hemming, John (1987) Indians and the frontier. In *Colonial Brazil*, Leslie Bethell (ed.), pp. 145–89 (Cambridge: Cambridge University Press).

Hendrickson, Carol (1991) Images of the Indian in Guatemala: the role of indigenous dress in Indian and ladino constructions. In *Nation-States and Indians in Latin America*, Greg Urban and Joel Sherzer (eds), pp. 286–306 (Austin: University of Texas Press).

Hendrickson, Carol (1995) *Weaving Identities: Construction of Dress and Self in a Highland Guatemala Town* (Austin: University of Texas Press).

Henfrey, Colin (1981) The hungry imagination: social formation, popular culture and ideology in Bahia. In *The Logic of Poverty: The Case of the Brazilian North-East*, Simon Mitchell (ed.), pp. 58–108 (London: Routledge and Kegan Paul).

Hernández Castillo, Rosalva Aída (2006) The indigenous movement in Mexico: between electoral politics and local resistance, *Latin American Perspectives* 33(2): 115–31.

Herskovits, Melville (1941) *The Myth of the Negro Past* (New York: Harper and Brothers).

Herskovits, Melville (1966) *The New World Negro*, Frances Herskovits (ed.) (London: Indiana University Press).

Heuman, Gad (ed.) (1986) *Out of the House of Bondage: Runaways, Resistance and Maronnage in Africa and the New World* (London: Frank Cass).

Hewitt de Alcántara, Cynthia (1984) *Anthropological Perspectives on Rural Mexico* (London: Routledge and Kegan Paul).

Hill, Jonathan D. (ed.) (1988) *Rethinking History and Myth: Indigenous South American Perspectives on the Past* (Urbana: University of Illinois Press).

Hill, Jonathan D. (ed.) (1996) *History, Power, and Identity: Ethnogenesis in the Americas, 1492–1992* (Iowa City: University of Iowa Press).

Hobsbawm, Eric and Terence Ranger (eds) (1983) *The Invention of Tradition* (Cambridge: Cambridge University Press).

Hodgen, Margaret (1964) *Early Anthropology in the Sixteenth and Seventeenth centuries* (Philadelphia: University of Pennsylvannia Press).

Hoetink, Harry (1969) Race relations in Curaçao and Surinam. In *Slavery in the New World: A Reader in Comparative History*, Laura Foner and Eugene Genovese (eds), pp. 178–88 (Englewood Cliffs, NJ: Prentice Hall).

Hoffmann, Odile (2004) *Communautés noires dans le Pacifique colombien. Innovations et dynamiques ethniques* (Paris: IRD, Karthala).

Hooker, Juliet (2005) Indigenous inclusion/black exclusion: race, ethnicity and multicultural citizenship in contemporary Latin America, *Journal of Latin American Studies* 37(2): 285–310.

Hooker, Juliet (2009) *Race and the Politics of Solidarity* (Oxford: Oxford University Press).

hooks, bell (1981) *Ain't I a Woman? Black Women and Feminism* (London: Pluto Press).

hooks, bell (1991) *Yearning: Race, Gender and Cultural Politics* (London: Turnaround Press.).

Horsman, Reginald (1981) *Manifest Destiny: The Origins of American Racial Anglo-Saxonism* (Cambridge, MA: Harvard University Press).

Howe, James (1991) An ideological triangle: San Blas Kuna culture, 1915–1925. In *Nation-States and Indians in Latin America*, Greg Urban and Joel Sherzer (eds), pp. 19–52 (Austin: University of Texas Press).

Howe, James (1998) *A People Who Would Not Kneel: Panama, the United States, and the San Blas Kuna* (Washington, DC: Smithsonian Institution Press).

Htun, Mala (2004) From 'racial democracy' to affirmative action: changing state policy on race in Brazil, *Latin American Research Review* 39(1): 60–89.

Hugh-Jones, Stephen (1989) Wãr bi and the white men: history and myth in northwest Amazonia. In *History and Ethnicity*, Elizabeth Tonkin, Maryon McDonald and Malcolm Chapman (eds), pp. 53–70 (London: Routledge).

Hulme, Peter (1986) *Colonial Encounters: Europe and the Native Caribbean, 1492–1797* (London: Methuen).

Hyam, Ronald (1990) *Empire and Sexuality: The British Experience* (Manchester: Manchester University Press).

Ianni, Octavio (1966) *Raças e clases sociais no Brazil* (Rio de Janerio: Civilizacão Brasileira).

Ianni, Octavio (1972) Race and class in Latin America. In *Readings in Race and Ethnic Relations*, Anthony H. Richmond (ed.), pp. 237–56 (Oxford: Pergamon).

Ireland, Rowan (1992) *Kingdom's Come: Religion and Politics in Brazil* (Pittsburgh, PA: University of Pittsburgh Press).

Irele, F. Abiola (2004) The Harlem Renaissance and the Negritude movement. In *The Cambridge History of African and Caribbean Literature*, F. Abiola Irele and Simon Gikandi (eds) pp. 759–84 (Cambridge: Cambridge University Press).

Isbell, Billie Jean (1978) *To Defend Ourselves: Ecology and Ritual in an Andean Village* (Austin: Institute of Latin American Studies, University of Texas).

Jackson, Jean (1991) Being and becoming an Indian in the Vaupés. In *Nation-states and Indians in Latin America*, Greg Urban and Joel Sherzer (eds), pp. 131–55 (Austin: University of Texas Press).

Jackson, Jean (1995) Culture, genuine and spurious: the politics of Indianness in the Vaupés, Colombia, *American Ethnologist* 22(1): 3–27.

Jackson, Jean E. and Kay B. Warren (2005) Indigenous movements in Latin America, 1992–2004: controversies, ironies, new directions. *Annual Review of Anthropology* 34(1): 549–73.

Jameson, Frederic (1991) *Postmodernism, or the Cultural Logic of Late Capitalism* (Durham, NC: Duke University Press).

Jaramillo Uribe, Jaime (1968) *Ensayos sobre historia social colombiana*, vol. 1: *La sociedad neogranadina* (Bogotá: Universidad Nacional).

Jaulin, Robert (1970) *La Paix blanche: introduction à l'étnocide* (Paris: Éditions du Seuil).

Jones, Eric L. (1981) *The European Miracle: Environments, Economies, and Geopolitics in the History of Europe and Asia* (Cambridge: Cambridge University Press).

Jordan, Winthrop (1969) American chiaroscuro: the status and definition of mulattoes in the British colonies. In *Slavery in the New World: A Reader in Comparative History*, Laura Foner and Eugene Genovese (eds), pp. 189–201 (Englewood Cliffs, NJ: Prentice Hall).

Jordan, Winthrop (1977) *White over Black: American Attitudes towards the Negro, 1550–1812* (New York: Norton).

Karasch, Mary C. (1987) *Slave Life in Rio De Janeiro, 1808–1850* (Princeton, NJ: Princeton University Press).

Katzew, Ilona (2004) *Casta Painting: Images of Race in Eighteenth-century Mexico* (New Haven, CT: Yale University Press).

Kay, Cristobal (1989) *Latin American Theories of Development and Underdevelopment* (London: Routledge).

Kearney, Michael (1996) Introduction (to Special Issue on Indigenous Ethnicity and Mobilization in Latin America), *Latin American Perspectives* 23(2): 5–16.

Kearney, Michael (2000) Transnational Oaxacan indigenous identity: the case of Mixtecs and Zapotecs, *Identities – Global Studies in Culture and Power* 7(2): 173–95.

Keith, Michael and Malcolm Cross (1993) Racism and the postmodern city. In *Racism, the City, and the State*, Michael Keith and Malcolm Cross (eds), pp. 1–30 (London: Routledge).

Keller, Evelyn Fox (1986) *Reflections on Gender and Science* (New Haven, CT: Yale University Press).

Kempadoo, Kamala (ed.) (1999) *Sun, Sex, and Gold: Tourism and Sex Work in the Caribbean* (Lanham, MD: Rowman and Littlefield).

Kent, Michael (2008) The making of customary territories: social change at the intersection of state and indigenous territorial politics on Lake Titicaca, Peru, *Journal of Latin American and Caribbean Anthropology* 13(2): 283–310.

Kizca, John (1995) Recent books on ethnohistory and ethnic relations in colonial Mexico, *Latin American Research Review* 30(3): 239–53.

Kizca, John (ed.) (1999) *The Indian in Latin American History: Resistance, Resilience, and Acculturation*, 2nd edn (Wilmington, DE: SR Books).

Klein, Herbert S. and Ben Vinson (2007) *African Slavery in Latin America and the Caribbean*, 2nd edn (Oxford: Oxford University Press).

Knight, Alan (1990) Racism, revolution and *indigenismo* in Mexico, 1910–1940. In *The Idea of Race in Latin America*, Richard Graham (ed.), pp. 71–113 (Austin: University of Texas Press).

Knowles, Caroline and Sharmila Mercer (1992) Feminism and antiracism: an exploration of the political possibilities. In *Race, Culture and Difference*, James Donald and Ali Rattansi (eds), pp. 104–25 (London: SAGE).

Koenig, Barbara A., Sandra Soo-Jin Lee and Sarah S. Richardson (eds) (2008) *Revisiting Race in a Genomic Age* (New Brunswick, NJ: Rutgers University Press).

Kovic, Christine (2008) Rights of the poor: progressive Catholicism and indigenous resistance in Chiapas. In *Human Rights in the Maya Region: Global Politics, Cultural Contentions and Moral Engagements*, Pedro Pitarch, Shannon Speed and Xochitl Leyva Solano (eds), pp. 257–77 (Durham, NC: Duke University Press).

Kraay, Hendrik (1998) Introduction: Afro-Bahia, 1790s–1990s. In *Afro-Brazilian Culture and Politics: Bahia, 1790s to 1990s*, Hendrik Kraay (ed.), pp. 3–29 (Armonk, NY: M.E. Sharpe).

Krotz, Esteban (1997) Anthropologies of the South: their rise, their silencing, their characteristics, *Critique of Anthropology* 17(3): 237–51.

Kuhn, Thomas (1970) *The Structure of Scientific Revolutions* (Chicago: University of Chicago Press).

Kuper, Leo and Michael G. Smith (eds) (1969) *Pluralism in Africa* (Berkeley: University of California Press).

Kutzinski, Vera (1993) *Sugar's Secrets: Race and the Erotics of Cuban Nationalism* (Charlottesville: University of Virginia Press).

Landers, Jane G. and Barry M. Robinson (eds) (2006) *Slaves, Subjects, and Subversives: Blacks in Colonial Latin America* (Albuquerque: University of New Mexico Press).

Landry, Donna and Gerald MacLean (1993) *Materialist Feminisms* (Oxford: Blackwell).

Langdon, E. Jean Matteson and Gerhard Baer (eds) (1992) *Portals of Power: Shamanism in South America* (Albuquerque: University of New Mexico Press).

Langer, Erick D. (ed.) (2003) *Contemporary Indigenous Movements in Latin America* (Wilmington, DE: Scholarly Resources Books).

Lao-Montes, Agustin (2007) Decolonial moves: trans-locating African diaspora spaces, *Cultural Studies* 21(2): 309–38.

Larson, Brooke, Olivia Harris and Enrique Tandeter (eds) (1995) *Ethnicity, Markets and Migration in the Andes: At the Crossroads of History and Anthropology* (Durham, NC: Duke University Press).

Lauderdale Graham, Sandra (2002) *Caetana Says No: Women's Stories from a Brazilian Slave Society* (Cambridge: Cambridge University Press).

Lazar, Sian (2008) *El Alto, Rebel City: Self and Citizenship in Andean Bolivia* (Durham, NC: Duke University Press).

Leiker, James N., Barbara Watkins, and Kim Warren (eds) (2007) *The First and the Forced: Essays on the Native American and African American Experience* (Lawrence: Hall Center for the Humanities, University of Kansas).

Lewis, Laura A. (2003) *Hall of Mirrors: Power, Witchcraft, and Caste in Colonial Mexico* (Durham, NC: Duke University Press).

Lewis, Oscar (1951) *Life in a Mexican Village: Tepoztlán Restudied* (Urbana: University of Illinois Press).

Leyva Solano, Xochitl (1998) The new Zapatista movement: political levels, actors and political discourse in contemporary Mexico. In *Encuentros Antropológicos: Politics, Identity and Mobility in Mexican Society*, Valentina Napolitano and Xochitl Leyva Solano (eds), pp. 35–55 (London: Institute of Latin American Studies).

Lieberman, Leonard and Larry T. Reynolds (eds) (1996) Race: the deconstruction of a scientific concept. In *Race and Other Misadventures: Essays in Honor of Ashley Montagu in his Ninetieth Year*, Larry T. Reynolds and Leonard Lieberman (eds), pp. 142–73 (Dix Hills, NY: General Hall Inc.).

Lima, Antonio Carlos de Souza (1991) On indigenism and nationality in Brazil. In *Nation-states and Indians in Latin America*, Greg Urban and Joel Sherzer (eds), pp. 236–58 (Austin: University of Texas Press).

Linger, Daniel Touro (1992) *Dangerous Encounters: Meanings of Violence in a Brazilian City* (Stanford, CA: Stanford University Press).

Lockhart, James and Stuart Schwartz (1983) *Early Latin America* (Cambridge: Cambridge University Press).

Lombardi, John V. (1974) Comparative slave systems in the Americas: a critical review. In *New Approaches to Latin American History*, Richard Graham and Peter Smith (eds), pp. 156–74 (Austin: University of Texas Press).

Long, Norman (1977) *An Introduction to the Sociology of Rural Development* (London: Tavistock).

Lovell, Peggy A. and Charles H. Wood (1998) Skin color, racial identity, and life chances in Brazil, *Latin American Perspectives* 25(3): 90–109.

Lucero, José Antonio (2006) Representing 'real Indians': the challenges of indigenous authenticity and strategic constructivism in Ecuador and Bolivia, *Latin American Research Review* 41(2): 31–56.

Lyons, Andrew (1996) The neotenic career of M.F. Ashley Montagu. In *Race and Other Misadventures: Essays in Honor of Ashley Montagu in his Ninetieth Year*, Larry T. Reynolds and Leonard Lieberman (eds), pp. 3–22 (Dix Hills, NY: General Hall Inc.).

MacDonald, John and Leatrice MacDonald (1978) The black family in the Americas: a review of the literature, *Sage Race Relations Abstracts* 3(1): 1–42.

McCaa, Robert (1984) *Calidad*, class and marriage in colonial Mexico: the case of Parral, 1780–1790, *Hispanic American Historical Review* 64(3): 477–501.

McCallum, Cecilia (2008) Víctimas egoístas: perspectivas sobre la sexualidad, raza, clase y adolescencia desde un hospital de maternidad en Salvador, Brasil. In *Raza, etnicidad y sexualidades: ciudadanía y multiculturalismo en América latina*, Peter Wade, Fernando Urrea Giraldo and Mara Viveros Vigoya (eds), pp. 137–66 (Bogotá: Instituto CES, Facultad de Ciencias Humanas, Universidad Nacional de Colombia).

McClintock, Anne (1993) Family feuds: gender, nationalism and the family, *Feminist Review* 44: 61–80.

McClintock, Anne (1995) *Imperial Leather: Race, Gender and Sexuality in the Colonial Contest* (London: Routledge).

McGarrity, Gayle and Osvaldo Cárdenas (1995) Cuba. In *No Longer Invisible: Afro-Latin Americans Today*, Minority Rights Group (ed.), pp. 77–108 (London: Minority Rights Group).

Maio, Marcos Chor (1999) O Projeto Unesco e a agenda das ciências sociais no Brasil dos anos 40 e 50, *Revista Brasilena de Ciências Socias* 14(41): 141–58.

Malinowski, Bronislaw and Julio de la fuente (1982) *Malinowski in Mexico: The Economics of a Mexican Market System*, edited and with and Introduction by Susan Drucker-Brown (London: Routledge and Kegan Paul. Original edition: Mexico, 1957).

Mallon, Florencia E. (1992) Indian communities, political cultures and the state in Latin America, 1780–1990, *Journal of Latin American Studies*, 24, *Quincentenary Supplement*: 35–53.

Mallon, Florencia E. (1995) *Peasant and Nation: The Making of Postcolonial Mexico and Peru* (Berkeley: University of California Press).

Manuel, Peter (1995) *Caribbean Currents: Caribbean Music from Rumba to Reggae* (Philadelphia, PA: Temple University Press).

Marable, Manning (1995) *Beyond Black and White* (London: Verso).

Marcus, George and Michael Fischer (1986) *Anthropology as Cultural Critique* (Chicago: University of Chicago Press).

Martínez, María Elena (2008) *Genealogical Fictions: Limpieza de Sangre, Religion, and Gender in Colonial Mexico* (Stanford, CA: Stanford University Press).

Martinez-Alier [Stolcke], Verena (1989) *Marriage, Colour and Class in Nineteenth-century Cuba: A Study of Racial Attitudes and Sexual Values in a Slave Society*, 2nd edn (Ann Arbor: University of Michigan Press).

Marx, Anthony (1998) *Making Race and Nation: A Comparison of South Africa, the United States, and Brazil* (Cambridge: Cambridge University Press).

Mason, Peter (1990) *Deconstructing America: Representations of the Other* (London: Routledge).

Matory, J. Lorand (1999) The English professors of Brazil: on the diasporic roots of the Yorùbá nation, *Comparative Studies in Society and History* 41(1): 72–103.

Matory, J. Lorand (2005) *Black Atlantic Religion: Tradition, Transnationalism, and Matriarchy in the Afro-Brazilian Candomblé* (Princeton, NJ: Princeton University Press).

Matory, J. Lorand (2006) The 'New World' surrounds an ocean: theorizing the live dialogue between African and African American cultures. In *Afro-Atlantic Dialogues: Anthropology in the Diaspora*, Kevin Yelvington (ed.), pp. 151–92 (Santa Fe, NM: School of American Research Press).

Mattoso, Kátia M. de Queirós (1986) *To Be a Slave in Brazil, 1550–1888* (New Brunswick, NJ: Rutgers University Press).

Mayr, Ernst (1982) *The Growth of Biological Thought: Diversity, Evolution and Inheritance* (Cambridge, MA: Harvard University Press).

Meek, Ronald (1976) *Social Science and the Ignoble Savage* (Cambridge: Cambridge University Press.).

Meertens, Donny (2009) Discriminación racial, desplazamiento y género en las sentencias de la Corte Constitucional. El racismo cotidiano en el banquillo, *Universitas Humanística* 66: 83–106.

Merchant, Carol (1983) *The Death of Nature: Women, Ecology and the Scientific Revolution* (San Francisco: Harper and Row).

Mignolo, Walter (2000) *Local Histories/Global Designs: Coloniality, Subaltern Knowledges, and Border Thinking* (Princeton, NJ: Princeton University Press).

Minna Stern, Alexandra (2003) From mestizophilia to biotypology: racialization and science in Mexico, 1920–1960. In *Race and Nation in Modern Latin America*, Nancy Appelbaum, Karin A. Rosemblatt and Anne S. Macpherson (eds), pp. 187–210 (Chapel Hill: University of North Carolina Press).

Mintz, Sidney and Richard Price (1976) *An Anthropological Approach to the Afro-American Past: A Caribbean Perspective* (Philadelphia, PA: Institute for the Study of Human Issues).

Mitchell, J. Clyde (1956) *The Kalela Dance: Aspects of Social Relationships among Urban Africans in Northern Rhodesia* (Manchester: Manchester University Press for the Rhodes-Livingstone Institute).

Mitchell, Timothy (1990) Everyday metaphors of power, *Theory and Society* 19(5): 545–77.

Modood, Tariq (2007) *Multiculturalism: A Civic Idea* (Cambridge: Polity).

Montejo, Esteban and Miguel Barnet (1993) *The Autobiography of a Runaway Slave*, trans. Jocasta Innes (London: Macmillan Caribbean).

Moore, Robin (1997) *Nationalizing Blackness: Afrocubanismo and Artistic Revolution in Havana, 1920–1940* (Pittsburgh, PA: University of Pittsburgh Press).

Moreno Figueroa, Mónica (2008) Historically-rooted transnationalism: slightedness and the experience of racism in Mexican families, *Journal of Intercultural Studies* 29(3): 283–97.

Mörner, Magnus (1967) *Race Mixture in the History of Latin America* (Boston, MA: Little Brown).

Moutinho, Laura (2004) *Razão, 'cor' e desejo: uma análise comparativa sobre relacionamentos afetivo-sexuais 'inter-raciais' no Brasil e África do Sul* (São Paulo: Editora da UNESP).

Nagel, Joane (2003) *Race, Ethnicity, and Sexuality: Intimate Intersections, Forbidden Frontiers* (Oxford: Oxford University Press).

Naro, Nancy Priscilla (ed.) (2002) *Blacks, Coloureds and National Identity in Nineteenth-century Latin America* (London: School of Advanced Study, Institute for the Study of the Americas).

Nash, Jennifer C. (2008) Re-thinking intersectionality, *Feminist Review* 89(1): 1–15.

Nash, June (1995) The reassertion of indigenous identity: Mayan responses to state intervention in Chiapas, *Latin American Research Review* 30(3): 7–41.

Nash, June (2001) *Mayan Visions: The Quest for Autonomy in an Age of Globalization* (London: Routledge).

Nash, Manning (1958) *Machine Age Maya: The Industrialization of a Guatemalan Community* (Mensha, WI: American Anthropological Association).

Nash, Manning (1970) The impact of mid-nineteenth-century economic change upon the indians of Middle America. In *Race and Class in Latin America*, Magnus Mörner (ed.), pp. 170–83 (New York: Columbia University Press).

Needell, Jeffrey D. (1995) Identity, race, gender, and modernity in the origins of Gilberto Freyre's *oeuvre*, *American Historical Review* 100(1): 51–77.

Nelson, Diane M. (1999) *A Finger in the Wound: Body Politics in Quincentennial Guatemala* (Berkeley: University of California Press).

Ng'weno, Bettina (2007a) Can ethnicity replace race? Afro-Colombians, indigeneity and the Colombian multicultural state, *Journal of Latin American and Caribbean Anthropology* 12(2): 414–40.

Ng'weno, Bettina (2007b) *Turf Wars: Territory and Citizenship in the Contemporary State* (Stanford, CA: Stanford University Press).

Nobles, Melissa (2000) *Shades of Citizenship: Race and the Census in Modern Politics* (Stanford, CA: Stanford University Press).

Nogueira, Oracy (1955) Preconceito racial de marca e preconceito racial de origem. In *Annais do XXXVI Congresso Internacional de Americanistas*, pp. 409–34 (São Paulo: Editora Anhembí).

Norget, Kristin (2004) 'Knowing where we enter': indigenous theology and the Catholic Church in Oaxaca, México. In *Resurgent Voices in Latin America: Indigenous Peoples, Political Mobilization, and Religious Change*, Edward L. Cleary and Timothy J. Steigenga (eds), pp. 154–86 (New Brunswick, NJ: Rutgers University Press).

Omi, Michael and Howard Winant (1986) *Racial Formation in the USA from the 1960s to the 1980s* (New York: Routledge).

Orlove, Benjamin (1998) Down to earth: race and substance in the Andes, *Bulletin of Latin American Research* 17(2): 207–22.

Ortiz, Fernando (1973 [1906]) *Hampa afrocubana: los negros brujos* (Miami: Ediciones Universal).

Ortiz, Fernando (1984) *Ensayos etnográficos*, edited by Miguel Barnet and Angel Fernández (Havana: Editorial de Ciencias Sociales).

Oslender, Ulrich (2008) Another history of violence: the production of 'geographies of terror' in Colombia's Pacific coast region, *Latin American Perspectives* 35(5): 77–102.

Pagden, Anthony (1982) *The Fall of Natural Man: The American Indian and the Origins of Comparative Ethnology* (Cambridge: Cambridge University Press).

Pagden, Anthony (1993) *European Encounters with the New World* (New Haven, CT: Yale University Press).

Paine, Robert (ed.) (1985) *Advocacy and Anthropology* (St Johns: Memorial University of Newfoundland).

Palmié, Stephan (1995) Against syncretism: 'Africanizing' and 'Cubanizing' discourses in North American *òrìsà* worship. In *Counterworks: Managing the Diversity of Knowledge*, Richard Fardon (ed.), pp. 73–104 (London: Routledge).

Parker, Andrew, Mary Russo, Doris Sommer and Patricia Yaeger (eds) (1992) *Nationalisms and Sexualities* (London: Routledge).

Peirano, Mariza (2008) Brazil: otherness in context. In *A Companion to Latin American Anthropology*, Deborah Poole (ed.), pp. 56–71 (Oxford: Blackwell Publishing).

Perlman, Janice (2005) The myth of marginality revisited: *favelas* in Rio de Janeiro, 1969–2003. World Bank. URL (accessed 21 August 2009): http://www.worldbank.org/urban/symposium2005/papers/perlman.pdf

Pierson, Donald (1942) *Negroes in Brazil: A Study of Race Contact at Bahia* (Chicago: University of Chicago Press).

Pieterse, J. Nederveen (1992) *White on Black: Images of Africa and Blacks in Western Popular Culture* (New Haven, CT: Yale University Press).

Pinheiro, Joceny (2009) Authors of authenticity: indigenous leadership and the politics of identity in the Brazilian northeast. PhD thesis, University of Manchester.

Pinho, Patricia (2006) Afro-aesthetics in Brazil. In *Beautiful/Ugly: African and Diaspora Aesthetics*, Sarah Nuttall (ed.), pp. 266–89 (Durham, NC: Duke University Press).

Platt, Tristan (1993) Simón Bolívar, the sun of justice and the Amerindian virgin – Andean conceptions of the *patria* in nineteenth-century Potosí, *Journal of Latin American Studies* 25(1): 159–85.

Platt, Tristan (1995) Ethnic calendars and market interventions among the *ayullus* of Lipes during the nineteenth century. In *Ethnicity, Markets, and Migration in the Andes: At the Crossroads of History and Anthropology*, Brooke Larson, Olivia Harris and Enrique Tandeter (eds), pp. 259–96 (Durham, NC: Duke University Press).

Poole, Deborah (1997) *Vision, Race and Modernity: A Visual Economy of the Andean Image World* (Princeton, NJ: Princeton University Press).

Poole, Deborah (ed.) (2008) *A Companion to Latin American Anthropology* (Oxford: Blackwell).

Porqueres i Gené, Enric (2007) Kinship language and the dynamics of race: the Basque case. In *Race, Ethnicity and Nation: Perspectives from Kinship and Genetics*, Peter Wade (ed.), pp. 125–44 (Oxford: Berghahn Books).

Postero, Nancy Grey (2007) *Now We Are Citizens: Indigenous Politics in Postmulticultural Bolivia* (Stanford, CA: Stanford University Press).

Postero, Nancy Grey and Leon Zamosc (eds) (2004) *Struggle for Indigenous Rights in Latin America* (Brighton: Sussex Academic Press).

Powers, Karen Vieira (2005) *Women in the Crucible of Conquest: The Gendered Genesis of Spanish American Society, 1500–1600* (Albuquerque: University of New Mexico Press).

Pravaz, Natasha (2003) Brazilian *mulatice*: performing race, gender, and the nation, *Journal of Latin American Anthropology* 8(1): 116–46.

Prescott, Laurence E. (1985) Jorge Artel frente a Nicolás Guillén: dos poetas mulatos ante la poesía negra hispanoamericana. In *Ensayos de literatura colombiana*, Raymond L. Williams (ed.), pp. 129–36 (Bogotá: Plaza y Janes).

Price, Richard (1979) Introduction' and Afterword. In *Maroon Societies: Rebel Slave Communities in the Americas*, 2nd edn, Richard Price (ed.), pp. 1–30 and 417–31 (Garden City, NY: Anchor Books).

Price, Richard (1983) *First Time: The Historical Vision of an Afro-American People* (Baltimore, MD: Johns Hopkins University Press).

Price, Richard (1990) *Alabi's World* (Baltimore, MD: Johns Hopkins University Press).

Price, Richard (2007) *Travels with Tooy: History, Memory, and the African American Imagination* (Chicago: University of Chicago Press).

Price, Sally (2001) *Primitive Art in Civilized Places*, 2nd edn (Chicago: University of Chicago Press).

Price, Sally and Richard Price (1999) *Maroon Arts: Cultural Vitality in the African Diaspora* (Boston, MA: Beacon Press).

Radcliffe, Sarah (1990) Ethnicity, patriarchy and incorporation into the nation: female migrants as domestic servants in southern Peru, *Environment and Planning D: Society and Space* 8: 379–93.

Radcliffe, Sarah (2008) Las mujeres indígenas ecuatorianas bajo la gobernabilidad multicultural y de género. In *Raza, etnicidad y sexualidades: ciudadanía y multiculturalismo en América latina*, Peter Wade, Fernando Urrea Giraldo and Mara Viveros Vigoya (eds), pp. 105–36 (Bogotá: Instituto CES, Facultad de Ciencias Humanas, Universidad Nacional de Colombia).

Radcliffe, Sarah, Nina Laurie and Robert Andolina (2002) Indigenous people and political transnationalism: globalization from below meets globalization from above? ESRC Transnational Communities Programme. URL (accessed 1 September 2009): www.transcomm.ox.ac.uk/working%20papers/WPTC-02–05%20 Radcliffe.pdf

Rahier, Jean (1999) Body politics in black and white: *señoras, mujeres, blanqueamiento* and Miss Esmeraldas 1997–1998, Ecuador, *Women and Performance: A Journal of Feminist Theory* 21: 103–19.

Ramírez, Susan Elizabeth (2009) Recent research on the Andes before Independence: ethnohistory, social history, and revolt and revolution, *History Compass* 7(3): 800–36.

Ramos, Alcida (1998) *Indigenism: Ethnic Politics in Brazil* (Madison: University of Wisconsin Press).

Rappaport, Joanne (1990) *The Politics of Memory: Native Historical Interpretation in the Colombian Andes* (Cambridge: Cambridge University Press).

Rappaport, Joanne (1994) *Cumbe Reborn: An Andean Ethnography of History* (Chicago: University of Chicago Press).

Rappaport, Joanne (2005) *Intercultural Utopias: Public Intellectuals, Cultural Experimentation and Ethnic Pluralism in Colombia* (Durham, NC: Duke University Press).

Rappaport, Joanne, and Robert V.H. Dover (1996) The construction of difference by native legislators: assessing the impact of the Colombian Constitution of 1991, *Journal of Latin American Anthropology* 1(2): 22–45.

Redfield, Robert (1930) *Tepoztlán: A Mexican Village* (Chicago: University of Chicago Press).

Redfield, Robert (1956) The relations between Indians and ladinos in Agua Escondida, Guatemala, *América Indígena* 16: 253–76.

Reily, Suzel Ana (1994) Macunaíma's music: national identity and ethnomusicological research in Brazil. In *Ethnicity, Identity and Music: The Musical Construction of Place*, Martin Stokes (ed.), pp. 71–96 (Oxford: Berg).

Reis, João José (1993) *Slave Rebellion in Brazil: The Muslim Uprising of 1835 in Bahia* (Baltimore, MD: Johns Hopkins University Press).

Renard, Marie-Christine (1994) Le Chiapas est aussi le Mexique: neo-zapatisme et changement politique, *Cahiers des Amériques Latines* 17: 5–23.

Restall, Matthew (2004) *Seven Myths of the Spanish Conquest* (New York: Oxford University Press).

Restall, Matthew (ed.) (2005) *Beyond Black and Red: African–Native Relations in Colonial Latin America* (Albuquerque: University of New Mexico Press).

Restrepo, Eduardo (2002) Políticas de la alteridad: etnización de 'comunidad negra' en el Pacífico sur colombiano, *Journal of Latin American Anthropology* 7(2): 34–58.

Restrepo, Eduardo and Arturo Escobar (2005) 'Other anthropologies and anthropology otherwise': steps to a world anthropologies framework, *Critique of Anthropology* 25(2): 99–129.

Rex, John (1986) Class analysis: a Weberian approach. In *Theories of Race and Ethnic Relations*, John Rex and David Mason (eds), pp. 64–83 (Cambridge: Cambridge University Press).

Reynolds, Larry T. and Leonard Lieberman (eds) (1996) *Race and Other Misadventures: Essays in Honor of Ashley Montagu in his Ninetieth Year* (Dix Hills, NY: General Hall Inc.).

Richard, Nelly (1997) Intersectando Latinoamérica con el latinoamericanismo: saberes académicos, práctica teórica y crítica cultural, *Revista Iberoaméricano* 63(180): 345–61.

Rivera Cusicanqui, Silvia (1993) Anthropology and society in the Andes: themes and issues, *Critique of Anthropology* 13(1): 77–96.

Roberts, Bryan (1974) The interrelationships between city and provinces in Peru and Guatemala. In *Anthropological Perspectives on Latin American Urbanization*, Wayne Cornelius and Felicity Trueblood (eds), pp. 207–36 (Beverly Hills, CA: SAGE).

Roberts, John Storm (1979) *The Latin Tinge: The Impact of Latin American Music on the United States* (New York: Oxford University Press).

Rodríguez, Clara E. (1994) Challenging racial hegemony: Puerto Ricans in the United States. In *Race*, Steven Gregory and Roger Sanjek (eds), pp. 131–45 (New Brunswick, NJ: Rutgers University Press).

Rodríguez, Clara E. (2000) *Changing Race: Latinos, the Census, and the History of Ethnicity in the United States* (New York: New York University Press).

Rodríguez-Mangual, Edna M. (2004) *Lydia Cabrera and the Construction of an Afro-Cuban Cultural Identity* (Chapel Hill: University of North Carolina Press).

Rostas, Susanna and André Droogers (eds) (1993) *The Popular Use of Popular Religion in Latin America* (Amsterdam: CEDLA).

Rouse, Roger (1995) Questions of identity: personhood and collectivity in transnational migration to the United States, *Critique of Anthropology* 15(4): 351–80.

Rout, Leslie (1976) *The African Experience in Spanish America: 1502 to the Present Day* (Cambridge: Cambridge University Press).

Russell-Wood, A.J.R. (1982) *The Black Man in Slavery and Freedom in Colonial Brazil* (London: St Antony's College and Macmillan).

Safa, Helen I. (2005) Challenging *mestizaje*: a gender perspective on indigenous and Afrodescendant movements in Latin America. *Critique of Anthropology* 25(3): 307–30.

Sagás, Ernesto (2004) From *ausentes* to dual nationals: the incorporation of transmigrants into Dominican politics. In *Dominican Migration: Transnational Perspectives*, Ernesto Sagás and Sintia E. Molina (eds), pp. 53–73 (Gainesville: University Press of Florida).

Sagás, Ernesto and Sintia E. Molina (eds) (2004) *Dominican Migration: Transnational Perspectives* (Gainesville: University Press of Florida).

Sahlins, Marshall (1993) Goodbye to tristes tropes: ethnography in the context of modern world history, *Journal of Modern History* 65: 1–25.

Sahlins, Marshall (1999) Two or three things that I know about culture, *Journal of the Royal Anthropological Institute* 5(3): 399–421.

Said, Edward (1985) *Orientalism: Western Concepts of the Orient* (Harmondsworth: Penguin).

Sanders, James (2004) *Contentious Republicans: Popular Politics, Race, and Class in Nineteenth-century Colombia* (Durham, NC: Duke University Press).

Sanford, Victoria (2004) Contesting displacement in Colombia: citizenship and state sovereignty at the margins. In *Anthropology in the Margins of the State*, Veena Das and Deborah Poole (eds), pp. 253–77 (Santa Fe, NM: School of American Research).

Sanjek, Roger (1971) Brazilian racial terms: some aspects of meaning and learning, *American Anthropologist* 73: 1126–44.

Sanjinés, Javier (2004) *Mestizaje Upside Down: Aesthetic Politics in Modern Bolivia* (Pittsburgh, PA: University of Pittsburgh Press).

Sansone, Livio (2003) *Blackness without Ethnicity: Constructing Race in Brazil* (Houndmills: Palgrave Macmillan).

Sansone, Livio, Eliseé Soumonni and Boubacar Barry (eds) (2008) *Africa, Brazil and the Construction of Trans-Atlantic Black Identities* (Trenton, NJ: Africa World Press).

Saunders, A.C. de C.M. (1982) *A Social History of Black Slaves and Freedmen in Portugal, 1441–1555* (Cambridge: Cambridge University Press).

Scherrer, Christian P. (1994) Regional autonomy in Eastern Nicaragua (1990–1994). In *Indigenous Peoples' Experiences with Self-Government*, Willem Assies and André Hoekema (eds), pp. 109–48 (Amsterdam: IWGIA and the University of Amsterdam).

Schryer, Frans J. (1990) *Ethnicity and Class Conflict in Rural Mexico* (Princeton, NJ: Princeton University Press).

Schwartz, Stuart B. (2002) Black Latin America: legacies of slavery, race, and African culture, *Hispanic American Historical Review* 82(3): 429–33.

Schwartzman, Luisa Farah (2009) Seeing like citizens: unofficial understandings of official racial categories in a Brazilian university, *Journal of Latin American Studies* 41(2): 221–50.

Schwarz, Roberto (1992) *Misplaced Ideas: Essays on Brazilian Culture*. Edited and with an introduction by John Gledson (London: Verso).

Scott, James (1985) *Weapons of the Weak: Everyday Forms of Peasant Resistance* (New Haven, CT: Yale University Press).

Seed, Patricia (1982) Social dimensions of race: Mexico City, 1753, *Hispanic American Historical Review* 62(4): 569–606.

Seigel, Micol (2009) *Uneven Encounters: Making Race and Nation in Brazil and the United States* (Durham, NC: Duke University Press).

Seligmann, Linda J. (2008) Agrarian reform and peasant studies: the Peruvian case. In *A Companion to Latin American Anthropology*, Deborah Poole (ed.), pp. 325–51 (Oxford: Blackwell Publishing).

Selka, Stephen (2007) *Religion and the Politics of Ethnic Identity in Bahia, Brazil* (Gainesville: University Press of Florida).

Selverston-Scher, Melina (2001) *Ethnopolitics in Ecuador: Indigenous Rights and the Strengthening of Democracy* (Miami, FL: North-South Center Press).

Sheriff, Robin E. (2001) *Dreaming Equality: Color, Race, and Racism in Urban Brazil* (New Brunswick, NJ: Rutgers University Press).

Sieder, Rachel (ed.) (2002) *Multiculturalism in Latin America: Indigenous Rights, Diversity and Democracy* (Houndmills: Palgrave Macmillan).

Sieder, Rachel, Alan Angell and Line Schjolden (eds) (2005) *The Judicialization of Politics in Latin America* (Houndmills: Palgrave Macmillan).

Silva, Denise Ferreira da (1998) Facts of blackness: Brazil is not (quite) the United States … And racial politics in Brazil?, *Social Identities* 4(2): 201–34.

Silva, Nelson do Valle (1985) Updating the cost of not being white in Brazil. In *Race, Class and Power in Brazil*, Pierre-Michel Fontaine (ed.), pp. 42–55 (Los Angeles: Center for Afro-American Studies, University of California).

Silva, Nelson do Valle and Carlos Hasenbalg (1999) Race and educational opportunity in Brazil. In *Race in Contemporary Brazil: From Indifference to Inequality*, Rebecca Reichmann (ed.), pp. 53–65 (Pennsylvania: Pennsylvania State University Press).

Silverblatt, Irene (2004) *Modern Inquisitions: Peru and the Colonial Origins of the Civilized World* (Durham, NC: Duke University Press).

Simmons, Kimberly Eison (2009) *Reconstructing Racial Identity and the African Past in the Dominican Republic* (Gainesville: University Press of Florida).

Simpson, Amelia (1993) *Xuxa: The Mega-marketing of Gender, Race and Modernity* (Philadelphia, PA: Temple University Press).

Sittón, Salomón Nahmad (2008) Mexico: anthropology and the nation-state. In *A Companion to Latin American Anthropology*, Deborah Poole (ed.), pp. 128–49 (Oxford: Blackwell Publishing).

Skidmore, Thomas (1972) Towards a comparative analysis of race relations since abolition in Brazil and the United States, *Journal of Latin American Studies* 4(1): 1–28.

Skidmore, Thomas (1974) *Black into White: Race and Nationality in Brazilian Thought* (New York: Oxford University Press).

Skidmore, Thomas (1993) Bi-racial USA vs. multi-racial Brazil: is the contrast still valid?, *Journal of Latin American Studies* 25: 373–86.

Skidmore, Thomas (2003) Racial mixture and affirmative action: the cases of Brazil and the United States, *American Historical Review* 108(5): 1391–6.

Smedley, Audrey (1993) *Race in North America: Origin and Evolution of a World View* (Oxford: Westview).

Smith, Carol A. (1997) The symbolics of blood: mestizaje in the Americas, *Identities: Global Studies in Power and Culture* 3(4): 495–521.

Smith, Carol A. (ed.) (1990) *Guatemalan Indians and the State, 1540–1988* (Austin: University of Texas Press).

Smith, Gavin (1999) *Confronting the Present: Towards a Politically Engaged Anthropology* (Oxford: Berg).

Smith, Gavin (2007) Hegemony. In *A Companion to the Anthropology of Politics*, David Nugent and Joan Vincent (eds), pp. 216–30 (Oxford: Blackwell).

Smith, Michael G. (1965) *The Plural Society in the British West Indies* (Berkeley: University of California Press).

Solaún, Mauricio and Sidney Kronus (1973) *Discrimination without Violence: Miscegenation and Racial Conflict in Latin America* (New York: John Wiley and Sons).

Solomos, John (1986) Varieties of Marxist conceptions of 'race', class and the state: a critical analysis. In *Theories of Race and Ethnic Relations*, John Rex and David Mason (eds), pp. 84–109 (Cambridge: Cambridge University Press).

Solomos, John (1989) *Race and Racism in Contemporary Britain* (London: Routledge).

Speed, Shannon (2005) Dangerous discourses: human rights and multiculturalism in neoliberal Mexico, *PoLAR: Political and Legal Anthropology Review* 28(1): 29–51.

Speed, Shannon and Xochitl Leyva Solano (2008) Global discourses on the local terrain: human rights in Chiapas. In *Human Rights in the Maya Region: Global Politics, Cultural Contentions and Moral Engagements*, Pedro Pitarch, Shannon Speed and Xochitl Leyva Solano (eds), pp. 207–31 (Durham, NC: Duke University Press).

Spivak, Gayatri Chakravorty (1999) *A Critique of Postcolonial Reason: Toward a History of the Vanishing Present* (Cambridge, MA: Harvard University Press).

Stavenhagen, Rodolfo (1975) *Social Classes in Agrarian Societies* (Garden City, NY: Anchor Books).

Stavenhagen, Rodolfo (1996) *Ethnic Conflicts and the Nation-State* (Houndmills: Macmillan; New York: St Martin's Press).

Stepan, Nancy (1982) *The Idea of Race in Science: Great Britain, 1800–1950* (London: Macmillan).

Stepan, Nancy (1991) *The Hour of Eugenics: Race, Gender and Nation in Latin America* (Ithaca, NY: Cornell University Press).

Stephen, Lynn (2002) *Zapata Lives! Histories and Cultural Politics in Southern Mexico* (Berkeley: University of California Press).

Stephens, Michelle Ann (2005) *Black Empire: The Masculine Global Imaginary of Caribbean Intellectuals in the United States, 1914–1962* (Durham, NC: Duke University Press).

Stern, Steve J. (ed.) (1987) *Resistance, Rebellion and Consciousness in the Andean Peasant World, 18th to 20th Centuries* (Madison: University of Wisconsin Press).

Stern, Steve J. (1993) *Peru's Indian Peoples and the Challenge of Spanish Conquest: Huamanga to 1640*, 2nd edn (Madison: University of Wisconsin Press).

Stern, Steve J. (1995) *The Secret History of Gender: Women, Men, and Power in Late Colonial Mexico* (Chapel Hill: University of North Carolina Press).

Stocking, George (1982) *Race, Culture and Evolution: Essays on the History of Anthropology*, 2nd edn (Chicago: University of Chicago Press).

Stoler, Ann Laura (2002) *Carnal Knowledge and Imperial Power: Race and the Intimate in Colonial Rule* (Berkeley: University of California Press).

Stone, John (1979) Introduction: internal colonialism in comparative perspective, *Ethnic and Racial Studies* 2(3): 253–9.

Streicker, Joel (1995) Policing boundaries: race, class, and gender in Cartagena, Colombia, *American Ethnologist* 22(1): 54–74.

Stutzman, Ronald (1981) *El mestizaje*: an all-inclusive ideology of exclusion. In *Cultural Transformations and Ethnicity in Modern Ecuador*, Norman E. Whitten (ed.), pp. 45–94. (Urbana: University of Illinois Press).

Tannenbaum, Frank (1948) *Slave and Citizen: The Negro in the Americas* (New York: Vintage Books).

Taussig, Michael (1980) *The Devil and Commodity Fetishism in South America* (Chapel Hill: University of North Carolina Press).

Taussig, Michael (1987) *Shamanism, Colonialism and the Wild Man: A Study in Terror and Healing* (Chicago: University of Chicago Press).

Tax, Sol (1942) Ethnic relations in Guatemala, *América Indígena* 2(4): 43–8.

Tax, Sol (1953) *Penny Capitalism: A Guatemalan Indian Economy* (Washington, DC: Smithsonian Institution).

Tax, Sol and Robert Hinshaw (1970) Panajachel a generation later. In *The Social Anthropology of Latin America: Essays in Honor of Ralph Leon Beals*, Walter Goldschmidt and Harry Hoijer (eds), pp. 175–98 (Los Angeles: Latin American Center, University of California).

Telles, Edward E. (2004) *Race in Another America: The Significance of Skin Color in Brazil* (Princeton, NJ: Princeton University Press).

Thompson, Alvin O. (2006) *Flight to Freedom: African Runaways and Maroons in the Americas* (Kingston, Jamaica: University of the West Indies Press).

Toplin, Robert (1971) Reinterpreting comparative race relations: the United States and Brazil, *Journal of Black Studies* 2(2): 135–56.

Toplin, Robert (1981) *Freedom and Prejudice: The Legacy of Slavery in the USA and Brazil* (Westport, CT: Greenwood Press).

Torgovnick, Mariana (1990) *Gone Primitive: Savage Intellects, Modern Lives* (Chicago: University of Chicago Press).

Treece, David (1990) Indigenous peoples in the Brazilian Amazon and the expansion of the economic frontier. In *The Future of Amazonia: Destruction or Sustainable Development?*, David Goodman and Anthony Hall (eds), pp. 264–87 (London: Macmillan).

Tumin, Melvin (1952) *Caste in a Peasant Society* (Princeton, NJ: Princeton University Press).

Turner, Bryan (ed.) (1990) *Theories of Modernity and Postmodernity* (London: SAGE).

Turner, Terence (1991) Representing, resisting, rethinking: historical transformations of Kayapo culture and anthropological consciousness. In *Colonial Situations: Essays on the Contextualization of Ethnographic Knowledge*, George Stocking (ed.), pp. 285–313 (Madison: University of Wisconsin Press).

Turner, Terence (1992) Defiant images: the Kayapo appropriation of video, *Anthropology Today* 8(6): 5–16.

Turra, Cleusa and Gustavo Venturi (1995) *Racismo cordial: a mais completa análise sobre o preconceito de cor no Brasil* (São Paulo: Ática).

Twinam, Ann (1999) *Public Lives, Private Secrets: Gender, Honor, Sexuality and Illegitimacy in Colonial Spanish America* (Stanford, CA: Stanford University Press).

Twine, France W. (1998) *Racism in a Racial Democracy: The Maintenance of White Supremacy in Brazil* (New Brunswick, NJ: Rutgers University Press).

Urban, Greg and Joel Sherzer (eds) (1991a) *Nation-states and Indians in Latin America* (Austin: University of Texas Press).

Urban, Greg and Joel Sherzer (1991b) Introduction: Indians, nation-states, and culture. In *Nation-states and Indians in Latin America*, Greg Urban and Joel Sherzer (eds), pp. 1–18 (Austin: University of Texas Press).

Urrea Giraldo, Fernando, Waldor Botero Arias, Hernán Darío Herrera Arce and José Ignacio Reyes Serna (2006) Afecto y elección de pareja en jóvenes de sectores populares de Cali, *Revista Estudos Feministas* 14: 117–48.

Van Cott, Donna Lee (2000) *The Friendly Liquidation of the Past: The Politics of Diversity in Latin America* (Pittsburgh, PA: University of Pittsburgh Press).

van den Berghe, Pierre (1967) *Race and racism* (New York: John Wiley and Sons).

van den Berghe, Pierre (1974a) Ethnic terms in Peruvian social science literature. In *Class and Ethnicity in Peru*, Pierre van den Berghe (ed.), pp. 12–22 (Leiden: E.J. Brill).

van den Berghe, Pierre (1974b) Introduction. In *Class and Ethnicity in Peru*, Pierre van den Berghe (ed.), pp. 1–11 (Leiden: E.J. Brill).

van den Berghe, Pierre (1975) Ethnicity and class in highland Peru. In *Ethnicity and Resource Competition in Plural Societies*, Leo Despres (ed.), pp. 71–85. (The Hague: Mouton).

Varese, Stefano (1996) The ethnopolitics of Indian resistance in Latin America, *Latin American Perspectives* 23(2): 58–71.

Vianna, Hermano (1999) *The Mystery of Samba: Popular Music and National Identity in Brazil*, trans. John Charles Chasteen (Chapel Hill: University of North Carolina Press).

Viveros Vigoya, Mara (2006) Políticas de sexualidad juvenil y diferencias étnico-raciales en Colombia, *Revista Estudos Feministas* 14(1): 149–69.

Viveros Vigoya, Mara (2008) Más que una cuestión de piel. Determinantes sociales y orientaciones subjetivas en los encuentros y desencuentros heterosexuales entre mujeres y hombres negros y non negros en Bogotá. In *Raza, etnicidad y sexualidades: ciudadanía y multiculturalismo en América latina*, Peter Wade, Fernando Urrea Giraldo and Mara Viveros Vigoya (eds), pp. 247–78 (Bogotá: Instituto CES, Facultad de Ciencias Humanas, Universidad Nacional de Colombia).

Wade, Peter (1986) Patterns of race in Colombia, *Bulletin of Latin American Research* 5(2): 1–19

Wade, Peter (1993a) *Blackness and Race Mixture: The Dynamics of Racial Identity in Colombia*. (Baltimore, MD: Johns Hopkins University Press).

Wade, Peter (1993b) 'Race', nature and culture, *Man* 28(1): 1–18.

Wade, Peter (1995) The cultural politics of blackness in Colombia, *American Ethnologist* 22(2): 342–58.

Wade, Peter (1999) Working culture: making cultural identities in Cali, Colombia, *Current Anthropology* 40(4): 449–71.

Wade, Peter (2000) *Music, Race and Nation: Música Tropical in Colombia* (Chicago: University of Chicago Press).

Wade, Peter (2002a) *Race, Nature and Culture: An Anthropological Perspective* (London: Pluto Press).

Wade, Peter (2002b) The Colombian Pacific in perspective, *Journal of Latin American Anthropology* 7(2): 2–33.

Wade, Peter (2004) Images of Latin American mestizaje and the politics of comparison, *Bulletin of Latin American Research* 23(1): 355–66.

Wade, Peter (2005) Rethinking *mestizaje*: ideology and lived experience, *Journal of Latin American Studies* 37: 1–19.

Wade, Peter (2006a) Afro-Latin studies: reflections on the field, *Latin American and Caribbean Ethnic Studies* 1(1): 105–24.

Wade, Peter (2006b) Understanding 'Africa' and 'blackness' in Colombia: music and the politics of culture. In *Afro-Atlantic Dialogues: Anthropology in the Diaspora*, Kevin Yelvington (ed.), pp. 351–78 (Santa Fe, NM: School of American Research Press).

Wade, Peter (2009a) Defining blackness in Colombia, *Journal de la Société des Américanistes* 95(1): 165–84.

Wade, Peter (2009b) *Race and Sex in Latin America* (London: Pluto Press).

Wagley, Charles (ed.) (1952) *Race and Class in Rural Brazil* (Paris: UNESCO).

Warren, Jonathan W. (2001) *Racial Revolutions: Antiracism and Indian Resurgence in Brazil* (Durham, NC: Duke University Press).

Warren, Kay B. (1998) *Indigenous Movements and Their Critics: Pan-Maya Activism in Guatemala* (Princeton, NJ: Princeton University Press).

Warren, Kay B. and Jean E. Jackson (eds) (2003) *Indigenous Movements, Self-representation, and the State in Latin America* (Austin: University of Texas Press).

Watanabe, John (1995) Unimagining the Maya: anthropologists, others and the inescapable hubris of authorship, *Bulletin of Latin American Research* 14(1): 25–46.

Weiner, Michael (1995) Discourses of race, nation and empire in pre-1945 Japan, *Ethnic and Racial Studies* 18(3): 433–56.

Weismantel, Mary (2001) *Cholas and Pishtacos: Stories of Race and Sex in the Andes* (Chicago: University of Chicago Press).

Wetherell, Margaret and Jonathan Potter (1992) *Mapping the Language of Racism: Discourse and the Legitimation of Exploitation* (London: Harvester Wheatsheaf).

Whitten, Norman (1965) *Class, Kinship and Power in an Ecuadorian Town* (Stanford, CA: Stanford University Press).

Whitten, Norman (1975) Jungle Quechua ethnicity: an Ecuadorian case study. In *Ethnicity and Resource Competition in Plural Societies*, Leo Despres (ed.), pp. 41–69 (The Hague: Mouton).

Whitten, Norman (1976) *Sacha Runa: Ethnicity and Adaptation of Ecuadorian Jungle Quichua* (Urbana: University of Illinois Press).

Whitten, Norman (ed.) (1981a) *Cultural Transformations and Ethnicity in Modern Ecuador* (Urbana: University of Illinois Press).

Whitten, Norman (1981b) Introduction. In *Cultural Transformations and Ethnicity in Modern Ecuador*, Norman E. Whitten (ed.), pp. 1–44 (Urbana: University of Illinois Press).

Whitten, Norman (1985) *Sicuanga Runa: The Other Side of Development in Amazonian Ecuador* (Urbana: University of Illinois Press).

Whitten, Norman (1986 [1974]) *Black Frontiersmen: A South American Case*, 2nd edn. (Prospect Heights, IL: Waveland Press).

Whitten, Norman and Arlene Torres (1992) Blackness in the Americas, *NACLA Report on the Americas* 15(4): 16–22.

Whitten, Norman and John Szwed (1970) Introduction. In *Afro-American Anthropology: Contemporary Perspectives*, Norman Whitten and John Szwed (eds), pp. 23–53 (New York: Free Press).

Whitten, Norman and Nina de Friedemann (1974) La cultura negra del litoral ecuatoriano y colombiano: un modelo de adaptación étnica, *Revista Colombiana de Antropología* 17: 75–115.

Whitten, Norman and Arlene Torres (eds) (1998) *Blackness in Latin America and the Caribbean: Social Dynamics and Cultural Transformations* (Bloomington: Indiana University Press).

Williams, Brackette (1989) A class act: anthropology and the race to nation across ethnic terrain, *Annual Review of Anthropology* 18: 401–44

Williams, Brackette (1991) *Stains on my Name, War in my Veins: Guyana and the Politics of Cultural Struggle* (Durham, NC: Duke University Press).

Williams, Raymond (1988) *Keywords* (London: Fontana).

Wilson, Richard (1995a) *Maya Resurgence in Guatemala: Q'echi' Experiences* (Norman: University of Oklahoma Press).

Wilson, Richard (1995b) Shifting frontiers: historical transformations of identities in Latin America, *Bulletin of Latin American Research* 14(1): 1–8.

Wilson, Richard (ed.) (1996) *Human Rights, Culture and Context: Anthropological Perspectives* (London: Pluto Press).

Wimmer, Andreas, and Nina Glick Schiller (2002) Methodological nationalism and beyond: nation-state building, migration and the social sciences, *Global Networks: A Journal of Transnational Affairs* 2: 301–34.

Winant, Howard (1992) Rethinking race in Brazil, *Journal of Latin American Studies* 24: 173–92.

Winant, Howard (1994) *Racial Conditions: Politics, Theory, Comparisons* (Minneapolis: University of Minnesota Press).

Wolf, Eric (1955) Types of Latin American peasantry: a preliminary discussion, *American Anthropologist* 57: 452–71.

Wolpe, Harold (1975) The theory of internal colonialism: the South African case. In *Beyond the Sociology of Development*, Ivar Oxaal, Tony Barnett and David Booth (eds), pp. 229–52 (London: Routledge and Kegan Paul).

Wright, Michelle M. (2004) *Becoming Black: Creating Identity in the African Diaspora* (Durham NC: Duke University Press).

Wright, Winthrop (1990) *Café con Leche: Race, Class and National Image in Venezuela* (Austin: University of Texas Press).

Yashar, Deborah (2005) *Contesting Citizenship in Latin America: The Rise of Indigenous Movements and the Postliberal Challenge* (Cambridge: Cambridge University Press).

Yelvington, Kevin (2001) The anthropology of Afro-Latin America and the Caribbean: diasporic dimensions, *Annual Review of Anthropology* 30: 227–60.

Yelvington, Kevin (ed.) (2006) *Afro-Atlantic Dialogues: Anthropology in the Diaspora* (Santa Fe, NM: School of American Research Press).

Young, Iris Marion (1990) *Justice and the Politics of Difference* (Princeton, NJ: Princeton University Press).

Young, Robert (1995) *Colonial Desire: Hybridity in Theory, Culture and Race* (London: Routledge).

Yuval-Davis, Nira and Floya Anthias (eds) (1989) *Woman-Nation-State* (London: Macmillan).

Zamosc, Leon (1994) Agrarian protest and the Indian movement in the Ecuadorian highlands, *Latin American Research Review* 29(3): 37–68.

Zanotta Machado, Lia (1994) Indigenous communitarianism as a critique of modernity and its juridical implications. In *Indigenous Peoples' Experiences with Self-government*, Willem Assies and André Hoekema (eds), pp. 73–91 (Amsterdam: IWGIA and the University of Amsterdam).

Index